THE NATURE AND NURTURE OF BEHAVIOR

Readings from

SCIENTIFIC AMERICAN

THE NATURE AND NURTURE
OF BEHAVIOR
Developmental Psychobiology

with introductions by
William T. Greenough
University of Illinois

W. H. Freeman and Company
San Francisco

Library of Congress Cataloging in Publication Data

Greenough, William T.   1944–   comp.
    The nature and nurture of behavior, developmental
psychobiology.

    1. Developmental psychobiology.   I. Scientific
American.   II. Title. [DNLM: 1. Behavior—
Collected works.   2. Psychology—Collected works.
BF 701 N285 1973]
RJ131.N33   155   72-11800
ISBN 0-7167-0868-X
ISBN 0-7167-0867-1 (pbk)

All of the SCIENTIFIC AMERICAN articles in
The Nature and Nurture of Behavior are available as
separate Offprints. For a complete list of more than
900 articles now available as Offprints, write to
W. H. Freeman and Company, 660 Market Street,
San Francisco, California 94104.

Printed in the United States of America

International Standard Book Number:
0-7167-0868-X (cloth)
0-7167-0867-1 (paper)

9 8 7 6 5 4

Cover Design from photographs by Sol Mednick

PREFACE

For at least as long as they have been writing down their ideas, philosophers and scientists have been fascinated by the development of living creatures. What began as a philosophical debate over the roles of innate versus environmental contributions to the final behaving organism has become an increasingly active area of scientific study. In recent years, controlled experimentation and the observation of natural processes, in both human and animal subjects, have led away from both nativist philosophical views (which stressed heredity over environment) and empiricist views (which stressed environment over heredity). Modern theoretical positions tend to view the development of behavior as a synthesis of both components, each indispensable to the attainment of normal patterns of behavior.

Research on the developmental process has come from a variety of disciplines. On the biological side, the past few decades have seen overwhelming advances in genetics, embryology, and the neurological sciences. While a great deal remains to be learned, we now understand much of how the fertilized ovum develops into specialized tissues that become further arranged into the functional organs of the final animal. Similarly, work in the behavioral sciences has done much to elucidate processes and stages in the development of behavior. At the interface of biological and behavioral approaches to development, developmental psychobiologists have begun to make exciting discoveries about the ways in which biological and behavioral development are related.

This short collection of readings is designed to present an overview to the developmental or child psychology student, or the biology student, of the research in this rapidly expanding area, where biological and psychological approaches to behavior development are beginning to meet. A glance at the list of authors of the readings in this book gives some idea of the diversity of subdisciplines that are contributing to this field. Psychologists, physiologists, ethologists, physicians, biologists, chemists, and anatomists are represented, along with others not easily classified.

There is similarly a variety in the species that the authors have chosen for their research. Obviously, many of the experiments in this volume could not have been carried out on human subjects, since they involve damage to the organism. But, beyond this, certain types of animals offer unique advantages in the study of certain developmental processes. This diversity in discipline and subjects is reflected in a healthy variety of opinion and methodology, which is not always found within individual fields of study. As the reader goes through the book, it will become apparent that the "principles" of developmental psychobiology, if they exist at all, are far from cut-and-dried. Differences of opinion, based on sound experimental data, will be evident among the selections. Nevertheless, a coherent theme emerges from this heterogeneous assortment. It is that behavior is invariably a result of a complex combination of intrinsic and experiential factors. In fact, to specify all of the hereditary and environmental contributions to any single action of an organism goes well beyond the limits of current or conceivable technology.

Of course the research described in this volume is not, with one or two exceptions, directed towards elucidating such components of specific behaviors. Rather, the common goal of the authors is to understand the role of inherent and acquired factors in the organization of basic behavioral processes. As an example, consider the diversity of approaches to the development of the visual system included among the selections. R. W. Sperry and D. H. Hubel examine the basic "wiring diagram" of different visual systems; T. G. R. Bower, and E. J. Gibson and R. D. Walk study the visual capacity of a variety of species prior to extensive postnatal experience; A. H. Riesen and R. L. Fantz examine the postnatal maturation of the visual system and the role of experience in its development; R. Held explores the integration of vision with other behavioral processes. While the species, the methods, and the theoretical viewpoints of these investigators differ widely, their combined efforts provide a harmonious view of the development of the visual system, including (a) the establishment of nerve connections between eye and brain, (b) developmental fine tuning, and (c) maintenance in the course of environmental experience.

Thus this collection of papers attempts to span the often-perceived gap between developmental biology and child psychology; the hope that this approach will be valuable to students of both disciplines has motivated the organization of this short reader.

August, 1972   WILLIAM T. GREENOUGH

CONTENTS

I PRENATAL DEVELOPMENT AND CAPACITY OF THE NEWBORN

II CRITICAL EVENTS IN THE SHAPING OF BASIC SYSTEMS

III ENVIRONMENTAL DETERMINANTS OF COMPLEX BEHAVIOR

Note on cross-references: References to articles included in this book are noted by the title of the article and the page on which it begins; references to articles that are available as Offprints, but are not included here, are noted by the article's title and Offprint number; references to articles published by SCIENTIFIC AMERICAN, but which are not available as Offprints, are noted by the title of the article and the month and year of its publication.

I

PRENATAL DEVELOPMENT AND CAPACITY OF THE NEWBORN

I

PRENATAL DEVELOPMENT AND CAPACITY OF THE NEWBORN

INTRODUCTION

The human infant at birth is suddenly exposed to a bewildering array of sights, sounds, bodily sensations, tastes, and smells. We really do not know what the child makes of this world—or the extent to which he can organize these complex patterns of stimulation into a coherent picture of his surroundings. We do know, if he has been born at the normal time, that all of his basic sensory capacities are functioning at least at a minimal level. He can see, hear, feel, taste, and smell aspects of his environment. For all of these sensory modalities, nerve connections exist such that stimulation of a receptor, such as the retina of the eye, causes a message to be carried along nerve pathways to trigger a response in the nerve-cell mass we call the brain.

R. W. Sperry, in "The Eye and the Brain," uses lower vertebrate species to study the way in which these nerve connections are established. His research is designed to determine how a developing nerve cell, sending a process from the eye, "knows" where in the brain the process should be connected. Although we do not expect vision in amphibians to be identical to that in humans (See, for example, Charles R. Michael, "Retinal Processing of Visual Images," *Scientific American,* May, 1969, Offprint 1143), the mechanisms through which the connections are established are likely to be similar.

Once the basic visual pathways have been laid down, nerve messages signalling stimulation of the eye by light can reach the brain. In higher mammals, however, information from various retinal points appears to be carried along parallel tracks to the visual centers of the brain. That is, the information received by the visual cortex does not consist of organized percepts, such as of a face or a nipple, but of an array of individual messages from each point on the retina. Somehow the visual cortex must organize this collection of inputs into a picture of the surrounding world, made up of objects, distances, and movement. David H. Hubel describes the way in which cortical nerve cells appear to carry out preliminary analysis of retinal input in his article, "The Visual Cortex of the Brain." Hubel, with his associate T. N. Wiesel, has reported that the "simple," "complex," and "hyper-complex" nerve cells they describe are found in newborn kittens at the time that their eyes first open. Thus normal visual experience does not seem to be necessary for their development. However, as we shall see in the later sections of this book, experience generally seems to be necessary to maintain them and to coordinate vision with the muscular activities necessary in dealing with the environment.

Electrical recording from brain cells can tell us that many of the connections necessary for normal vision are already established in the newborn, but it cannot tell us whether the infant can use them in behavior. Eleanor J. Gibson and Richard D. Walk describe one of the methods they have used to test the visual ability of the infant in their article, "The 'Visual Cliff.'" These studies of depth perception emphasize an important point which must be kept in mind when the development of sensory and motor capacity of different species is compared: just as the range of behavioral capacities of the adult has evolved to meet the requirements of his natural environment, so the extent to which these capacities are developed at birth, and the rate at which they mature thereafter, will depend upon the demands of the postnatal environment. The young kitten, who will be nursed and protected by his mother for several weeks after birth, is born with its eyes closed and does not begin to use vision until they open more than a week later. The newly hatched chick, on the other hand, must successfully peck for food within hours after its birth; hence both vision and visuomotor integration are highly developed at the time of hatching.

This might imply that cats require postnatal environmental experience for the development of their visual ability while chickens do not. Alternatively, it might suggest that the point in development at which birth occurs differs for the two types of organisms: those that have to cope with the world at birth develop to a more mature state before they are born. For these animals, prenatal experience may contribute to the development of advanced postnatal abilities. For example, many years ago the noted behaviorist Zing-Yang Kuo reported naturalistic observations of developing chick embryos that suggested that the precocial development of the ability to peck for food might be aided by stimulation of the neck muscles by the rhythmic beating of the heart beneath them in the latter stages of development.

The term "environment," then, describes both the conditions that surround the developing embryo before birth (or hatching) and those that surround the neonate when it emerges from the egg or womb. It includes not only the sensory stimuli activating the organism's receptors and the objects towards which his muscular responses are directed but also those aspects necessary to the organism's metabolic processes. The metabolic component whose absence is most rapidly felt is, of course, oxygen. As William F. Windle points out in "Brain Damage by Asphyxia at Birth," although modern medical techniques have greatly reduced the frequency of injury or death to both mother and infant, certain practices have actually increased the possibility that the infant will be deprived of oxygen during delivery. While infants show a remarkable ability to recover from extensive oxygen deprivation, severe anoxia can lead to permanent disability or death.

In the final selection of this section we return to the question proposed at the outset—to what extent are the newborn human child's sensations organized into an accurate perception of the world around him? T. G. R. Bower, in "The Visual World of Infants," uses a clever social-reward training system to induce infants to reveal their knowledge of the visual environment. Bower finds that very young children, who have had minimal opportunity to learn about their visual world from experience, demonstrate visual capacities that were previously thought to be learned only after the child was old enough to compare visual experience with the experiences of touching and moving about objects. Although it is clear that the capacity for visual-information processing in these children is considerably below that of an adult, this and the preceding articles indicate that much of the ability to understand what we see is developed at, or very shortly after, birth. Hence the newborn can no longer be thought of as a *tabula rasa*, entirely molded by experience. Clearly, the genetic material, acting in concert with the prenatal environment, provides a solid foundation upon which postnatal experience may build.

SUGGESTED READINGS

Gibson, E. J. *Principles of perceptual learning and development.* New York: Appleton-Century-Crofts, 1969.

Hubel, D. H., and Wiesel, T. N. Receptive fields of cells in striate cortex of very young, visually inexperienced kittens. *Journal of Neurophysiology,* Vol. 26, pages 994–1002, 1963.

Hubel, D. H., and Wiesel, T. N. The period of susceptibility to the physiological effects of unilateral eye closure in kittens. *Journal of Physiology,* Vol. 206, pages 419–436, 1970.

Kuo, Z.-Y. Ontogeny of embryonic behavior in aves: IV. The influence of embryonic movements upon behavior after hatching. *Journal of Comparative Psychology,* Vol. 14, pages 109–122, 1932.

Further Readings From *Scientific American*

Bower, T. G. R. The object in the world of the infant. *Scientific American,* October, 1971 (Offprint 539).

Gesell, A. Infant vision. *Scientific American,* February, 1950 (Offprint 401).

Sperry, R. W. The growth of nerve circuits. *Scientific American,* November, 1959 (Offprint 72).

Thomas, A., Chess, S., and Birch, H. G. The origin of personality, "*Scientific American,* August, 1970 (Offprint 529).

1

THE EYE AND THE BRAIN

R. W. SPERRY
May 1956

If the optic nerve of a newt is cut and its eye is turned through 180 degrees, the nerve regenerates and the animal sees upside down. Such results deeply affect our picture of how the nervous system develops

Probably no question about the behavior of living things holds greater general interest than the age-old issue: Heredity versus Learning. And none perhaps is more difficult to investigate in any clear-cut way. Most behavior has elements of both inheritance and training; yet each must make a distinct contribution. The problem is to separate the contributions. We can take vision as a case in point. An animal, it is often said, must learn to see. It is born with eyes, but it matures in the use of them. The question is: Just where does its inborn seeing ability end and learning begin? To put the matter another way: Exactly what equipment and instinctive skills are we born with?

This article is an account of experiments which have given some new insight into the heredity-learning question. The behavior studied is vision, and the story begins 31 years ago.

In 1925 Robert Matthey, a zoologist of the University of Geneva, delivered to the Society of Biology in Paris an astonishing report. He had severed the optic nerve in adult newts, or salamanders, and they had later recovered their vision! New nerve fibers had sprouted from the cut stump and had managed to grow back to the visual centers of the brain. That an adult animal could regenerate the optic nerve (and even, as Matthey reported later, the retina of the eye) was surprising enough, but that it could also re-establish the complex network of nerve-fiber connections between the eye and a multitude of precisely located points in the brain seemed to border on the incredible. And yet this was the only possible explanation, for without question the newts had regained normal vision. They would stalk a moving worm separated from them by a glass wall in their aquarium; they were able to see a small object distinctly and follow its movements accurately.

A long series of confirmations of Matthey's discovery followed. He transplanted an eyeball from one newt to another, with good recovery of vision. Leon S. Stone and his co-workers at Yale University transplanted eyes successfully from one species of salamander to another, and grafted the same eye in four successive individuals in turn, each of which was able to use the eye to regain its vision. Eventually experimenters found that fishes, frogs and toads (but not mammals) also could regenerate the optic nerve and recover vision if the nerve was cut carefully without damage to the main artery to the retina.

The optic nerve of a fish has tens of thousands of fibers, most or all of which must connect with a specific part of the visual area of the brain if the image on the retina is to be projected accurately to the brain. The newt, whose retina is less fine-grained than a fish's, has fewer optic fibers, but still a great many. The system is analogous to a distributor's map with thousands of strings leading from a focal point to thousands of specific spots on the map. How can an animal whose optic fibers have all been cut near the focal point re-establish this intricate and precisely patterned system of connections? Matthey found that the regenerating fibers wound back into the

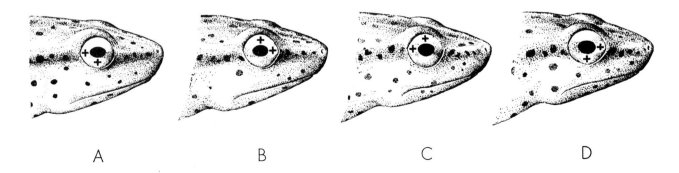

A   B   C   D

EYE OF THE NEWT was turned in various ways by the experiments described in this article. In A the normal position of the eye is marked with crosses. In B the eye has been turned so that its front-back and up-down axes are inverted. In C the eye on the opposite side of the head has been transplanted to the side shown with its up-down axis inverted. In D the eye on the opposite side of the head has been transplanted to the side shown with its front-back axis inverted. In each case the operation is done on both eyes.

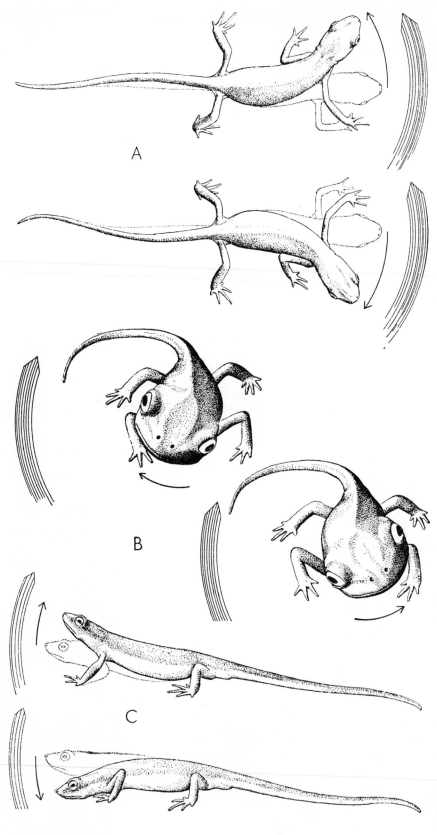

A

B

C

RESPONSE OF THE NEWT to moving objects varies with the operations depicted on the preceding page. The first newt in each of the three pairs of animals on this page is normal. When an object *(thick arrows)* is moved past the newt, the animal turns its head in the same direction *(thin arrows)*. The second newt in each pair represents the behavior of the animal after one or more of the operations. The response of the second newt in A corresponds to operations B and D on the preceding page; in B, to operations B and C; in C, to C and D.

brain in what looked like a hopelessly mixed up snarl. Yet somehow, from this chaos, the original orderly system of communications was restored.

Two possible explanations have been considered. The one that was long regarded as the more plausible is that the connections are formed again by some kind of learning process. According to this theory, as the cut nerve regenerates a host of new fibers, branching and crawling all over the brain, the animal learns through experience to make use of the fiber linkages that happen to be established correctly, and any worthless connections atrophy from disuse.

The second theory is that each fiber is actually specific and somehow manages to arrive at its proper destination in the brain and reform the connection. This implies some kind of affinity, presumably chemical, between each individual optic fiber and matching nerve cells in the brain's visual lobe. The idea that each of the many thousands of nerve fibers involved has a different character seemed so fantastic that it was not very widely accepted.

These were the questions we undertook to test: Does the newt relearn to see, or does its heredity, forming and organizing its regenerated fibers according to a genetic pattern, automatically restore orderly vision?

Our first experiment was to turn the eye of the newt upside down—to find out whether this rotation of the eyeball would produce upside-down vision, and if so, whether the inverted vision could be corrected by experience and training. We cut the eyeball free of the eyelids and muscles, leaving the optic nerve and main blood vessels intact, then turned the eyeball by 180 degrees. The tissues rapidly healed and the eyeball stayed fixed in the new position.

The vision of animals operated on this way was then tested. Their responses showed very clearly that their vision was reversed. When a piece of bait was held above the newt's head, it would begin digging into the pebbles and sand on the bottom of the aquarium. When the lure was presented in front of its head, it would turn around and start searching in the rear; when the bait was behind it, the animal would lunge forward. (Since its eyes are on the side of the head, a newt can see objects behind it.) As color-adapting animals, the newts with upside-down eyes even adjusted their color to the brightness above them instead of to the dark background of the aquarium bottom. Besides seeing everything upside down and backward, the animals kept turning in circles, as if the whole visual field appeared to be whirling about them. Human subjects who have worn experimental lenses that invert the visual field have reported that any movement of the head or eyes tends to make everything seem to whirl around them.

The operated newts never relearned to see normally during the experiment. Some were kept with their eyes inverted for as long as two years, but showed no significant improvement. However, when rotated eyes were turned back to the normal position by surgery, the animals at once resumed normal behavior. There was no evidence that their long experience with inverted vision had brought about any change in the functioning of the central nervous system.

A second experiment bore out further the now growing suspicion that learning probably was not responsible for the recovery of vision by newts whose optic nerves had been cut. This time we rotated the eyeball and severed the optic nerve as well. The object was to find out whether the regenerating nerve fibers would give the newt normal vision, inverted vision or just a confused blur.

During the period of nerve regeneration the animals were blind. The first visual responses began to reappear about 25 to 30 days after the nerve had been cut. From the beginning these responses were systematically reversed in the same way as those produced by eye rotation alone. In other words, the animals again responded as if everything was seen upside down and backward. In these animals also the reversed vision remained permanently uncorrected by experience.

In another series of experiments we cut the optic nerves of the two eyes and switched their connections to the brain. Normally each optic nerve crosses to the side of the brain opposite the eye. We connected the cut nerve to the brain lobe on the same side. The result was to make the animals behave after regeneration as if the right and left halves of the visual field were reversed. That is, the animals responded to anything seen through one eye as if it were being viewed through the other eye. This switch too was permanent, uncorrected by experience. Frogs and toads responded to the experiment in the same way as newts.

By rotating the eyeball less than 180 degrees (*e.g.*, a 90-degree turn), and by combining eye transplantation from one side to the other with various degrees of rotation, we produced many

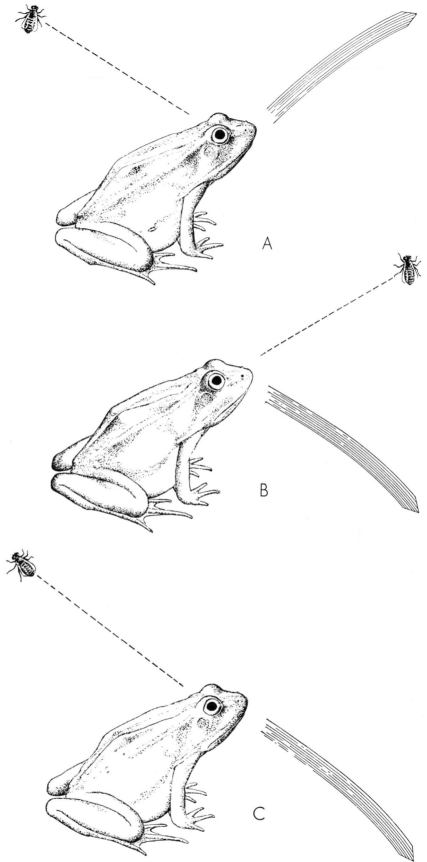

SAME OPERATIONS ON A FROG produce these effects when the animal strikes at a fly. In A the fly is above and behind a frog whose eyes have been turned by operation D on page 5; the animal strikes in the direction shown by the thick arrow. In B the eyes of the frog have been turned by operation C. In C the eyes of the frog have been turned by operation B.

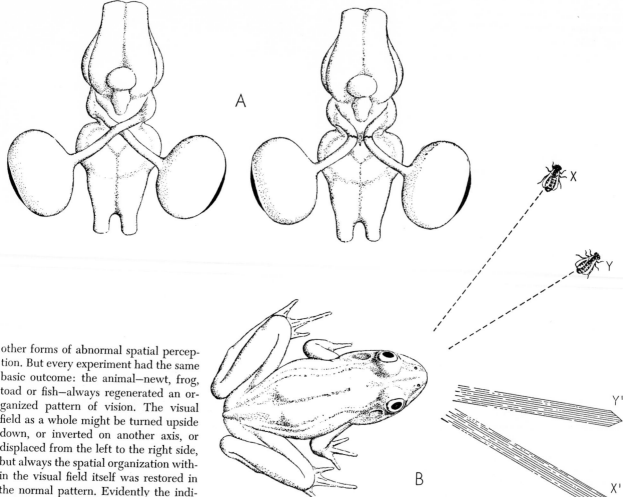

OPERATION ON THE OPTIC NERVES of a frog produced the effect shown at the lower right. At upper left the eyes of the frog are joined to the brain by the optic nerves. In the operation, which is depicted at top center, the nerves were cut and rejoined so that they did not cross. When a fly was at X, the frog struck at X'; when it was at Y, the frog struck at Y'.

other forms of abnormal spatial perception. But every experiment had the same basic outcome: the animal—newt, frog, toad or fish—always regenerated an organized pattern of vision. The visual field as a whole might be turned upside down, or inverted on another axis, or displaced from the left to the right side, but always the spatial organization within the visual field itself was restored in the normal pattern. Evidently the individual neı ve fibers from the retina, after regeneration, all regained their original relative spatial functions in projecting the picture to the brain.

This orderly restoration of the spatial relations could hardly be based on any kind of learning or adaptation, under the conditions of our experiments. Animals don't *learn* to see things upside down and backward or reversed from left to right: reversed vision is more disadvantageous than no vision at all. The results clearly demonstrated that the orderly recovery of correct functional relations on the part of the ingrowing fibers was not achieved through function and experience, but rather was predetermined in the growth process itself.

Apparently the tangle of regenerating fibers was sorted out in the brain so as to restore the orderly maplike projection of the retina upon the optic lobe. If we destroyed a small part of the optic lobe after such regeneration, the animal had a blind spot in the corresponding part of its visual field, just as would be the case in normal animals. It was as if each regenerated fiber did indeed make a connection with a spot in the brain matching a corresponding spot in the retina.

It follows that optic fibers arising from different points in the retina must differ from one another in some way. If the ingrowing optic fibers were indistinguishable from one another, there would be no way in which they could re-establish their different functional connections in an orderly pattern. Each optic fiber must be endowed with some quality, presumably chemical, that marks it as having originated from a particular spot of the retinal field. And the matching spot at its terminus in the brain must have an exactly complementary quality. Presumably an ingrowing fiber will attach itself only to the particular brain cells that match its chemical flavor, so to speak. This chemical specificity seems to lie, as certain further experiments indicate, in a biaxial type of differentiation which produces unique arrays of chemical properties at the junction places.

Such chemical matching would account for recognition on contact, but how does a fiber find its way to its destination? There is good reason to believe that the regenerating fibers employ a shotgun approach. Each fiber puts forth many branches as it grows into the brain, and the brain cells likewise have widespreading branches. Thus the chances are exceedingly good that a given fiber will eventually make contact with its partner cells. We can picture the advancing tip of a fiber making a host of contacts as it invades the dense tangle of brain cells and their treelike expansions. The great majority of these contacts come to nothing, but eventually the growing tip encounters a type of cell surface for which it has a specific chemical affinity and to which it adheres. A chemical reaction then causes the fiber tip to stop advancing and to form a lasting functional union with the group of cells, presumably roughly circular in formation, which constitutes the spot in the brain matching the fiber's source spot in the retina.

The experiments on vision have been found to apply equally to other parts of the central nervous system. Normal function can be recovered through regeneration by general sensory nerves in the spinal cord, by the vestibular nerve in the ear mediating the sense of equilibrium and by other sensory and motor nerve circuits.

All the experiments point to one conclusion: the theory of inherent chemical affinities among the nerve fibers and cells is able to account for the kinds of behavior tested better than any hypothetical mechanism based on experience and learning. There is no direct proof of the theory, for no one has yet seen evidence of the chemical affinity type of reaction among nerves under the microscope. But an ever-growing accumulation of experimental findings continues to add support to the chemical theory.

We return to our original question: How big a role does heredity play in behavior? The experiments cited here show that in the lower vertebrates, at least, many features of visual perception—the sense of direction and location in space, the organization of patterns, the sense of position of the visual field as a whole, the perception of motion, and the like—are built into the organism and do not have to be learned. More general experiments suggest that the organization of pathways and associations in the central nervous system must be ascribed for the most part to inherent developmental patterning, not to experience. Of the thousands of circuit connections in the brain that have been described, not one can demonstrably be attributed to learning. Whatever the neural changes induced in the brain by experience, they are extremely inconspicuous. In the higher animals they are probably located mainly in the more remote byways of the cerebral cortex. In any case they are superimposed upon an already elaborate innate organization.

The whole idea of instincts and the inheritance of behavior traits is becoming much more palatable than it was 15 years ago, when we lacked a satisfactory basis for explaining the organization of inborn behavior. Today we can give more weight to heredity than we did then. Every animal comes into the world with inherited behavior patterns of its species. Much of its behavior is a product of evolution, just as its biological structure is.

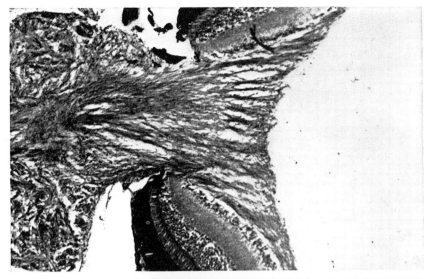

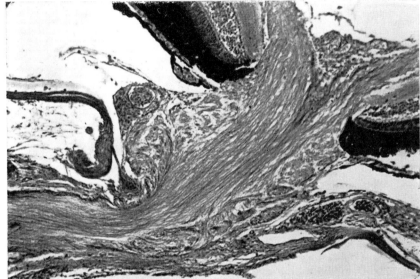

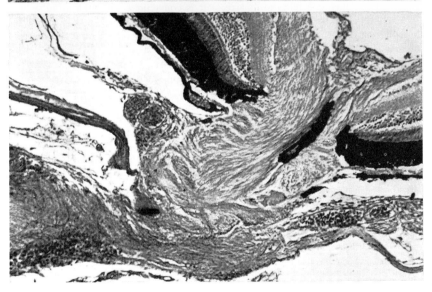

OPTIC NERVE of *Bathygobius soporator*, a fish of the goby family, was cut and allowed to regenerate. The regenerated nerve is shown in these three photomicrographic sections. In each photograph the eye is toward the right and the nerve runs from right to left. The top photograph shows a section of one nerve; the bottom two photographs show different sections of the same nerve. In all three sections the nerve fibers are tangled. Despite this apparent disorganization the fishes from which the sections were taken could see normally.

2

THE VISUAL CORTEX OF THE BRAIN

DAVID H. HUBEL
November 1963

A start toward understanding how it analyzes images on the retina can be made through studies of the responses that individual cells in the visual system of the cat give to varying patterns of light

An image of the outside world striking the retina of the eye activates a most intricate process that results in vision: the transformation of the retinal image into a perception. The transformation occurs partly in the retina but mostly in the brain, and it is, as one can recognize instantly by considering how modest in comparison is the achievement of a camera, a task of impressive magnitude.

The process begins with the responses of some 130 million light-sensitive receptor cells in each retina. From these cells messages are transmitted to other retinal cells and then sent on to the brain, where they must be analyzed and interpreted. To get an idea of the magnitude of the task, think what is involved in watching a moving animal, such as a horse. At a glance one takes in its size, form, color and rate of movement. From tiny differences in the two retinal images there results a three-dimensional picture. Somehow the brain manages to compare this picture with previous impressions; recognition occurs and then any appropriate action can be taken.

The organization of the visual system —a large, intricately connected population of nerve cells in the retina and brain —is still poorly understood. In recent years, however, various studies have begun to reveal something of the arrangement and function of these cells. A decade ago Stephen W. Kuffler, working with cats at the Johns Hopkins Hospital, discovered that some analysis of visual patterns takes place outside the brain, in the nerve cells of the retina. My colleague Torsten N. Wiesel and I at the Harvard Medical School, exploring the first stages of the processing that occurs in the brain of the cat, have mapped the visual pathway a little further: to what appears to be the sixth step from the retina to the cortex of the cerebrum. This kind of

work falls far short of providing a full understanding of vision, but it does convey some idea of the mechanisms and circuitry of the visual system.

In broad outline the visual pathway is clearly defined [*see bottom illustration on opposite page*]. From the retina of each eye visual messages travel along the optic nerve, which consists of about a million nerve fibers. At the junction known as the chiasm about half of the nerves cross over into opposite hemispheres of the brain, the other nerves remaining on the same side. The optic nerve fibers lead to the first way stations in the brain: a pair of cell clusters called the lateral geniculate bodies. From here new fibers course back through the brain to the visual area of the cerebral cortex. It is convenient, although admittedly a gross oversimplification, to think of the pathway from retina to cortex as consisting of six types of nerve cells, of which three are in the retina, one is in the geniculate body and two are in the cortex.

Nerve cells, or neurons, transmit messages in the form of brief electrochemical impulses. These travel along the outer membrane of the cell, notably along the membrane of its long principal fiber, the axon. It is possible to obtain an electrical record of impulses of a single nerve cell by placing a fine electrode near the cell body or one of its fibers. Such measurements have shown that impulses travel along the nerves at velocities of between half a meter and 100 meters per second. The impulses in a given fiber all have about the same amplitude; the strength of the stimuli that give rise to them is reflected not in amplitude but in frequency.

At its terminus the fiber of a nerve cell makes contact with another nerve cell (or with a muscle cell or gland

cell), forming the junction called the synapse. At most synapses an impulse on reaching the end of a fiber causes the release of a small amount of a specific substance, which diffuses outward to the membrane of the next cell. There the substance either excites the cell or inhibits it. In excitation the substance acts to bring the cell into a state in which it is more likely to "fire"; in inhibition the substance acts to prevent firing. For most synapses the substances that act as transmitters are unknown. Moreover, there is no sure way to determine from microscopic appearances alone whether a synapse is excitatory or inhibitory.

It is at the synapses that the modification and analysis of nerve messages take place. The kind of analysis depends partly on the nature of the synapse: on how many nerve fibers converge on a single cell and on how the excitatory and inhibitory endings distribute themselves. In most parts of the nervous system the anatomy is too intricate to reveal much about function. One way to circumvent this difficulty is to record impulses with microelectrodes in anesthetized animals, first from the fibers coming into a structure of neurons and then from the neurons themselves, or from the fibers they send onward. Comparison of the behavior of incoming and outgoing fibers provides a basis for learning what the structure does. Through such exploration of the different parts of the brain concerned with vision one can hope to build up some idea of how the entire visual system works.

That is what Wiesel and I have undertaken, mainly through studies of the visual system of the cat. In our experiments the anesthetized animal faces a wide screen 1.5 meters away, and we shine various patterns of white light on the screen with a projector. Simultaneously we penetrate the visual portion of the cortex with microelectrodes. In that way we can record the responses of individual cells to the light patterns. Sometimes it takes many hours to find the region of the retina with which a particular visual cell is linked and to work out the optimum stimuli for that cell. The reader should bear in mind the relation between each visual cell—no matter how far along the visual pathway it may be—and the retina. It requires an image on the retina to evoke a meaningful response in any visual cell, however indirect and complex the linkage may be.

The retina is a complicated structure, in both its anatomy and its physiology, and the description I shall give is highly simplified. Light coming through the lens of the eye falls on the mosaic of receptor cells in the retina. The receptor cells do not send impulses directly through the optic nerve but instead connect with a set of retinal cells called bipolar cells. These in turn connect with retinal ganglion cells, and it is the latter set of cells, the third in the visual pathway, that sends its fibers—the optic nerve fibers—to the brain.

This series of cells and synapses is no simple bucket brigade for impulses: a receptor may send nerve endings to more than one bipolar cell, and several receptors may converge on one bipolar cell. The same holds for the synapses between the bipolar cells and the retinal ganglion cells. Stimulating a single receptor by light might therefore be expected to have an influence on many bipolar or ganglion cells; conversely, it should be possible to influence one bipolar or retinal ganglion cell from a number of receptors and hence from a substantial area of the retina.

The area of receptor mosaic in the retina feeding into a single visual cell is called the receptive field of the cell. This term is applied to any cell in the visual system to refer to the area of retina with which the cell is connected—the retinal area that on stimulation produces a response from the cell.

Any of the synapses with a particular cell may be excitatory or inhibitory, so that stimulation of a particular point on the retina may either increase or decrease the cell's firing rate. Moreover, a single cell may receive several excitatory and inhibitory impulses at once, with the result that it will respond according to the net effect of these inputs. In considering the behavior of a single cell an observer should remember that it is just one of a huge popu-

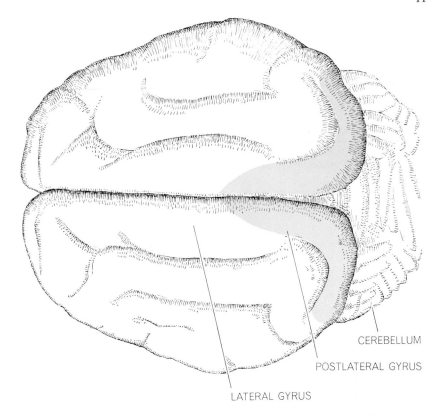

CORTEX OF CAT'S BRAIN is depicted as it would be seen from the top. The colored region indicates the cortical area that deals at least in a preliminary way with vision.

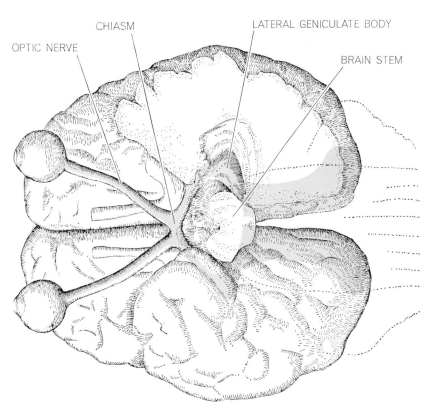

VISUAL SYSTEM appears in this representation of the human brain as viewed from below. Visual pathway from retinas to cortex via the lateral geniculate body is shown in color.

12

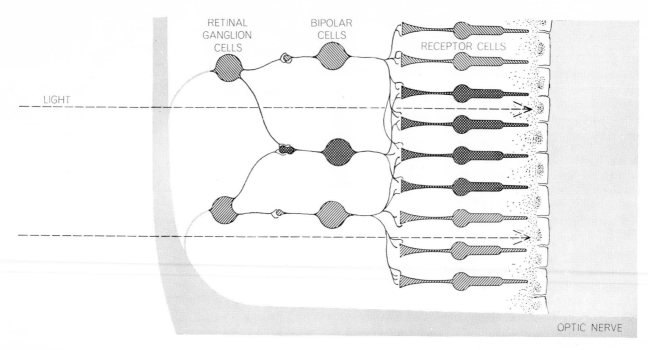

STRUCTURE OF RETINA is depicted schematically. Images fall on the receptor cells, of which there are about 130 million in each retina. Some analysis of an image occurs as the receptors transmit messages to the retinal ganglion cells via the bipolar cells. A group of receptors funnels into a particular ganglion cell, as indicated by the shading; that group forms the ganglion cell's receptive field. Inasmuch as the fields of several ganglion cells overlap, one receptor may send messages to several ganglion cells.

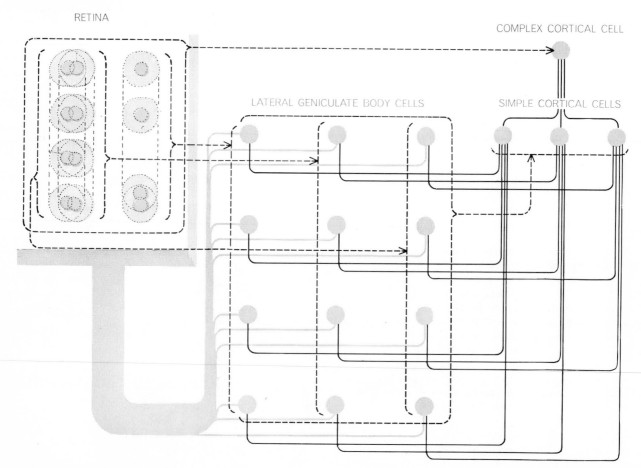

VISUAL PROCESSING BY BRAIN begins in the lateral geniculate body, which continues the analysis made by retinal cells. In the cortex "simple" cells respond strongly to line stimuli, provided that the position and orientation of the line are suitable for a particular cell. "Complex" cells respond well to line stimuli, but the position of the line is not critical and the cell continues to respond even if a properly oriented stimulus is moved, as long as it remains in the cell's receptive field. Broken lines indicate how receptive fields of all these cells overlap on the retina; solid lines, how several cells at one stage affect a single cell at the next stage.

lation of cells: a stimulus that excites one cell will undoubtedly excite many others, meanwhile inhibiting yet another array of cells and leaving others entirely unaffected.

For many years it has been known that retinal ganglion cells fire at a fairly steady rate even in the absence of any stimulation. Kuffler was the first to observe how the retinal ganglion cells of mammals are influenced by small spots of light. He found that the resting discharges of a cell were intensified or diminished by light in a small and more or less circular region of the retina. That region was of course the cell's receptive field. Depending on where in the field a spot of light fell, either of two responses could be produced. One was an "on" response, in which the cell's firing rate increased under the stimulus of light. The other was an "off" response, in which the stimulus of light decreased the cell's firing rate. Moreover, turning the light off usually evoked a burst of impulses from the cell. Kuffler called the retinal regions from which these responses could be evoked "on" regions and "off" regions.

On mapping the receptive fields of a large number of retinal ganglion cells into "on" and "off" regions, Kuffler discovered that there were two distinct cell types. In one the receptive field consisted of a small circular "on" area and a surrounding zone that gave "off" responses. Kuffler termed this an "on"-center cell. The second type, which he called "off"-center, had just the reverse form of field—an "off" center and an "on" periphery [*see top illustration on this page*]. For a given cell the effects of light varied markedly according to the place in which the light struck the receptive field. Two spots of light shone on separate parts of an "on" area produced a more vigorous "on" response than either spot alone, whereas if one spot was shone on an "on" area and the other on an "off" area, the two effects tended to neutralize each other, resulting in a very weak "on" or "off" response. In an "on"-center cell, illuminating the entire central "on" region evoked a maximum response; a smaller or larger spot of light was less effective.

Lighting up the whole retina diffusely, even though it may affect every receptor in the retina, does not affect a retinal ganglion cell nearly so strongly as a small circular spot of exactly the right size placed so as to cover precisely the receptive-field center. The main concern of these cells seems to be the contrast in illumination between one retinal region and surrounding regions.

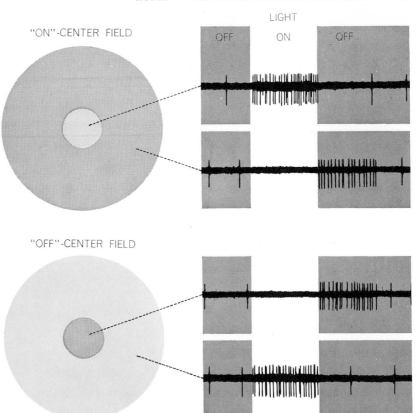

CONCENTRIC FIELDS are characteristic of retinal ganglion cells and of geniculate cells. At top an oscilloscope recording shows strong firing by an "on"-center type of cell when a spot of light strikes the field center; if the spot hits an "off" area, the firing is suppressed until the light goes off. At bottom are responses of another cell of the "off"-center type.

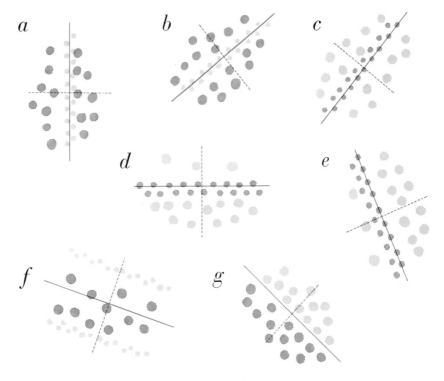

SIMPLE CORTICAL CELLS have receptive fields of various types. In all of them the "on" and "off" areas, represented by colored and gray dots respectively, are separated by straight boundaries. Orientations of fields vary, as indicated particularly at *a* and *b*. In the cat's visual system such fields are generally one millimeter or less in diameter.

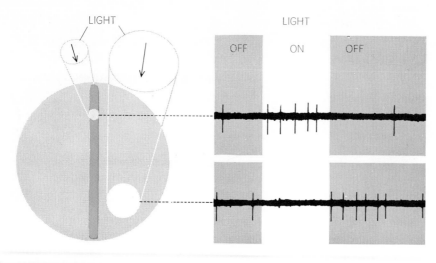

RESPONSE IS WEAK when a circular spot of light is shone on receptive field of a simple cortical cell. Such spots get a vigorous response from retinal and geniculate cells. This cell has a receptive field of type shown at *a* in bottom illustration on preceding page.

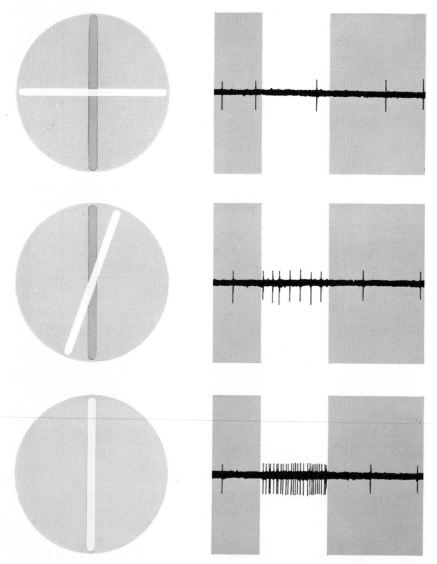

IMPORTANCE OF ORIENTATION to simple cortical cells is indicated by varying responses to a slit of light from a cell preferring a vertical orientation. Horizontal slit *(top)* produces no response, slight tilt a weak response, vertical slit a strong response.

Retinal ganglion cells differ greatly in the size of their receptive-field centers. Cells near the fovea (the part of the retina serving the center of gaze) are specialized for precise discrimination; in the monkey the field centers of these cells may be about the same size as a single cone—an area subtending a few minutes of arc at the cornea. On the other hand, some cells far out in the retinal periphery have field centers up to a millimeter or so in diameter. (In man one millimeter of retina corresponds to an arc of about three degrees in the 180-degree visual field.) Cells with such large receptive-field centers are probably specialized for work in very dim light, since they can sum up messages from a large number of receptors.

Given this knowledge of the kind of visual information brought to the brain by the optic nerve, our first problem was to learn how the messages were handled at the first central way station, the lateral geniculate body. Compared with the retina, the geniculate body is a relatively simple structure. In a sense there is only one synapse involved, since the incoming optic nerve fibers end in cells that send their fibers directly to the visual cortex. Yet in the cat many optic nerve fibers converge on each geniculate cell, and it is reasonable to expect some change in the visual messages from the optic nerve to the geniculate cells.

When we came to study the geniculate body, we found that the cells have many of the characteristics Kuffler described for retinal ganglion cells. Each geniculate cell is driven from a circumscribed retinal region (the receptive field) and has either an "on" center or an "off" center, with an opposing periphery. There are, however, differences between geniculate cells and retinal ganglion cells, the most important of which is the greatly enhanced capacity of the periphery of a geniculate cell's receptive field to cancel the effects of the center. This means that the lateral geniculate cells must be even more specialized than retinal ganglion cells in responding to spatial differences in retinal illumination rather than to the illumination itself. The lateral geniculate body, in short, has the function of increasing the disparity—already present in retinal ganglion cells—between responses to a small, centered spot and to diffuse light.

In contrast to the comparatively simple lateral geniculate body, the cerebral cortex is a structure of stupendous complexity. The cells of this great plate of

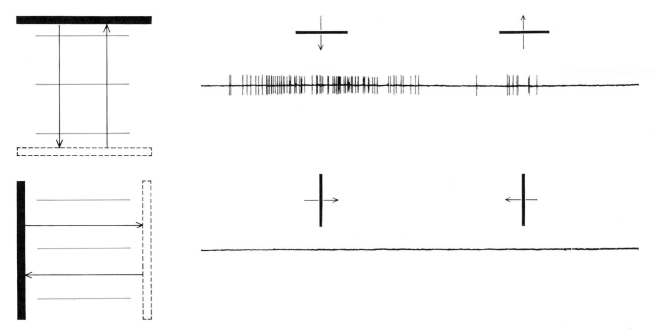

COMPLEX CORTICAL CELL responded vigorously to slow downward movement of a dark, horizontal bar. Upward movement of bar produced a weak response and horizontal movement of a vertical bar produced no response. For other shapes, orientations and movements there are other complex cells showing maximum response. Such cells may figure in perception of form and movement.

gray matter—a structure that would be about 20 square feet in area and a tenth of an inch thick if flattened out—are arranged in a number of more or less distinct layers. The millions of fibers that come in from the lateral geniculate body connect with cortical cells in the layer that is fourth from the top. From here the information is sooner or later disseminated to all layers of the cortex by rich interconnections between them. Many of the cells, particularly those of the third and fifth layers, send their fibers out of the cortex, projecting to centers deep in the brain or passing over to nearby cortical areas for further processing of the visual messages. Our problem was to learn how the information the visual cortex sends out differs from what it takes in.

Most connections between cortical cells are in a direction perpendicular to the surface; side-to-side connections are generally quite short. One might therefore predict that impulses arriving at a particular area of the cortex would exert their effects quite locally. Moreover, the retinas project to the visual cortex (via the lateral geniculate body) in a systematic topologic manner; that is, a given area of cortex gets its input ultimately from a circumscribed area of retina. These two observations suggest that a given cortical cell should have a small receptive field; it should be influenced from a circumscribed retinal region only, just as a geniculate or retinal ganglion cell is. Beyond this the anatomy provides no hint of what the cortex does

with the information it receives about an image on the retina.

In the face of the anatomical complexity of the cortex, it would have been surprising if the cells had proved to have the concentric receptive fields characteristic of cells in the retina and the lateral geniculate body. Indeed, in the cat we have observed no cortical cells with concentric receptive fields; instead there are many different cell types, with fields markedly different from anything seen in the retinal and geniculate cells.

The many varieties of cortical cells may, however, be classified by function into two large groups. One we have called "simple"; the function of these cells is to respond to line stimuli—such shapes as slits, which we define as light lines on a dark background; dark bars (dark lines on a light background), and edges (straight-line boundaries between light and dark regions). Whether or not a given cell responds depends on the orientation of the shape and its position on the cell's receptive field. A bar shone vertically on the screen may activate a given cell, whereas the same cell will fail to respond (but others will respond) if the bar is displaced to one side or moved appreciably out of the vertical. The second group of cortical cells we have called "complex"; they too respond best to bars, slits or edges, provided that, as with simple cells, the shape is suitably oriented for the particular cell under observation. Complex cells, how-

ever, are not so discriminating as to the exact position of the stimulus, provided that it is properly oriented. Moreover, unlike simple cells, they respond with sustained firing to moving lines.

From the preference of simple and complex cells for specific orientation of light stimuli, it follows that there must be a multiplicity of cell types to handle the great number of possible positions and orientations. Wiesel and I have found a large variety of cortical cell responses, even though the number of individual cells we have studied runs only into the hundreds compared with the millions that exist. Among simple cells, the retinal region over which a cell can be influenced—the receptive field—is, like the fields of retinal and geniculate cells, divided into "on" and "off" areas. In simple cells, however, these areas are far from being circularly symmetrical. In a typical example the receptive field consists of a very long and narrow "on" area, which is adjoined on each side by larger "off" regions. The magnitude of an "on" response depends, as with retinal and geniculate cells, on how much either type of region is covered by the stimulating light. A long, narrow slit that just fills the elongated "on" region produces a powerful "on" response. Stimulation with the slit in a different orientation produces a much weaker effect, because the slit is now no longer illuminating all the "on" region but instead includes some of the antagonistic "off" region. A slit at right angles to the optimum orientation for a

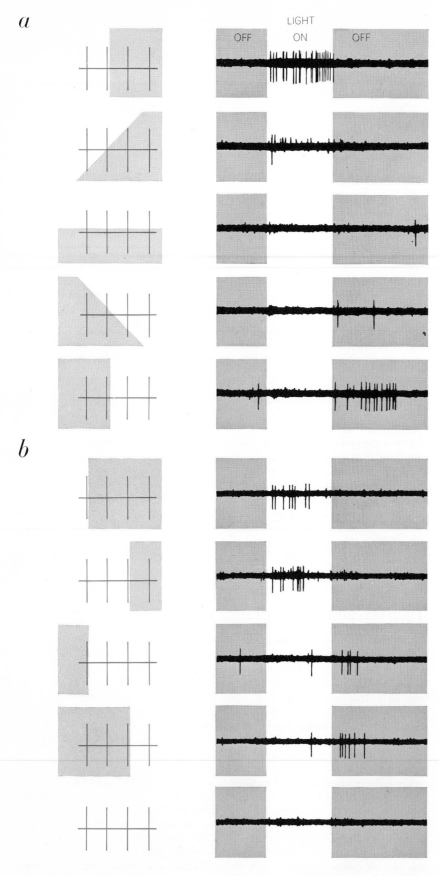

a

LIGHT

OFF   ON   OFF

b

SINGLE COMPLEX CELL showed varying responses to an edge projected on the cell's receptive field in the retina. In group *a* the stimulus was presented in differing orientations. In group *b* all the edges were vertical and all but the last evoked responses regardless of where in the receptive field the light struck. When a large rectangle of light covered entire receptive field, however, as shown at bottom, cell failed to respond.

cell of this type is usually completely ineffective.

In the simple cortical cells the process of pitting these two antagonistic parts of a receptive field against each other is carried still further than it is in the lateral geniculate body. As a rule a large spot of light—or what amounts to the same thing, diffuse light covering the whole retina—evokes no response at all in simple cortical cells. Here the "on" and "off" effects apparently balance out with great precision.

Some other common types of simple receptive fields include an "on" center with a large "off" area to one side and a small one to the other; an "on" and an "off" area side by side; a narrow "off" center with "on" sides; a wide "on" center with narrow "off" sides. All these fields have in common that the border or borders separating "on" and "off" regions are straight and parallel rather than circular [*see bottom illustration on page 13*]. The most efficient stimuli—slits, edges or dark bars—all involve straight lines. Each cell responds best to a particular orientation of line; other orientations produce less vigorous responses, and usually the orientation perpendicular to the optimum evokes no response at all. A particular cell's optimum, which we term the receptive-field orientation, is thus a property built into the cell by its connections. In general the receptive-field orientation differs from one cell to the next, and it may be vertical, horizontal or oblique. We have no evidence that any one orientation, such as vertical or horizontal, is more common than any other.

How can one explain this specificity of simple cortical cells? We are inclined to think they receive their input directly from the incoming lateral geniculate fibers. We suppose a typical simple cell has for its input a large number of lateral geniculate cells whose "on" centers are arranged along a straight line; a spot of light shone anywhere along that line will activate some of the geniculate cells and lead to activation of the cortical cell. A light shone over the entire area will activate all the geniculate cells and have a tremendous final impact on the cortical cell [*see bottom illustration on page 12*].

One can now begin to grasp the significance of the great number of cells in the visual cortex. Each cell seems to have its own specific duties; it takes care of one restricted part of the retina, responds best to one particular shape of stimulus and to one particular orientation. To look at the problem from the opposite direction, for each stimulus—each area of the retina stimulated, each type of line (edge, slit or bar) and each orientation of stimulus—there is a particular set of simple cortical cells that will respond; changing any of the stimulus arrangements will cause a whole new population of cells to respond. The number of populations responding successively as the eye watches a slowly rotating propeller is scarcely imaginable.

Such a profound rearrangement and analysis of the incoming messages might seem enough of a task for a single structure, but it turns out to be only part of what happens in the cortex. The next major transformation involves the cortical cells that occupy what is probably the sixth step in the visual pathway: the complex cells, which are also present in this cortical region and to some extent intermixed with the simple cells.

Complex cells are like simple ones in several ways. A cell responds to a stimulus only within a restricted region of retina: the receptive field. It responds best to the line stimuli (slits, edges or dark bars) and the stimulus must be oriented to suit the cell. But complex fields, unlike the simple ones, cannot be mapped into antagonistic "on" and "off" regions.

A typical complex cell we studied happened to fire to a vertical edge, and it gave "on" or "off" responses depending on whether light was to the left or to the right. Other orientations were almost completely without effect [see illustration on opposite page]. These responses are just what could be expected from a simple cell with a receptive field consisting of an excitatory area separated from an inhibitory one by a vertical boundary. In this case, however, the cell had an additional property that could not be explained by such an arrangement. A vertical edge evoked responses anywhere within the receptive field, "on" responses with light to the left, "off" responses with light to the right. Such behavior cannot be understood in terms of antagonistic "on" and "off" subdivisions of the receptive field, and when we explored the field with small spots we found no such regions. Instead the spot either produced responses at both "on" and "off" or evoked no responses at all.

Complex cells, then, respond like simple cells to one particular aspect of the stimulus, namely its orientation. But when the stimulus is moved, without changing the orientation, a complex cell differs from its simple counterpart chiefly in responding with sustained firing. The firing continues as the stimulus is moved over a substantial retinal area, usually the entire receptive field of the cell, whereas a simple cell will respond to movement only as the stimulus crosses a very narrow boundary separating "on" and "off" regions.

It is difficult to explain this behavior by any scheme in which geniculate cells project directly to complex cells. On the other hand, the findings can be explained fairly well by the supposition that a complex cell receives its input from a large number of simple cells. This supposition requires only that the simple cells have the same field orientation and be all of the same general type. A complex cell responding to vertical edges, for example, would thus receive fibers from simple cells that have vertically oriented receptive fields. All such a scheme needs to have added is the requirement that the retinal positions of these simple fields be arranged throughout the area occupied by the complex field.

The main difficulty with such a scheme is that it presupposes an enormous degree of cortical organization. What a vast network of connections must be needed if a single complex cell is to receive fibers from just the right simple cells, all with the appropriate field arrangements, tilts and positions! Yet there is unexpected and compelling evidence that such a system of connections exists. It comes from a study of what can be called the functional architecture of the cortex. By penetrating with a microelectrode through the cortex in many directions, perhaps many times in a single tiny region of the brain, we learned that the cells are arranged not in a haphazard manner but with a high degree of order. The physiological results show that functionally the cortex is subdivided like a beehive into tiny columns, or segments [see illustration on next page], each of which extends from the surface to the white matter lower in the brain. A column is de-

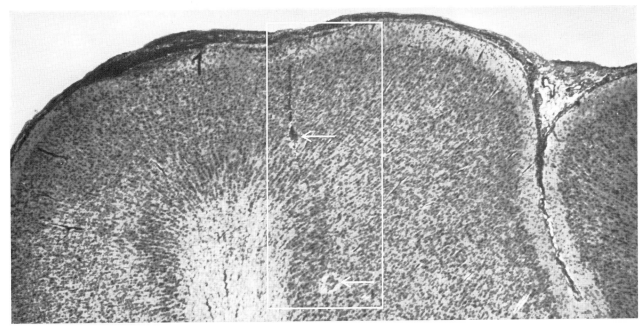

SECTION OF CAT'S VISUAL CORTEX shows track of microelectrode penetration and, at arrows, two points along the track where lesions were made so that it would be possible to ascertain later where the tip of the electrode was at certain times. This section of cortex is from a single gyrus, or fold of the brain; it was six millimeters wide and is shown here enlarged 30 diameters.

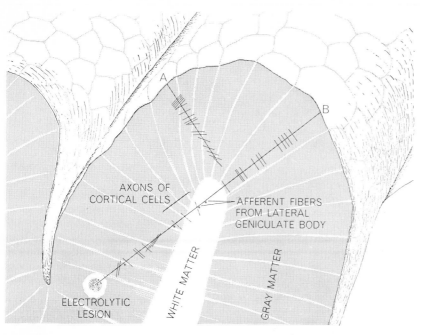

FUNCTIONAL ARRANGEMENT of cells in visual cortex resembled columns, although columnar structure is not apparent under a microscope. Lines *A* and *B* show paths of two microelectrode penetrations; colored lines show receptive-field orientations encountered. Cells in a single column had same orientation; change of orientation showed new column.

fined not by any anatomically obvious wall—no columns are visible under the microscope—but by the fact that the thousands of cells it contains all have the same receptive-field orientation. The evidence for this is that in a typical microelectrode penetration through the cortex the cells—recorded in sequence as the electrode is pushed ahead—all have the same field orientation, provided that the penetration is made in a direction perpendicular to the surface of the cortical segment. If the penetration is oblique, as we pass from column to column we record several cells with one field orientation, then a new sequence of cells with a new orientation, and then still another.

The columns are irregular in cross-sectional shape, and on the average they are about half a millimeter across. In respects other than receptive-field orientation the cells in a particular column tend to differ; some are simple, others complex; some respond to slits, others prefer dark bars or edges.

Returning to the proposed scheme for explaining the properties of complex cells, one sees that gathered together in a single column are the very cells one should expect to be interconnected: cells whose fields have the same orientation and the same general retinal position, although not the same position. Furthermore, it is known from the anatomy that there are rich interconnections between neighboring cells, and the preponderance of these connections in a vertical direction fits well with the long, narrow, more or less cylindrical shape of the columns. This means that a column may be looked on as an independent functional unit of cortex, in which simple cells receive connections from lateral geniculate cells and send projections to complex cells.

It is possible to get an inkling of the part these different cell types play in vision by considering what must be happening in the brain when one looks at a form, such as, to take a relatively simple example, a black square on a white background. Suppose the eyes fix on some arbitrary point to the left of the square. On the reasonably safe assumption that the human visual cortex works something like the cat's and the monkey's, it can be predicted that the near edge of the square will activate a particular group of simple cells, namely cells that prefer edges with light to the left and dark to the right and whose fields are oriented vertically and are so placed on the retina that the boundary between "on" and "off" regions falls exactly along the image of the near edge of the square. Other populations of cells will obviously be called into action by the other three edges of the square. All the cell populations will change if the eye strays from the point fixed on, or if the square is moved while the eye remains stationary, or if the square is rotated.

In the same way each edge will activate a population of complex cells, again cells that prefer edges in a specific orientation. But a given complex cell, unlike a simple cell, will continue to be activated when the eye moves or when the form moves, if the movement is not so large that the edge passes entirely outside the receptive field of the cell, and if there is no rotation. This means that the populations of complex cells affected by the whole square will be to some extent independent of the exact position of the image of the square on the retina.

Each of the cortical columns contains thousands of cells, some with simple fields and some with complex. Evidently the visual cortex analyzes an enormous amount of information, with each small region of visual field represented over and over again in column after column, first for one receptive-field orientation and then for another.

In sum, the visual cortex appears to have a rich assortment of functions. It rearranges the input from the lateral geniculate body in a way that makes lines and contours the most important stimuli. What appears to be a first step in perceptual generalization results from the response of cortical cells to the orientation of a stimulus, apart from its exact retinal position. Movement is also an important stimulus factor; its rate and direction must both be specified if a cell is to be effectively driven.

One cannot expect to "explain" vision, however, from a knowledge of the behavior of a single set of cells, geniculate or cortical, any more than one could understand a wood-pulp mill from an examination of the machine that cuts the logs into chips. We are now studying how still "higher" structures build on the information they receive from these cortical cells, rearranging it to produce an even greater complexity of response.

In all of this work we have been particularly encouraged to find that the areas we study can be understood in terms of comparatively simple concepts such as the nerve impulse, convergence of many nerves on a single cell, excitation and inhibition. Moreover, if the connections suggested by these studies are remotely close to reality, one can conclude that at least some parts of the brain can be followed relatively easily, without necessarily requiring higher mathematics, computers or a knowledge of network theories.

3

THE "VISUAL CLIFF"

ELEANOR J. GIBSON AND RICHARD D. WALK
April 1960

*This simple apparatus is used to investigate depth
perception in different animals. All species thus far
tested seem able to perceive and avoid a sharp drop
as soon as they can move about*

Human infants at the creeping and toddling stage are notoriously prone to falls from more or less high places. They must be kept from going over the brink by side panels on their cribs, gates on stairways and the vigilance of adults. As their muscular coordination matures they begin to avoid such accidents on their own. Common sense might suggest that the child learns to recognize falling-off places by experience—that is, by falling and hurting himself. But is experience really the teacher? Or is the ability to perceive and avoid a brink part of the child's original endowment?

Answers to these questions will throw light on the genesis of space perception in general. Height perception is a special case of distance perception: information in the light reaching the eye provides stimuli that can be utilized for the discrimination both of depth and of receding distance on the level. At what stage of development can an animal respond effectively to these stimuli? Does the onset of such response vary with animals of different species and habitats?

At Cornell University we have been investigating these problems by means of a simple experimental setup that we call a visual cliff. The cliff is a simulated one and hence makes it possible not only to control the optical and other stimuli (auditory and tactual, for instance) but also to protect the experimental subjects. It consists of a board laid across a large sheet of heavy glass which is supported a foot or more above the floor. On one side of the board a sheet of patterned material is placed flush against the undersurface of the glass, giving the glass the appearance as well as the substance of solidity. On the other side a sheet of the same material is laid upon the floor; this side of the board thus becomes the visual cliff.

We tested 36 infants ranging in age from six months to 14 months on the visual cliff. Each child was placed upon the center board, and his mother called him to her from the cliff side and the shallow side successively. All of the 27 infants who moved off the board crawled out on the shallow side at least once; only three of them crept off the brink onto the glass suspended above the pattern on the floor. Many of the infants crawled away from the mother when she called to them from the cliff side; others cried when she stood there, because they could not come to her without crossing an apparent chasm. The experiment thus demonstrated that most human infants can discriminate depth as soon as they can crawl.

The behavior of the children in this situation gave clear evidence of their dependence on vision. Often they would peer down through the glass on the deep side and then back away. Others would pat the glass with their hands, yet despite this tactual assurance of solidity would refuse to cross. It was equally clear that their perception of depth had matured more rapidly than had their locomotor abilities. Many supported themselves on the glass over the deep side as they maneuvered awkwardly on the board; some even backed out onto the glass as they started toward the mother on the shallow side. Were it not for the glass some of the children would have fallen off the board. Evidently infants should not be left close to a brink, no matter how well they may discriminate depth.

This experiment does not prove that the human infant's perception and avoidance of the cliff are innate. Such an interpretation is supported, however, by the experiments with nonhuman infants. On the visual cliff we have observed the behavior of chicks, turtles, rats, lambs, kids, pigs, kittens and dogs. These animals showed various reactions, each of which proved to be characteristic of their species. In each case the reaction is plainly related to the role of vision in the survival of the species, and the varied patterns of behavior suggest something about the role of vision in evolution.

In the chick, for example, depth perception manifests itself with special rapidity. At an age of less than 24 hours the chick can be tested on the visual cliff. It never makes a "mistake" and always hops off the board on the shallow side. Without doubt this finding is related to the fact that the chick, unlike many other young birds, must scratch for itself a few hours after it is hatched.

Kids and lambs, like chicks, can be tested on the visual cliff as soon as they can stand. The response of these animals is equally predictable. No goat or lamb ever stepped onto the glass of the deep side, even at one day of age. When one of these animals was placed upon the glass on the deep side, it displayed characteristic stereotyped behavior. It would refuse to put its feet down and would back up into a posture of defense, its front legs rigid and its hind legs limp. In this state of immobility it could be pushed forward across the glass until its head and field of vision crossed the edge of the surrounding solid surface, whereupon it would relax and spring forward upon the surface.

At the Cornell Behavior Farm a group of experimenters has carried these experiments with kids and goats a step further. They fixed the patterned material to a sheet of plywood and were thus able to adjust the "depth" of the deep side. With the pattern held immediately beneath the glass, the animal would move about the glass freely. With the optical floor dropped more than a foot below the glass, the animal would immediately freeze into its defensive posture. Despite repeated experience of the tactual solidity of the glass, the animals never learned

to function without optical support. Their sense of security or danger continued to depend upon the visual cues that give them their perception of depth.

The rat, in contrast, does not depend predominantly upon visual cues. Its nocturnal habits lead it to seek food largely

by smell, when moving about in the dark, it responds to tactual cues from the stiff whiskers (vibrissae) on its snout. Hooded rats tested on the visual cliff show little preference for the shallow side so long as they can feel the glass with their vibrissae. Placed upon the

KITTEN'S DEPTH PERCEPTION also manifests itself at an early age. Though the animal displays no alarm on the shallow side (*top*), it "freezes" when placed on the glass over the deep side (*bottom*); in some cases it will crawl aimlessly backward in a circle.

glass over the deep side, they move about normally. But when we raise the center board several inches, so that the glass is out of reach of their whiskers, they evince good visual depth-discrimination: 95 to 100 per cent of them descend on the shallow side.

Cats, like rats, are nocturnal animals, sensitive to tactual cues from their vibrissae. But the cat, as a predator, must rely more strongly on its sight. Kittens proved to have excellent depth-discrimination. At four weeks—about the earliest age that a kitten can move about with any facility—they invariably choose the shallow side of the cliff. On the glass over the deep side, they either freeze or circle aimlessly backward until they reach the center board [see illustrations on preceding page].

The animals that showed the poorest performance in our series were the turtles. The late Robert M. Yerkes of Harvard University found in 1904 that aquatic turtles have somewhat poorer depth-discrimination than land turtles. On the visual cliff one might expect an aquatic turtle to respond to the reflections from the glass as it might to water and so prefer the deep side. They showed no such preference: 76 per cent of the aquatic turtles crawled off the board on the shallow side. The relatively large minority that choose the deep side suggests either that this turtle has poorer depth-discrimination than other animals, or that its natural habitat gives it less occasion to "fear" a fall.

All of these observations square with what is known about the life history and ecological niche of each of the animals tested. The survival of a species requires that its members develop discrimination of depth by the time they take up independent locomotion, whether at one day (the chick and the goat), three to four weeks (the rat and the cat) or six to 10 months (the human infant). That such a vital capacity does not depend on possibly fatal accidents of learning in the lives of individuals is consistent with evolutionary theory.

To make sure that no hidden bias was concealed in the design of the visual cliff we conducted a number of control experiments. In one of them we eliminated reflections from the glass by lighting the patterned surfaces from below the glass (to accomplish this we dropped the pattern below the glass on both sides, but more on one side than on the other). The animals—hooded rats—still consistently chose the shallow side. As a test of the role of the patterned surface we

GOATS SHOW DEPTH PERCEPTION at an age of only one day. A kid walks freely on the shallow side (*top*); on the deep side (*middle*) it leaps the "chasm" to safety (*bottom*).

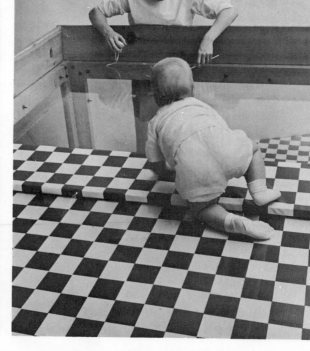

CHILD'S DEPTH PERCEPTION is tested on the visual cliff. The apparatus consists of a board laid across a sheet of heavy glass, with a patterned material directly beneath the glass on one side and several feet below it on the other. Placed on the center board (*top left*), the child crawls to its mother across the "shallow" side (*top right*). Called from the "deep" side, he pats the glass (*bottom left*), but despite this tactual evidence that the "cliff" is in fact a solid surface he refuses to cross over to the mother (*bottom right*).

replaced it on either side of the centerboard with a homogeneous gray surface. Confronted with this choice, the rats showed no preference for either the shallow or the deep side. We also eliminated the optical difference between the two sides of the board by placing the patterned surface directly against the undersurface of the glass on each side. The rats then descended without preference to either side. When we lowered the pattern 10 inches below the glass on each side, they stayed on the board.

We set out next to determine which of two visual cues plays the decisive role in depth perception. To an eye above the center board the optical pattern on the two sides differs in at least two important respects. On the deep side distance decreases the size and spacing of the pattern elements projected on the retina. "Motion parallax," on the other hand, causes the pattern elements on the shallow side to move more rapidly across the field of vision when the animal moves its position on the board or moves its head, just as nearby objects seen from a moving car appear to pass by more quickly than distant ones [*see illustration on following page*]. To eliminate the potential distance cue provided by pattern density we increased the size and spacing of the pattern elements on the deep side in proportion to its distance from the eye [*see top illustration at right*]. With only the cue of motion parallax to guide them, adult rats still preferred the shallow side, though not so strongly as in the standard experiment. Infant rats chose the shallow side nearly 100 per cent of the time under both conditions, as did day-old chicks. Evidently both species can discriminate depth by differential motion alone, with no aid from texture density and probably little help from other cues. The perception of distance by binocular parallax, which doubtless plays an important part in human behavior, would not seem to have a significant role, for example, in the depth perception of chicks and rats.

To eliminate the cue of motion parallax we placed the patterned material directly against the glass on either side of the board but used smaller and more densely spaced pattern-elements on the cliff side. Both young and adult hooded rats preferred the side with the larger pattern, which evidently "signified" a nearer surface. Day-old chicks, however, showed no preference for the larger pattern. It may be that learning plays some part in the preference exhibited by the

rats, since the young rats were tested at a somewhat older age than the chicks. This supposition is supported by the results of our experiments with animals reared in the dark.

The effects of early experience and of such deprivations as dark-rearing represent important clues to the relative roles of maturation and learning in animal behavior. The first experiments along this line were performed by K. S. Lashley and James T. Russell at the University of Chicago in 1934. They tested light-reared and dark-reared rats on a "jumping stand" from which they induced animals to leap toward a platform placed at varying distances. Upon finding that both groups of animals jumped with a force closely correlated with distance, they concluded that depth perception in rats is innate. Other investi-

gators have pointed out, however, that the dark-reared rats required a certain amount of "pretraining" in the light before they could be made to jump. Since the visual-cliff technique requires no pretraining, we employed it to test groups of light-reared and dark-reared hooded rats. At the age of 90 days both groups showed the same preference for the shallow side of the apparatus, confirming Lashley's and Russell's conclusion.

Recalling our findings in the young rat, we then took up the question of whether the dark-reared rats relied upon motion parallax or upon contrast in texture density to discriminate depth. When the animals were confronted with the visual cliff, cued only by motion parallax, they preferred the shallow side, as had the light-reared animals. When the

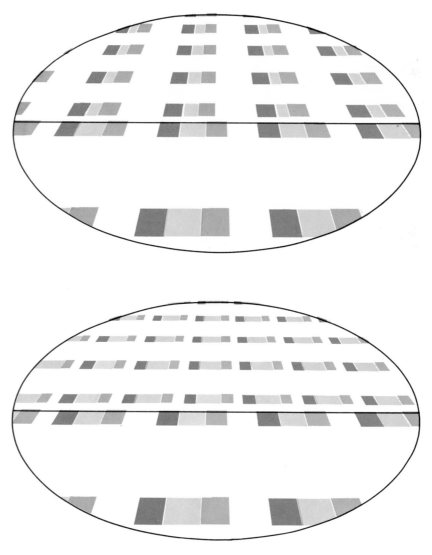

SEPARATION OF VISUAL CUES is shown in these diagrams. Pattern density is held constant (*top*) by using a larger pattern on the low side of the cliff; the drop in optical motion (motion parallax) remains. Motion parallax is equalized (*bottom*) by placing patterns at same level; the smaller pattern on one side preserves difference in spacing.

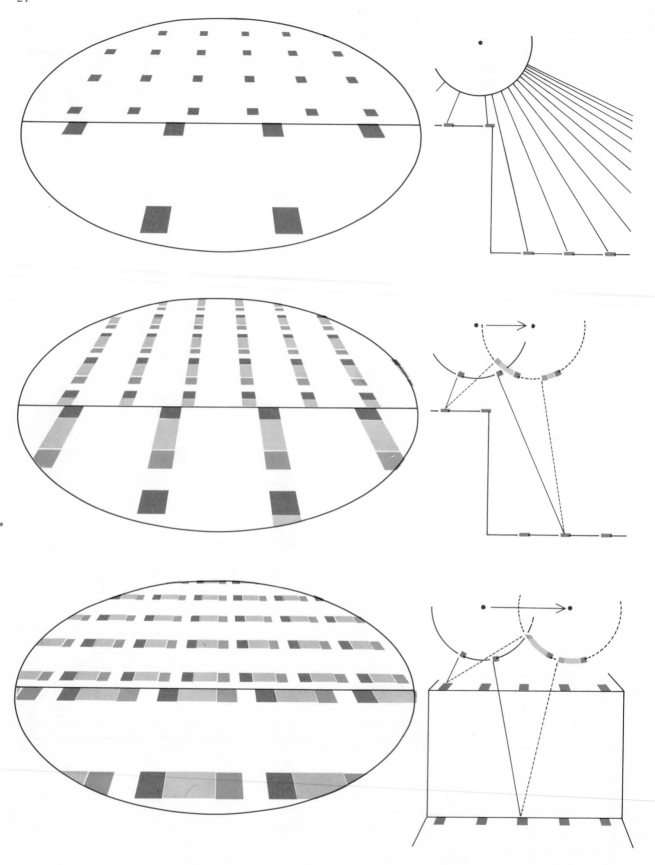

TWO TYPES OF VISUAL DEPTH-CUE are diagrammed schematically on this page. Ellipses approximate the visual field of an animal standing near the edge of the cliff and looking toward it; diagrams at right give the geometrical explanation of differences in the fields. The spacing of the pattern elements (*solid color*) decreases sharply beyond the edge of the cliff (*top*). The optical motion (*shaded color*) of the elements as the animal moves forward (*center*) or sideways (*bottom*) shows a similar drop-off.

IMPORTANCE OF PATTERN in depth perception is shown in these photographs. Of two patterns set at the same depth, normal rats almost invariably preferred the larger (*top row and bottom* *left*), presumably because it "signified" a nearer and therefore safer surface. Confronted with two patternless surfaces set at different depths, the animals displayed no preference (*bottom right*).

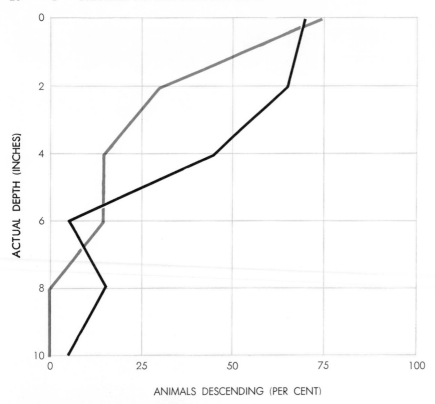

CONTROL EXPERIMENT measured the effect on rats of reflections on the glass of the apparatus. The percentage of animals leaving the center board decreased with increasing depth in much the same way, whether glass was present (*black curve*) or not (*colored curve*).

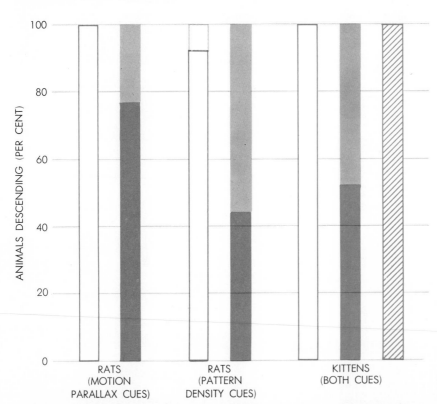

DARK-REARING EXPERIMENTS reveal the order in which different depth-cues are utilized as animals mature. Animals reared in the light (*open bars*) all strongly preferred the shallow side (*color*) to the deep side (*gray*). Dark-reared rats (*solid bars*), utilizing motion parallax alone, still preferred the shallow side; pattern density alone elicited no preference. Dark-reared kittens also showed no preference, because of temporary blindness. After seven days in the light all of them chose the shallow side (*hatched bar*).

choice was cued by pattern density, however, they departed from the pattern of the normal animals and showed no significant preference [*see bottom illustration at left*]. The behavior of dark-reared rats thus resembles that of the day-old chicks, which also lack visual experience. It seems likely, therefore, that of the two cues only motion parallax is an innate cue for depth discrimination. Responses to differential pattern-density may be learned later.

One cannot automatically extrapolate these results to other species. But experiments with dark-reared kittens indicate that in these animals, too, depth perception matures independently of trial and error learning. In the kitten, however, light is necessary for normal visual maturation. Kittens reared in the dark to the age of 27 days at first crawled or fell off the center board equally often on the deep and shallow sides. Placed upon the glass over the deep side, they did not back in a circle like normal kittens but showed the same behavior that they had exhibited on the shallow side. Other investigators have observed equivalent behavior in dark-reared kittens; they bump into obstacles, lack normal eye movement and appear to "stare" straight ahead. These difficulties pass after a few days in the light. We accordingly tested the kittens every day. By the end of a week they were performing in every respect like normal kittens. They showed the same unanimous preference for the shallow side. Placed upon the glass over the deep side, they balked and circled backward to a visually secure surface. Repeated descents to the deep side, and placement upon the glass during their "blind" period, had not taught them that the deep side was "safe." Instead they avoided it more and more consistently. The initial blindness of dark-reared kittens makes them ideal subjects for studying the maturation of depth perception. With further study it should be possible to determine which cues they respond to first and what kinds of visual experience accelerate or retard the process of maturation.

From our first few years of work with the visual cliff we are ready to venture the rather broad conclusion that a seeing animal will be able to discriminate depth when its locomotion is adequate, even when locomotion begins at birth. But many experiments remain to be done, especially on the role of different cues and on the effects of different kinds of early visual experience.

4

BRAIN DAMAGE BY ASPHYXIA AT BIRTH

WILLIAM F. WINDLE
October 1969

In both monkey and human infants handicaps that arise from such asphyxia seem to disappear with time. Experiments with monkeys, however, demonstrate that asphyxia permanently damages the brain

Birth is a normal physiological event. Most animals that bear live young pay no more heed to it than they do to their everyday activities. The human animal is exceptional. He has come to look on the time of birth as one of the most critical in the life of both mother and child, and rightly so. There are many things that can go wrong with the delivery of the human infant. Not the least of the hazards is asphyxia that can lead to brain damage and possibly cerebral palsy and mental retardation. It is this hazard that I shall discuss here.

Asphyxia is a condition resulting from a disturbance of the respiratory mechanism. It has been defined as a state of suspended animation due to a lack of oxygen in the blood. In the fetus at birth it involves more than a lack of oxygen (hypoxemia). The blood of an asphyxiated newborn infant may not only contain virtually no oxygen but also contain excessive amounts of carbon dioxide and lactic acid, which lower its pH (that is, make it acid). The infant's heartbeat will have slowed, its blood pressure may be alarmingly reduced and it cannot begin to breathe. This combination of events is termed asphyxia neonatorum. When such asphyxia occurs, immediate resuscitation measures are of course imperative. Several stages of birth asphyxia are recognized. The hypoxemia is not always prolonged to the point where spontaneous efforts to breathe stop (terminal apnea). When asphyxiation stops short of apnea, the infant will not need resuscitation and its body functions may be only temporarily depressed.

Asphyxia neonatorum is an unnatural event that in human infants may come about because of unavoidable conditions. Among them is the fact that the human infant has a large head. Evolution has given man a highly developed

brain and a skull that attains such a size at the end of gestation that its delivery is an unusual biological problem. Today many women have come to fear childbirth and to demand relief from their physician. Sometimes the well-being of the fetus is unwittingly placed in jeopardy in ensuring the mother's comfort and peace of mind. Not all factors that complicate the delivery of the human infant are clearly perceived; some, however, are recognizable and can be avoided.

The role of asphyxia neonatorum in brain damage has been debated for more than a century. As early as 1861 an English physician, W. J. Little, suggested a relationship between asphyxia during birth and neurological and mental disorders of infancy. His view was accepted by few and had little impact on medical practice, although from time to time it was advocated by others. This long debate illustrates what little influence retrospective clinical observations have had on medical opinion. In 1957 C. J. Bailey, speaking at a Puerto Rico conference titled "Neurological and Psychological Deficits of Asphyxia Neonatorum," pointed out that retrospective clinical studies can never logically answer the question of whether asphyxia at birth causes brain damage resulting in symptoms of cerebral palsy and mental retardation or whether other factors causing cerebral palsy and mental retardation also induce asphyxia. Any child with cerebral palsy or mental retardation who also presents a history of asphyxia at birth can be used as an example to support either proposition. The answer can be found only by experiment.

Over the past 15 years much experimental work has been done on asphyxia neonatorum. Obviously such investigations cannot be pursued with the

human fetus; controlled experiments with animals have been designed. These experiments, in conjunction with clinical observations, have made us better able to evaluate the role of asphyxia neonatorum in brain damage and propose measures of prevention.

Earlier experiments had been conducted on asphyxia at birth in guinea pigs. Brain damage and impairment of learning ability were found, but the asphyxia required was severe and the relevance of experiments with rodents to findings in human infants was questioned. Therefore when adequate facilities and support became available workers in the field turned their attention to nonhuman primates. The experiments I shall review here were conducted in two National Institutes of Health laboratories (one in Bethesda, Md., and the other in San Juan, Puerto Rico) and more recently at the New York University Medical Center.

We chose the rhesus monkey (*Macaca mulatta*) for studying fetal physiology and its experimental alteration. We used more than 500 fetal and newborn monkeys, about a fifth of which were asphyxiated during birth. Before I turn to the experiments it will be helpful to compare the monkey's birth with the birth of the human infant. There are marked differences that bear on the relevance of comparisons between the two, but there are also many similarities.

Spontaneous neurological deficits are practically unknown among rhesus monkeys born in their natural habitat or in colonies housed in laboratories. In this respect the monkeys differ from human beings. There are a good many defective human offspring and, more important, the techniques of modern medicine can keep them alive. If defective monkeys are conceived, they die at birth and disappear from the monkey population.

Most monkey births occur at night, as is the case with human beings. Labor is short: an hour or less. The female squats and drops the infant on the ground. During delivery most of the blood in the placenta passes to the infant and, as the uterus continues to contract after birth, the placenta is expelled. Thereupon the female severs the umbilical cord with her teeth and, like most other mammals, eats much of the placenta. Human infants are born in much the same way in many parts of the world. The woman delivers, often unassisted, in the squatting position, and the infant, being below her, recovers most of the blood from the vessels of the placenta and the umbilical cord. I would not recommend that women revert to primitive ways, certainly not to chewing the umbilical cord to sever it (a practice that is still encountered in some places). Nevertheless, in any delivery it is important to keep the umbilical cord intact until the placenta has been delivered. To clamp the cord immediately is equivalent to subjecting the infant to a massive hemorrhage, because almost a fourth of the fetal blood is in the placental circuit at birth. Depriving

the infant of that much blood can be a factor in exacerbating an incipient hypoxemia and can thus contribute to the danger of asphyxial brain damage.

In advanced countries, of course, the supine position of delivery is used to enable the attending physician or midwife to observe the birth conveniently and to assist if necessary. The squatting position, in addition to allowing the infant to receive the placental blood from above, has other advantages over the supine position. It avoids compression of the blood vessels supplying the placenta, which occurs in the supine patient when the gravid uterus tilts back against the pelvis. Delivery while the woman is lying on her side, however, can also avoid such compression and prevent the infant's oxygen supply from being sharply reduced. Doubtless this position would be more acceptable to American women than the squatting one.

Monkeys offer a number of benefits in experiments on asphyxia at birth. Many of the variables that cannot be avoided in human births can be controlled. Anesthetic drugs that might affect the infant's ability to begin breath-

ing need not be administered. The production of asphyxia can be timed with some accuracy and terminated at precisely the desired moment. Most important, after observations of the behavior of a monkey that has been asphyxiated and resuscitated have been completed, the brain of the monkey can be prepared for histological examination, thus providing the kind of neuropathological material that can rarely be obtained from human subjects.

We began our experiments by inducing asphyxia in infant monkeys near the end of gestation (which lasts about six months). The fetus and its surrounding membranes were removed by Cesarean section after the mother had been given a local anesthetic. Stimulated by the asphyxia imposed by its removal from the mother, the fetus attempted to breathe while it was still enveloped in the surrounding membranes. These respiratory movements continued for eight or nine minutes. When they had stopped, the membranes were opened, a tube was inserted into the monkey's trachea and at a predetermined time artificial respiration with oxygen was started. This was continued until the infant monkey began

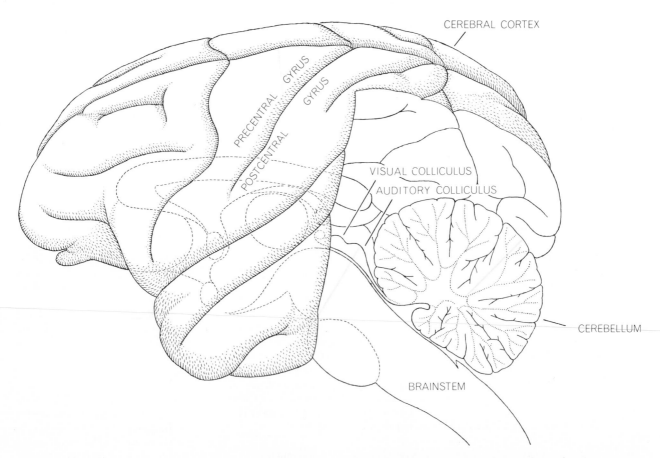

INJURIES of the monkey brain are produced by asphyxiation for varying periods. Lines (*color*) indicate regions that are often severely damaged by asphyxiation during birth. Asphyxia lasting more than 12 minutes creates lesions in the auditory colliculus and in deeper brain structures but does not affect the visual colliculus. It also causes degeneration of cells in the cerebellum and sometimes in the precentral gyrus of the cerebral cortex, a part of the brain concerned with such functions as memory and learning.

to breathe. In some experiments asphyxiation was halted before the monkey's efforts to breathe had stopped, so that no resuscitation was required. Other monkeys were delivered by Cesarean section but were not asphyxiated; these animals and some that were born spontaneously served as controls.

The period of asphyxiation ranged from four minutes to more than 21 minutes. Some of the more severely asphyxiated monkeys died soon after birth. Others were killed for neuropathological studies after as little as a few days and as much as several years. A few are still living more than 10 years after asphyxiation.

Both the experimental monkeys and the controls were raised by technicians, when necessary in an oxygen-enriched atmosphere. Periodically the animals were examined and given tests to evaluate their neurological status. The experimental procedures and the monkeys' behavior and reactions were recorded with motion pictures, which proved invaluable for later review. For the neuropathological studies each brain was sliced into as many as 5,000 sections for microscopic examination. Sections were also made at representative levels of the spinal cord.

One of our first aims was to find out how short a period of asphyxia will leave a mark and how long a period is compatible with survival. In two monkeys that had been asphyxiated for only six minutes at birth and had not needed resuscitation we detected what we termed "minimal" structural brain damage, but there was no appreciable deficit in function. At the other extreme was a monkey that had been asphyxiated for more than 21 minutes at birth and had been in coma until it was killed after three days. Nearly all parts of its brain showed severe damage. Most of our observations were made on the brains of animals that had been asphyxiated for eight minutes or more. (More than eight minutes must elapse during asphyxiation before resuscitation becomes necessary.) We found no lesions in the brains of the control monkeys.

In monkeys that had been asphyxiated for eight to 12 minutes there was loss of nerve cells in the thalamus and the inferior colliculus of the midbrain (both are centers that receive nerve impulses concerned with general body sensations and hearing and relay them to the appropriate higher centers) and in some other groups of cells in the brain stem. Symmetrical lesions were produced on both sides of the brain. They were sharp-

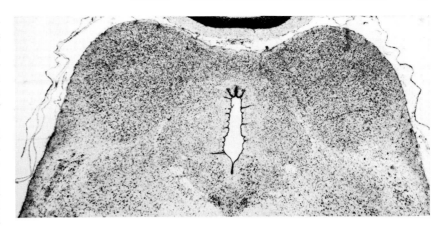

NORMAL COLLICULUS consists of densely packed nerve cells that relay nerve impulses related to hearing originating in the structures of the ear to the higher brain centers.

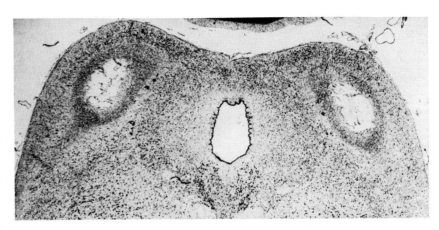

DAMAGED COLLICULUS from a monkey that was asphyxiated during birth nearly five years previously is pitted by cavities (left and right) left by cells that disintegrated.

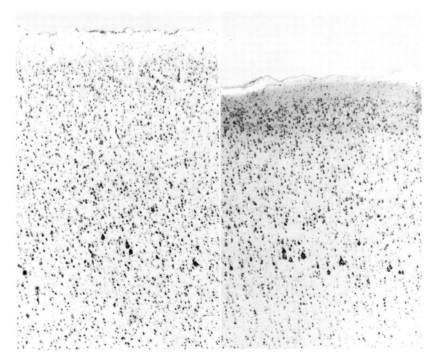

PRECENTRAL GYRUS normally consists of a thick structure of cells (left) organized into layers. Asphyxia at birth causes the precentral gyrus to atrophy (right), because cells in this structure are linked to those in the thalamus by fibers. When asphyxia destroys the cells of the thalamus, both the linking fibers and cells of gyrus degenerate and disappear.

ly circumscribed by unaffected tissue and showed no hemorrhages. Most other parts of the brain, including the motor components of the spinal cord, the cerebellum and the cerebral cortex, were also unaffected.

Monkeys asphyxiated at birth whose brains were affected in this pattern displayed abnormal neurological signs after resuscitation. They had trouble righting themselves and for a time could not move about easily. Their limb movements were uncoordinated. All of them had trouble feeding because they could not suck. These abnormalities eventually disappeared, often within a few days and at most within a few weeks. The electroencephalogram of the monkeys, when it was affected at all by such asphyxia, quickly became normal.

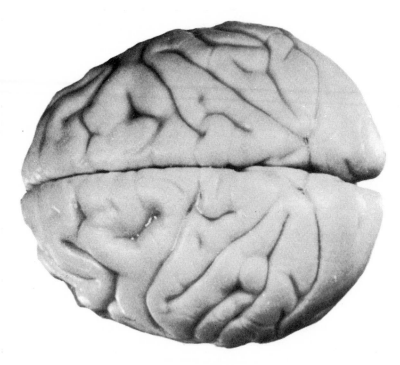

NORMAL BRAIN of a rhesus monkey that was not asphyxiated has a fully developed cerebral cortex. The convolutions of the cortex have a characteristically rounded form.

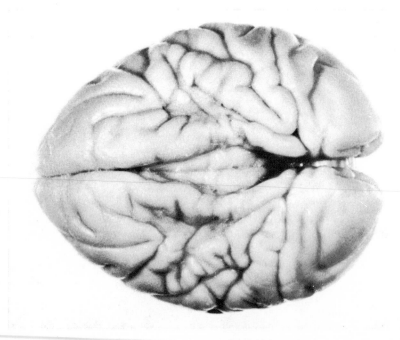

ABNORMAL BRAIN of a three-month-old monkey that had been asphyxiated and revived, but suffered respiratory distress, is shriveled because lack of oxygen killed tissue.

These monkeys may be comparable to human infants who encounter some degree of asphyxia at birth, have low Apgar scores (an index of the newborn infant's general condition) but recover without apparent neurological deficit. It is generally believed that such infants are normal. If one could inspect their brains as we examined the brains of our monkeys, one would probably find the same kind of lesions. It is no longer acceptable to assume that the human fetus or newborn infant is so resistant to oxygen deficiency that it will escape harm from a short exposure to asphyxia neonatorum. If the infant's brain can be compared to the monkey's, asphyxia of such duration that resuscitation was required will certainly have damaged it. The damage, although it is minimal, will be permanent even when it is clinically noticeable for only a short time or when it produces no symptoms at all. What effect such minimal brain damage will have as the child matures is not known.

Asphyxia lasting more than 12 minutes during the monkey's birth damaged brain structures more extensively and caused more pronounced functional deficits. The basic lesions of the thalamus, the inferior colliculus and the brain stem were more severe. They consisted of regions where nerve cells had degenerated and in time had been replaced by scars surrounded by normal tissue. Furthermore, there were new centers of destruction in the basal ganglia, the cerebellum and the spinal cord. The cerebral cortex and the primary motor nuclei remained less damaged than other regions. (This was true even in the brain of the monkey that had sustained more than 21 minutes of asphyxia.) The white matter in the brain and the spinal cord was not affected directly, although tracts of nerve fibers associated with cells that had been destroyed by asphyxia had themselves degenerated.

All the monkeys that had been asphyxiated during birth for more than 12 minutes and had to be resuscitated exhibited functional deficits that persisted for some time. Many required intensive nursing care. The most seriously injured animals presented symptoms resembling those encountered in human beings with cerebral palsy.

The amount of brain damage and the extent of functional loss were sometimes increased by complicating factors associated with asphyxia neonatorum or arising afterward. Some of these factors are premature birth, postnatal respiratory distress accompanied by so-called hyaline membrane disease, cerebral hemorrhages, swelling of the brain and the neuropathological condition known as kernicterus.

Inadequacy of lung function is often encountered in prematurely born infants. The establishment and maintenance of breathing depends on the immediate expansion and activation of the alveoli, or air sacs. The lungs attain a state of development that can support breathing well in advance of a normal full-term birth. There is a point in time, however, before which full efficiency of the pulmonary mechanism has not been attained, and if birth occurs prematurely, the lungs cannot adequately oxygenate the blood. The infant turns blue and enters a state of respiratory distress.

Postnatal respiratory distress in the monkey resembles such distress in human infants. It is manifested by rapid gasping and by inward movement of the edges of the rib cage, often accompanied by audible grunts. The monkey is pale and, even when it is kept in an atmosphere enriched with oxygen, its respiration occasionally fails and it turns blue. Respiratory distress arose spontaneously in only four out of 90 of our nonasphyxiated infant monkeys, and three of these were so premature that their lungs were incapable of normal function. In contrast, the incidence of respiratory distress was high (50 percent) among 68 monkeys that had suffered asphyxia neonatorum or other kinds of experimentally induced crisis.

Some of the monkeys exhibiting respiratory distress and requiring intensive nursing care in incubators supplied with oxygen showed evidence of added neurological deficits. When their brains were examined later, certain regions of the cerebral cortex were found to have undergone marked degeneration. Thus it appears that postnatal respiratory distress can increase the brain damage of asphyxia neonatorum, and although it is not the primary cause of damage in such disorders as cerebral palsy and mental retardation, it is surely an important contributing factor.

When the lungs of some of the monkeys that had failed to survive were examined, membranes were found in the alveoli similar to those seen in some human infants who are said to have died of hyaline membrane disease. Such membranes interfere with the normal exchange of carbon dioxide and oxygen in the alveoli. They were not encountered in the lungs of monkeys that had not been asphyxiated. The formation of hyaline membranes appears to be a manifestation of abnormal pulmonary function. This condition is therefore not really a

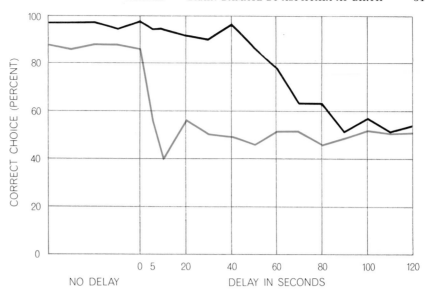

TEST PERFORMANCE shows that monkeys with atrophied brain tissue have a diminished ability to remember. In this test experimental and control monkeys watched through a plastic window as a food pellet was placed in one of two covered containers. The window was then opened so that the monkey could take the food. If the opening of the window was delayed for five seconds or more, the monkeys that had suffered asphyxia 10 years earlier (*colored curve*) reached for the food receptacle only about 50 percent of the time, a record that was no better than what would have been expected on the basis of random choice.

disease but an effect of the asphyxia. It can be prevented but not cured.

As for the complicating factor of cerebral hemorrhage, it is widely believed asphyxia neonatorum produces little hemorrhages in the brain, because they are sometimes found after death in human infants who had suffered asphyxia at birth. The belief that hemorrhages in the brain are the result of asphyxiation is so firmly held in some places (notably France) that if an infant is found dead in its crib with its face up, and if postmortem examination by the medical examiner discloses hemorrhages, the death is likely to be considered homicide by suffocation. Experimental findings in monkeys place brain hemorrhages of the newborn in a different light.

The asphyxiation of monkeys produced no hemorrhages, large or small. The duration of asphyxia made no difference; hemorrhages were absent from the brain of the one monkey that had been resuscitated after more than 21 minutes of asphyxia. Even monkeys asphyxiated so long that they could not be resuscitated showed no cerebral hemorrhages. On the other hand, little hemorrhages were sometimes found in the brains of asphyxiated monkeys that had been resuscitated but then for one reason or another, days or even weeks later, had difficulties in breathing that led gradually to their death. Hemorrhages of this kind must be caused by factors other than the lack of oxygen.

Premature birth is said to enhance the likelihood of cerebral hemorrhage. Traumatic delivery may also be an important cause of such hemorrhage. We observed brain hemorrhages in a monkey whose head had had to be extracted manually during a breech birth (a feet-first delivery). Human infants may be more susceptible to traumatic birth injury and brain hemorrhage than monkeys because of their larger heads. The use of drugs to strengthen uterine contractions and hasten delivery can cause bleeding from the vessels of the brain. Oxytocin administered to a gravid monkey to induce labor was responsible for hemorrhages in such deep-seated fetal brain structures as the globus pallidus.

Some neuropathologists believe swelling, or edema, of the brain is a primary cause of brain lesions. Other investigators have reported that edema of the fetal brain was induced by experimental interference with the passage of oxygen across the placenta in monkeys. Our experimental asphyxiation of monkeys during birth, however, did not result in any swelling that could be identified at any time after their resuscitation. It seems probable that edema of the brain at birth is not an important cause of brain damage.

Kernicterus is characterized by groups of nerve cells with a canary yellow color. This condition is related to high levels in the blood of the bile pigment bilirubin. A high bilirubin level (hyperbilirubinemia) is manifested by jaundice and

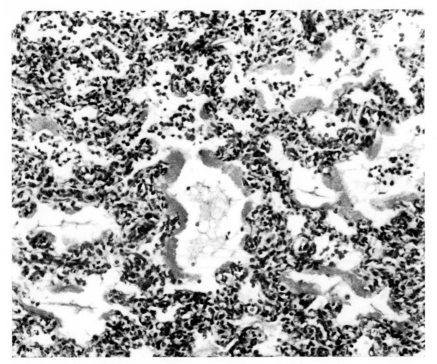

HYALINE MEMBRANE appears as a dark lining inside the lung sacs in this micrograph. It is widely believed the hyaline membrane causes asphyxia at birth. The author proposes that, rather than being a cause of asphyxia, the membrane is the result of asphyxia.

occurs in infants with such disorders as Rh incompatibility. Sometimes extraordinary efforts are made to ameliorate hyperbilirubinemia in human infants in the belief that the excessive amount of bilirubin can produce brain damage. We found no experimental evidence that hyperbilirubinemia per se causes the lesions that have been associated with kernicterus.

When the level of bilirubin was experimentally elevated in the blood of newborn monkeys, a marked jaundice developed, but no kernicterus. An episode of asphyxia during birth superimposed on hyperbilirubinemia did, however, bring about a full-blown kernicterus. It is true that hyperbilirubinemia is associated with the reduced ability of tissues to utilize oxygen, and that it can thus compound the metabolic disturbances caused by asphyxia or other conditions. These observations suggest that when hyperbilirubinemia is present, the emphasis should be placed less on relieving the jaundice than on avoiding or preventing asphyxia. Maneuvers aimed at eliminating or reducing excess bilirubin in blood of the fetus may only exacerbate other conditions that may give rise to asphyxia. Such maneuvers may produce the same brain damage or even worse damage but without the telltale yellow color of kernicterus.

Most of our experiments on asphyxia neonatorum in monkeys were designed

with the hope of avoiding these various complicating conditions. One of our major concerns was to determine what effects asphyxia neonatorum might have on the individual as he matured. It is known that children with some forms of brain damage arising from difficulties at birth show improvement over a period of time. Credit is often given to intensive therapy, but many instances of spontaneous improvement are known.

The briefly asphyxiated infant monkeys with minimal brain damage lost their signs of neurological deficit. Even those whose brains had been severely damaged by more prolonged asphyxiation, including several that had experienced other difficulties after birth, exhibited substantial improvement in their physical condition in due course. The extent of this "recovery" was surprising because no replacement of the nerve cells destroyed by asphyxia neonatorum could be expected. Only after we had made thorough histological studies of the brains of the animals that had been allowed to reach adolescence or adulthood did the significance of the apparent recovery become clear.

Seventeen monkeys were selected for a study of changes in neurological status over a period of time. All of them had shown marked neurological deficits on the first day after resuscitation. Seven of them had turned blue after birth, and two had been in coma. None could suck,

and six showed impaired swallowing. All 17 monkeys tended to be lethargic. They could not right themselves but lay on their side and made uncoordinated flailing movements of their arms and legs when they were disturbed. Normal newborn monkeys can right themselves and crawl in a few hours; a few can stand, although they are unsteady when they try to walk.

During the first week or two it was necessary to keep most of these asphyxiated monkeys in incubators in order to control their body temperature and to be able to administer oxygen on occasion. Some required nursing care around the clock. They slept most of the time but made random movements when they were handled. When they awoke, their crying was weak. Three of them had minor seizures of forelimbs and five had generalized seizures of the trunk and the extremities, accompanied in two cases by salivation and vocalization.

By the end of the first or second week the condition of most of the monkeys showed some improvement. Although they could not right themselves, they maintained a sprawling attitude when they were placed in the prone position. They did not move, however, until they had been stimulated. Then their attempts to progress forward were weak, their limb movements being uncoordinated and tremulous. They could not localize sounds. They were still quite helpless.

Some of the early neurological deficits gradually disappeared or were masked as the monkeys matured. The adjustment to handicaps began to be evident during the first month. Normal monkeys a month old are active, alert and highly emotional. They run, climb and jump, and are more advanced in many ways than human children three or four years old. The month-old asphyxiated monkeys, on the other hand, were dull, slow and generally inactive. They lacked curiosity about surrounding objects and were undisturbed by strange environments. Their motor functions were not normal. Their limb movements were imperfectly coordinated, their forelimbs often acting independently of their hindquarters. Some of the infant monkeys had marked peculiarities of locomotion. They hopped forward like a rabbit, using their hind limbs as a pivot. One monkey had such marked spasticity of the forelimbs that it used its limbs as crutches in hopping. Some of the month-old monkeys still had difficulty sucking. Seizures were no longer seen and electroencephalograms showed few abnormalities.

In most cases the functional defects

gradually became less noticeable. The daily care of one animal, however, was so burdensome that it was killed at 10 months. The rest were permitted to live until adolescence or maturity; five of them are still alive nine to 11 years after asphyxiation at birth. This is about a third of their normal life-span.

The adjustment of the monkeys to the neurological deficits of infancy reached a plateau after three or four years. The residual deficits of the surviving animals are now inadequate manual dexterity and a reduced level of spontaneous activity. The monkeys find it difficult to pick up small morsels of food and prefer to feed themselves as dogs do. They can run, climb and jump when forced, but usually they do not choose to do so. They simply do not engage in all the activities of normal rhesus monkeys. Nevertheless, casual inspection of them in their cages reveals little or nothing of an abnormal nature. This was the case in all of the monkeys that had survived for a long period, including the 12 that were killed for brain studies.

Sections of these brains showed the same pattern of lesions found in the brains of the monkeys killed a few days to a few months after resuscitation. The original lesions of asphyxia appeared as shrunken scars or even cavities. There was no evidence of structural "repair" of the brain tissue. Indeed, there was more loss than we had encountered in the brains of asphyxiated monkeys killed soon after birth. A widespread depletion of nerve-cell populations in regions that had not been affected by the initial asphyxiation had developed. This was particularly noticeable in certain regions of the cerebral cortex, but it was also encountered in parts of the thalamus, the basal ganglia and the brain stem, and in the dorsal regions of the spinal cord. The cell loss was not accompanied by scar formation, as it had been after the primary asphyxia lesions. Nerve cells of these initially intact regions simply were not there. It is probable that their disappearance from the cerebral cortex had come about because nerve cells in the thalamus had been destroyed by the asphyxia at birth and their nerve fibers, which radiate from the thalamus to the cortex, had degenerated. The nerve cells of the cortex on which these fibers had terminated atrophied and disappeared.

The monkeys that showed this secondary brain damage had been severely affected by the primary losses incurred with asphyxia neonatorum, and early in life they had exhibited symptoms com-

parable to human neurological disorders, including cerebral palsy. The symptoms gradually lessened, and in time most of them disappeared. (This is strikingly evident in our motion-picture records.) In view of the extensive nerve-cell loss that had been sustained by the brain it is remarkable that so few physical handicaps persisted. The main structural defects involved centers that process signals from the environment and others that control the association and integration of information. The motor elements withstood the effects of asphyxia neonatorum to a greater degree. This leads one to wonder if such functions as memory and learning were affected by the physical damage so apparent in the microscope slides.

In undertaking to answer this question Jeri A. Sechzer tested four of the surviving experimental monkeys against four similarly reared normal monkeys for their ability to execute a standard delayed-response test. The testing was done in their home cage, to the front of which a special device had been attached. Through a plastic window the monkeys could watch the experimenter place a banana-flavored food pellet in one of two closed wells. After a delay of between five and 120 seconds the window was raised and the monkey was expected to open the correct well to get the reward of food. The study clearly demonstrated a memory deficit in the

monkeys eight to 10 years after asphyxia [see illustration on page 31].

How can these findings in monkeys be related to human infants who survive asphyxia neonatorum and initially have alarming neurological deficits? Significant data on the question are now available from the Collaborative Perinatal Research Program supported by the National Institutes of Health. Approximately 1.5 percent of all the infants who had been born on the obstetrical services of the 14 participating U.S. medical institutions were found to have neurological abnormalities at the end of their first year. If the neurological examinations had been conducted before the infants were a year old, the number with detectable deficits would undoubtedly have been much greater; for example, 21 percent of the infants in the study had low Apgar scores at birth.

The findings were not considered to be particularly alarming because most of these children seemed to be normal by the time they were four years old. It may be wishful thinking, however, to conclude that all is well with such a child because he does not have a physical handicap. It is commonly recognized that improvement can be expected after a distressful birth. A child with a slight brain defect often appears no different from a normal child. His intelligence quotient may lie in the range considered

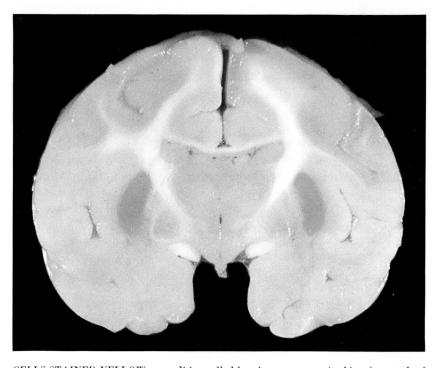

CELLS STAINED YELLOW, a condition called kernicterus, appear in this micrograph of tissue from monkey brain. It was thought that such staining, produced by excessive amounts of the bile pigment bilirubin in the blood, damaged brain cells. It appears, however, that only those cells that are already damaged by asphyxia at birth become stained with pigment.

NORMAL RHESUS MONKEY assumes an alert, crouching stance soon after birth. Curious and playful, it can feed itself easily by sucking on a bottle. At about three months the infant monkey will be more advanced than a human child three or four years old.

ABNORMAL RHESUS MONKEY was experimentally subjected to asphyxia at birth. Like a child suffering from cerebral palsy, this monkey is unable to use its arms and legs normally. It sprawls, and it will not move unless prodded. It is also unable to feed itself.

normal, but one never knows how much higher it would have been if his brain had escaped damage in the uterus or during birth. The brain-damaged monkeys also overcame most of their neurological deficits at roughly comparable stages of development. The difference is that we know that the brain of a "recovered" monkey is structurally damaged, whereas we only assume on clinical grounds that the brain of a "recovered" human infant is normal. There can now be little doubt that the brain of such an infant also harbors lesions. The few postmortem studies of the brains of human infants who suffered asphyxia at birth have revealed damage similar to that sustained by the asphyxiated monkeys.

The monkey experiments described in this article have taught us that birth asphyxia lasting long enough to make resuscitation necessary always damages the brain. This could be proved, however, only by histological examination. A great many human infants have to be resuscitated at birth. We assume that their brains too have been damaged. There is reason to believe that the number of human beings in the U.S. with minimal brain damage due to asphyxia at birth is much larger than has been thought. Need this continue to be so? Perhaps it is time to reexamine current practices of childbirth with a view to avoiding conditions that give rise to asphyxia and brain damage.

AZTEC FIGURINE of Ixcuina, the goddess of childbirth, illustrates the squatting position of delivery that is observed in some primitive societies today. It may be that this position is less likely to cause asphyxia of the infant than the supine position of delivery.

5

THE VISUAL WORLD OF INFANTS

T. G. R. BOWER
December 1966

Does an infant see things in the same general way adults do, or must he learn to do so? The question is taken up by means of conditioning experiments with infants, in which the reward is a cheery "peekaboo"

What does an infant see as he gazes at the world around him—an ordered array of stable objects or a random flux of evanescent shadows? There are proponents of both answers. Some psychologists have maintained that the ability to perceive the world is as much a part of man's genetic endowment as the ability to breathe; others have contended that perception is an acquired capacity, wholly dependent on experience and learning. The nativists have argued that a baby sees about what adults see; empiricists have held that an infant's visual world must be—in William James's words—"buzzing confusion."

At the heart of the argument there is a genuine scientific question: how to account for the discrepancy between the richness of perception and the poverty of its apparent cause—the momentary retinal image. First of all, there is the problem of space perception. The world as perceived seems to have one more dimension—the dimension of depth—than the retinal image does. Then there are the spatial "constancies," the tendency of an object to retain its size regardless of changes in viewing distance (even though the size of the retinal image changes) and to retain its shape even when its orientation (and therefore its retinal image) is changed. In other words, perception seems faithful to the object rather than to its retinal image.

Most psychologists have given empiricist answers to the problems of space perception and constancy. They have assumed that the infant's perceptual world mirrors the sequence of momentary retinal images that creates it. The chaotic two-dimensional ensemble of changing shapes is slowly ordered, in this view, by various mechanisms. The retinal image contains many cues to depth; for exam-

ple, far-off objects are projected lower on the retina than nearby objects (which is why they appear higher to us). Supposedly a baby learns that it must crawl or reach farther to get to such a higher image, and so comes to correlate relative height with relative distance. A similar correlation is presumably made in the case of the many other distance cues.

Once these theories have accounted for space perception they must go on to endow infants with the constancies. The oldest theory of constancy learning stems from Hermann von Helmholtz. He argued that by seeing an object at different distances and in a variety of orientations one learns the set of retinal projections that characterize it, so that on encountering a familiar retinal projection one can infer the size, shape, distance and orientation of the object producing it. According to this theory, however, there could be no constancy with an unfamiliar object. To avoid this prediction a different (but still empiricist) theory was developed from a suggestion made by the Gestalt psychologist Kurt Koffka. It assumes that a child who has acquired space perception will notice that there is a predictable relation between the distance of an image and its size, and a predictable relation between the orientation of an image and its shape. Once these relations have been inferred the child should be able to predict the size an image would have if its distance were changed and the shape it would have if its orientation were changed. The child could achieve shape constancy by predicting what shape a slanted image would have if it were rotated to lie directly across his line of sight. This means that the constancies could be attained with any object, familiar or not.

Note that this theory makes an asser-

tion about the course of perceptual development that is also an assertion about the sequence of events in perception: Before an infant can attain size and shape constancy he must be able to register distance or orientation and projective size or shape; before an adult can compute true size or shape he must register projective size and shape and distance and orientation. There were many attempts to validate this theory of development by testing adult subjects. In a typical experiment adults were shown shapes in various orientations and asked to report true shape, projective shape and orientation. If the theory were correct, one should be able to predict a subject's true-shape judgments from the other two. This turned out to be impossible. Subjects' judgments of true shape were often far more accurate than any deduction from their judgments of projective shape and slant could have been; they often got the true shape right and, say, the orientation completely wrong. This apparent disproof of the theory was explained away by supposing the process of deduction from retinal projection and orientation to true shape had become so automatic with long practice that the premises of the deduction had become subconscious.

So-called completion effects are another puzzle created by the characteristics of the retinal image. If one object is partly occluded by another, the two-dimensional retinal image of the first object is transformed in bizarre ways. Koffka argued that when an adult looks at a book on a table, he can see the table under the book. Similarly, if one looks at a triangle with a pencil across it, one can still see that there is a triangle under the pencil. In the retinal image, of course, there is a gap in the table and a gap in the triangle. Empiricists argue that experience and learning are necessary for these retinal deficiencies to be corrected. They argue that one *learns* the shape of a triangle, after which, on seeing a partly covered triangle, one can infer what the hidden parts look like.

This short review of problems will give the reader some idea of what the perceptual world of the infant should be if empiricist theory is correct. William James's description of it as buzzing confusion is then too mild; it should be a chaotic, frightening flux in which nothing stays constant, in which sizes, shapes and edges change, disappear and reappear in a confusing flow. Yet the theories described above are at least serious attempts to handle the problems of space perception, spatial constancies and completion effects. Nativist theories in contrast make a rather poor showing. Too often a nativist theory has merely been an argument against empiricism, not an attempt at genuine explanation.

The nativism-empiricism issue has remained open largely because there have seemed to be no ways to investigate the perceptual world of infants. How is one to get an answer from an organism as helpless as a young human infant, capable of few responses of any kind and of even fewer spatially directed responses? One obvious solution is the use of the operant-conditioning methods that were devised by B. F. Skinner: one selects some response from an organism's repertory and delivers some "reinforcing" agent contingent on the occurrence of that response. If reinforcement is delivered only in the presence of a certain stimulus, the response soon occurs only in the presence of that "conditioned" stimulus. It is then possible, among other things, to introduce new stimuli to be discriminated from the conditioned stimulus. Using manipulations of this kind, one can discover a great deal about the perceptual worlds of pigeons, fishes and even worms.

For some years, first at Cornell University and more recently at Harvard University, I have been applying operant-conditioning techniques to investigate perception in human infants. The major block to applying these methods to infants had been the necessity of a reinforcing agent. The agent is ordinarily either food or water, and it is usually withheld for some time before the experiment; a pigeon working for grain is kept at 80 percent of its normal body weight. One could hardly inflict such privation on infants. Fortunately less drastic methods are available. As

OPERANT-CONDITIONING technique requires that an infant be trained to respond to the presentation of a certain stimulus. In this experiment in shape perception the stimuli are plywood rectangles and trapezoids placed at various angles to the infant's line of sight. The object is to see how well the infant can differentiate among the shapes and orientations.

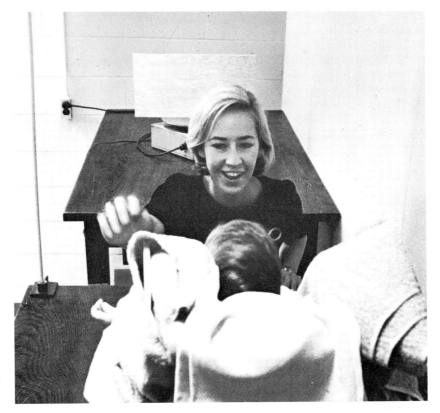

"REINFORCEMENT," part of the training program, is delivered when the infant responds correctly. The usual reinforcement in animal experiments is food or water. The author uses a "peekaboo": as shown, an experimenter pops up, cooing and smiling, then disappears.

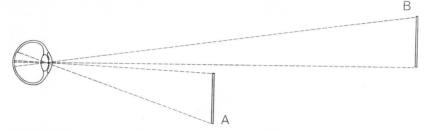

RETINAL IMAGE varies with distance. Objects *A* and *B* are the same size but *A* projects a larger image on the retina. In spite of this, adults usually see such objects as being the same size. One of the author's objectives was to see if infants too have this "size constancy."

Skinner pointed out, any change in surroundings, even the simple rustling of a newspaper, seems to reinforce an infant's responses. The reinforcement we use is a little game that adults often play with infants called "peekaboo": the adult pops out in front of the infant, smiling and nodding, and speaks to him (sometimes patting him on the tummy if he is unresponsive) and then quickly disappears from view. Infants between two and 20 weeks old seem to find this event highly reinforcing and will respond for 20 minutes at a time to make it occur. The situation can be made even more reinforcing by altering the schedule of reinforcement.

A lesser problem is deciding what response to use. Infants have few responses available; most of these require substantial effort and would quickly tire the subject of an experiment. The one used in the present investigations is a turn of the head. The infant reclines with his head between two yielding pads. By turning his head as little as half an inch to the left or right he closes a microswitch that operates a recorder. This response re-

quires scant effort; even infants as young as two weeks old can give 400 such responses with no apparent fatigue.

The first experiment carried out with these techniques was aimed at discovering whether or not infants can perceive distance and are capable of size constancy. An infant between six and eight weeks old, too young to be capable of the spatial behavior of reaching and crawling, reclined in an infant seat on a table, with the peekabooing experimenter crouching in front of him and the stimuli beyond the experimenter. A translucent screen could be raised for rest periods and stimulus changes. The conditioned stimulus in the first experiment was a white cube 30 centimeters (12 inches) on a side, placed one meter from the infant's eyes.

After training an infant to respond only in the presence of the cube, we gradually changed the reinforcement schedule to a variable one in which every fifth response, on the average, was reinforced. After one experimental hour on this schedule we began perceptual test-

ing by introducing three new stimuli. These were the 30-centimeter cube placed three meters away, a 90-centimeter cube placed one meter away and the same 90-centimeter cube placed three meters away. These three stimuli and the conditioned stimulus were each presented for four 30-second periods in counterbalanced order and the number of responses elicited by each stimulus was recorded. During the testing period no reinforcement was given.

On any theory, the conditioned stimulus could be expected to elicit more responses than any of the other stimuli. The stimulus eliciting the next highest number of responses should be the one that appears to the infant to be most like the conditioned stimulus. If the empiricist hypothesis that infants do not perceive distance and do not have size constancy is correct, the stimulus that should have appeared most similar was the third stimulus, the 90-centimeter cube placed three meters away; it was three times the height and width of the conditioned stimulus but also three times as far away, so that it projected a retinal image of the same size. If infants can perceive distance but still lack size constancy, stimulus 3 should still have seemed more like the conditioned stimulus than stimulus 1, the 30-centimeter cube at three meters. Both were at the same distance, but stimulus 3 projected a retinal image with the same area as the conditioned stimulus, whereas stimulus 1 projected an image with only one-ninth the area. If the infants had been unable to discriminate distance at all, stimulus 2 would have elicited as many responses as stimulus 1, since stimulus 2 projected an image with nine times the area of the conditioned stimulus and stimulus 1 projected an image one-ninth as large. If they had been sensitive to distance or its cues but had lacked size constancy, stimulus 2 would have elicited more responses than stimulus 1, since stimulus 2 was at the same distance as the conditioned stimulus. If, on the other hand, the infants had been able to perceive distance and had size constancy, stimuli 1 and 2 should have elicited about the same number of responses, since stimulus 1 differed from the conditioned stimulus in distance and stimulus 2 differed in size; stimulus 3 should have elicited the lowest number of responses, since it differed from the conditioned stimulus in both size and distance [see *illustration at left*].

To sum up the predictions, according to empiricism stimulus 3 should be as effective as or more effective than stimu-

	CONDITIONED STIMULUS	TEST STIMULI		
		1	2	3
TRUE SIZE				
TRUE DISTANCE	1	3	1	3
RETINAL SIZE				
RETINAL DISTANCE CUES		DIFFERENT	SAME	DIFFERENT

SIZE CONSTANCY was investigated with cubes of different sizes placed at different distances from the infants. The conditioned stimulus was 30 centimeters on a side and one meter away, test stimuli 30 or 90 centimeters on a side and one or three meters away. The chart shows how test stimuli were related to the conditioned stimulus in various respects.

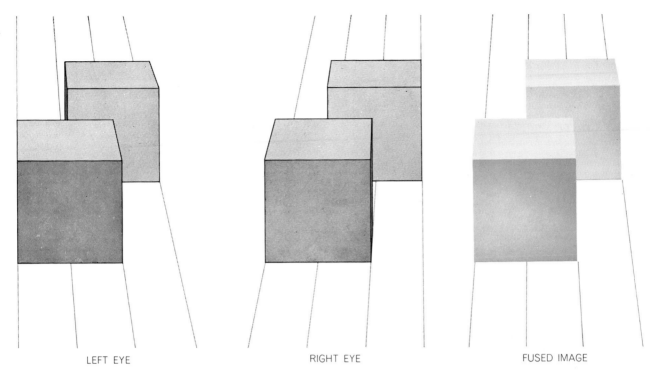

LEFT EYE   RIGHT EYE   FUSED IMAGE

BINOCULAR PARALLAX is one of two "primary" cues to distance. Because the right and left eyes are some distance apart, each registers a somewhat different view of the same scene. In the two drawings at the left the lower, or nearer, cube is farther to the left in the right eye's view than in the left eye's view. If the two images are combined stereoscopically (with the aid of a prism to superpose one image on the other, for example), the scene acquires a third dimension. The result is simulated by the drawing at the right.

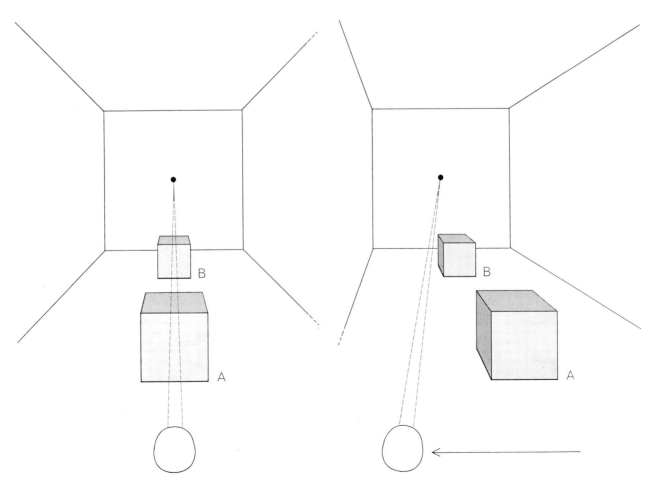

MOTION PARALLAX also provides different perspectives that vary with distance. If the head moves left and the eyes are kept fixed on a distant point, the nearer object (A) appears to move to the right farther and faster than the more distant object (B) does.

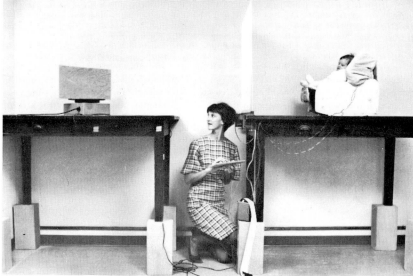

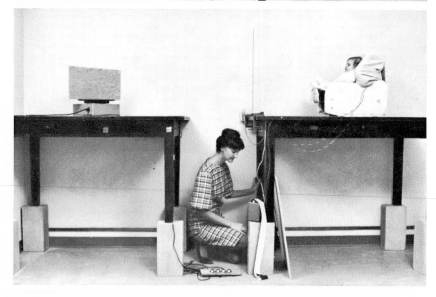

EXPERIMENTAL PROCEDURE begins with conditioning. The infant is trained to respond to a rectangle seen in a certain orientation and the response is reinforced by a "peekaboo" (*top*). Then a screen is interposed between the infant and the stimulus area while the experimenter changes the orientation (*center*). With the screen removed, the experimenter watches a recorder to see whether or not the infant responds to the test stimulus (*bottom*).

lus 2, which should in turn get more responses than stimulus 1; if retinal distance cues are not taken into account, 3 should be clearly superior to 2. According to nativism the order should be the reverse: more responses to 1 than to 2, more to 2 than to 3. What happened was that the conditioned stimulus elicited an average of 98 responses; stimulus 1, 58 responses; stimulus 2, 54 responses, and stimulus 3, 22 responses. It therefore seems that the retinal image theory cannot be correct. These infants' responses were affected by real size and real distance, not by retinal size or by retinal distance cues.

What stimulus variables were being used by these infants to gauge depth? Two cues, binocular parallax and motion parallax, are called "primary" because they are the most reliable of all the cues. The first of these is available because a human being's eyes are set some distance apart and therefore receive slightly different views of the same scene. This binocular disparity produces an immediate impression of distance, at least in adults. Motion parallax is a similar cue: by moving one's head from side to side, one picks up a sequence of slightly differing perspectives of a scene. Moreover, near objects are displaced farther and faster than far objects. Are binocular parallax and motion parallax "primary" in a developmental sense, however? The presumptive cause of perception is the momentary retinal image of a single eye. As soon as two eyes are introduced for binocular parallax there arises the problem of integrating the two images; as soon as a sequence of images is brought in for motion parallax there is the question of how the visual system integrates multiple images spread out over time. Since these presumably complex integration processes must come into play before the two kinds of parallax can acquire spatial meaning, it is little wonder that these variables have seemed poor candidates for development early in infancy. This drawback does not apply to the host of pictorial cues that are implicit in the momentary retinal image of a single eye. These are the cues—shading, perspective, texture and so on—a painter exploits to produce the illusion of depth on a canvas without benefit of the parallaxes. It has seemed possible that these cues are recognized early in development as having differential value and so become endowed early with spatial meaning.

To discover which cues should be called primary, we tested three new groups of infants on the size-constancy test. Infants in one group wore a patch over one eye so that they could not register binocular parallax but could register only motion parallax and pictorial cues. A second group viewed, instead of the real cubes, projected slides that were rich in pictorial cues but lacked both binocular and motion parallax entirely. A third group of infants wore specially constructed stereoscopic goggles and viewed projected stereograms of the various scenes; their presentation contained binocular parallax and pictorial cues but lacked motion parallax. The results were interesting. The monocular group performed just as the unrestricted group of the first experiment had. The conditioned stimulus elicited an average of 101 responses; stimulus 1 (the same cube farther away), 60 responses; stimulus 2 (the large cube at the distance of the conditioned stimulus), an average of 53 responses; stimulus 3 (the large cube set to be projectively equivalent to the conditioned stimulus), only 22 responses. The infants who viewed the slides performed quite differently: they produced 94 responses to the conditioned stimulus, 52 to stimulus 1, 44 to stimulus 2 and 96 to stimulus 3. Their behavior suggested that their responses were determined solely by the projective size of the cubes

RESPONSE in these experiments was a head-turning motion that operated a switch in the cushions at the infant's head. At first the infants gave exaggerated responses (*left*); later they responded more economically, keeping their eyes on the stimulus (*right*).

PLEASURE at the peekaboo reinforcement was manifest (*left*), and was sufficient to keep infants responding up to 20 minutes between reinforcements. The problem in experiments with infants is boredom; after a while even the peekaboo loses its charm (*right*).

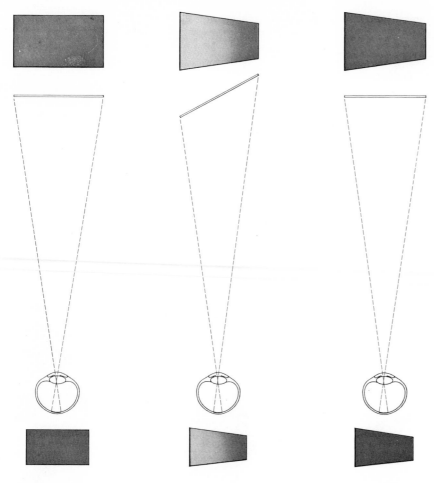

SHAPE CONSTANCY is illustrated by shapes in different orientations. A rectangle presented in the parallel plane (*left*) projects a rectangular image on the retina (*bottom*) and is seen as a rectangle. Presented at a slant, it projects a trapezoidal image (*center*), yet is usually seen as a rectangle. A trapezoid in the parallel plane projects the same shape (*right*).

in the various presentations; the pictorial distance cues in the slides were obviously not even being detected (or stimulus 3 could not have elicited as many responses as the conditioned stimulus), much less serving as cues to distance and size constancy. The infants in the stereogram group were different again. Their responses suggested some size constancy but less than the responses of either the unrestricted infants or the monocular group did. The values were: conditioned

stimulus, 94 responses; stimulus 1, 44 responses; stimulus 2, 40 responses, and stimulus 3, 32 responses. It therefore appeared that motion parallax was the most effective cue to depth, followed by binocular parallax. The static pictorial cues in the retinal image seemed to be of no value.

A second set of experiments was carried out to investigate shape constancy and slant perception. The sub-

jects were infants between 50 and 60 days old. The conditioned stimulus in this investigation was a wooden rectangle 25 by 50 centimeters (about 10 by 20 inches) placed two meters away and turned 45 degrees from the "fronto-parallel plane," a plane at a right angle to their line of sight. The test stimuli were (1) the same rectangle placed in the infant's parallel plane, or at a right angle to the line of sight; (2) a trapezoid, placed in the parallel plane, that projected a retinal image of the same shape as the rectangle in the 45-degree position, and (3) this same trapezoid placed in the 45-degree position. The three test stimuli differed from the conditioned stimulus as shown in the bottom illustration on this page.

If infants are capable of shape constancy, stimulus 1 should be more effective than stimulus 3, which should be about the same as stimulus 2. If they are controlled by retinal shape only, on the other hand, stimulus 2 should get more responses than 3 or 1. The results were that the conditioned stimulus elicited an average of 51 responses; stimulus 1, the same rectangle in a different orientation, elicited 45.13 responses; stimulus 2, which projected the same retinal image as the conditioned stimulus, elicited only 28.50 responses, and stimulus 3 elicited 26 responses. There was no doubt that these infants had learned to respond to real shape, not retinal shape. Statistical analysis showed, moreover, that there was no significant difference between the number of responses elicited by the conditioned stimulus and the number elicited by test stimulus 1. It therefore appeared that the infants were responding to true shape and displaying shape constancy *without* having discriminated between different orientations of the same object.

This last result was extremely puzzling and we modified the experiment to examine it in more detail. There were three groups of infants aged 50 to 60 days, each with a different set of stimuli. One group was trained with the rectangle turned five degrees away from the parallel position. The three test stimuli were the same rectangle turned 15 degrees, 30 degrees and 45 degrees from the parallel plane. The second group of infants was trained with a trapezoid placed in the parallel plane whose shape was projectively equivalent to the rectangle in its five-degree position. The three test stimuli were trapezoids set up in the parallel position and projectively equal to the three test stimuli used for the first group. For the third group the

STIMULUS	REAL SHAPE	ORIENTATION	RETINAL SHAPE
1	SAME	DIFFERENT	DIFFERENT
2	DIFFERENT	DIFFERENT	SAME
3	DIFFERENT	SAME	DIFFERENT

TEST STIMULI in the first shape-constancy experiment described in the text differed from the conditioned stimulus as shown. Retinal shape was expected to be the governing factor.

rectangles used for the first group were hidden by a screen with a rectangular hole cut in it so that the body of the rectangle was visible but its edges were not; the only information available on the difference between the conditioned stimulus and the test stimuli was therefore given by variations in orientation. To summarize the three viewing conditions, the stimuli viewed by group 1 varied in projective shape and orientation, with real shape constant. Those viewed by group 2 varied in real shape and projective shape, with orientation constant. Those viewed by group 3 varied in orientation only, with real shape and projective shape remaining constant.

This was a multipurpose experiment. It was intended, first of all, to discover whether or not infants can discriminate among different orientations of the same shape; hence group 1. If the answer to that question were negative, the experiment should show whether or not such infants could discriminate orientation as such; hence group 3. Moreover, a comparison of group 1 with groups 2 and 3 would bear on the idea, mentioned earlier, that spatial constancies are attained by a prediction from one retinal image in a perceived orientation to another image in another orientation. If it were true that infants see an object in space as a projective shape with an orientation, the infants in group 1 would give far fewer responses to the test stimuli than the infants in the other two groups, since the first group, viewing an object rotated in space, would have both projective shape and orientation available to differentiate test stimuli from conditioned stimulus, whereas the other two groups would have only one of these differentiating variables at their disposal.

On the contrary, the infants in group 1 showed the poorest discrimination; they responded as if the three test stimuli looked the same as the conditioned stimulus. The infants in groups 2 and 3 showed good discrimination, indicating that variations in real shape (and therefore in projective shape) can be registered by infants and that variations in orientation can also be registered. The poor discrimination shown by group 1 can only mean that real shape—which was the same in all four of the stimuli—was perceptually more salient than either orientation or projective shape. This finding seems very important, since it is a blow not only against empiricism but also against the idea (common to nativists and empiricists) that perception of simple variables is in some way developmentally earlier than perception of complex variables.

A third set of experiments was concerned with completion problems. Again the subjects were infants between 50 and 60 days old. The conditioned stimulus was a black wire triangle with a black iron bar placed across it. After training as before, four wire test stimuli were presented [*see illustration on this page*]. The complete triangle elicited an average of 42 responses. The other test stimuli elicited 18.25, 17.25 and 20 responses respectively. This can only mean that these infants saw the conditioned stimulus as a triangle with a bar over it. Since none of these infants had ever seen a triangle before the experiment, and since during the experiment it was only seen with a bar over it, the empiricist reliance on learning and experience cannot be justified. In a second experiment in which slides of these triangular objects were presented rather than the wire objects, the result was quite different: there was no preference for one test figure over any other. As in the case of space perception, the infants' performance appeared to depend not on static retinal cues but rather on the information contained in variables, such as motion parallax, that are available only to a mobile organism viewing a three-dimensional array.

Our investigation was originally directed to the nativism-empiricism controversy. The eight-week-old infants certainly were more capable of depth discrimination, orientation discrimination, size constancy, shape constancy and completion than an empiricist would have predicted. On the other hand, the babies were also less capable than a strict nativist would have predicted. They could not discriminate pictorial cues and they could not maintain shape constancy and orientation discrimination simultaneously. It cannot be stated, therefore, that the experiments have resolved the issue one way or another. Nor do they seem merely to indicate that the true position is a compromise—that there are some innate abilities and that these are

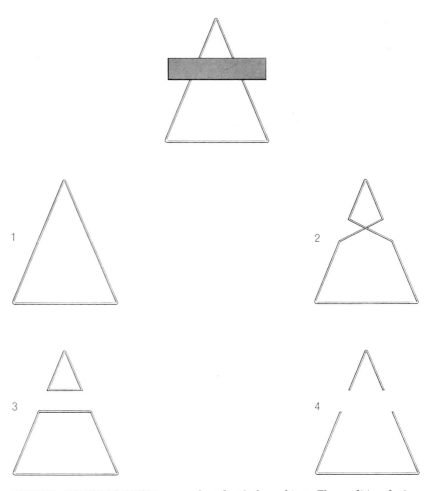

COMPLETION EXPERIMENT was conducted with these objects. The conditioned stimulus was a triangle with a bar attached to it, thus interrupting its shape. Of the test stimuli, *3* and *4* are more like the conditioned stimulus than *1* and *2* are. Actually infants seem to complete objects as adults do, as shown by the fact that *1* was the most effective stimulus.

elaborated by experience and learning. My impression is rather that these studies have added to the growing body of evidence that the whole controversy is based on false premises.

The most notable set of false premises stems from the belief that perception is caused by the momentary retinal image. What the experiments seem to show is that evolution has tuned the human perceptual system to register not the low-grade information in momentary retinal images but rather the high-fidelity information in sequences of images or in simultaneous complexes of images—the kind of information given by motion parallax and binocular parallax. The infants in these studies were obviously able to register variables containing complex information. Yet they were unable to use the information in the slide presentations of the first and third sets of experiments. This failure must surely mean that infants are not sensitive to the kind of information that can be frozen on the plane of a picture or locked into a momentary retinal image. A similar conclusion can be drawn from the fact that in none of these experiments did retinal similarity seem to make for more responses. Rather than being the most primitive kind of perceptual ability, it would seem, the ability to register the information in a retinal image may be a highly sophisticated attainment and may indeed have to be learned.

These results suggest a theory of perceptual and perceptual-motor development. It is obvious that an adult is capable of some responses these infants apparently lacked. For example, the infants in the second shape-constancy experiment seemed to be unable to register real shape and orientation simultaneously but able to register orientation in the case of a surface without limiting contours. The most plausible hypothesis is to assume that infants have a lower processing capacity than adults—that their perceptual systems can handle simultaneously only a fraction of the information they register. Infants can register the real shape of an object and they can also register its orientation. If they have limited processing capacity, however, they may be able to process only one of these variables even when both are present and are registered. This makes sense of the discrepancy between the behavior of group 1 and that of group 3 in the shape-constancy experiment. The infants of group 1 were presented with a real shape in various orientations, but they could process only the shape, which remained invariant, and so their discrimination appeared poor. Those in group 3 viewed a surface whose retinal shape stayed the same but whose orientation varied, and by choosing to process orientation and ignore retinal shape they were able to show good discrimination.

If capacity is limited, it also seems plausible that the infant perceptual system should give priority to information that has definite survival value. On this reasoning one would expect the shape of an object to have greater priority than its orientation and the orientation of a surface to have greater priority than its shape. Objects must be responded to, and their shape will often indicate the proper response, whereas surfaces are things to be landed on or used as supports, and their orientation is surely their most important attribute. One would also predict low priority for retinal shape and size, variables that are of no survival value except to a representational artist.

This evolutionarily oriented line of reasoning may also help one to understand the problem of perceptual-motor learning. The fact that infants will initially misreach has often been taken to show that they cannot perceive depth. If they can in fact perceive depth, the misreaching remains to be explained. A clue to an explanation is given by the fact that the most obvious change in an infant as he develops is a change in size. It seems likely that an infant who misreaches does so not because of poor depth perception but because he simply does not know how long his arm is. Since arm length is going to change drastically during development, it would be uneconomical—indeed, positively maladaptive—if the perceptual-motor system were geared at birth for a particular arm length.

The overall picture of perceptual development that is emerging is very different from traditional ones. It has long been assumed that perceptual development is a process of construction—that at birth infants receive through their senses fragmentary information that is elaborated and built on to produce the ordered perceptual world of the adult. The theory emerging from our studies and others not reported here is based on evidence that infants can in fact register most of the information an adult can register but can handle less of the information than adults can. Through maturation they presumably develop the requisite information-processing capacity. If this view is correct, the visual world of the infant may well be overwhelming at times, but it is probably not the meaningless buzz it has long been thought to be.

II

CRITICAL EVENTS IN THE SHAPING OF BASIC SYSTEMS

II

CRITICAL EVENTS IN THE SHAPING OF BASIC SYSTEMS

INTRODUCTION

Although we should view birth as a point on the continum of development rather than as the beginning of behavioral development, we must realize that it is an important point, particularly for higher organisms, who deal with their environment in more intricate ways. Most mammalian infants are born with a considerable degree of readiness for dealing with the environment, but they still require environmental experience for the full development of their behavioral capacity. Of course we all realize that the animal must, during its life, learn about many properties of its environment, such as its sources of food and safety. But in addition to the process of learning about the environment, there seem to be a number of cases in which basic systems of the organism, which will allow it to interact with its surroundings, are fine-tuned by stimuli present in the surroundings during the organism's early development. Since the organism is maturing quite rapidly during the period following its birth, the time span during which certain types of environmental events have their maximal effect on development is often quite short. Such a limited time span, during which the organism is most sensitive (or at all sensitive) to some aspect of its environment, is often called a "critical period."

The degree to which the period is "critical" may vary considerably from species to species and from system to system within species. For example, the developing kitten, between 4 and 8 weeks after birth, is particularly sensitive to visual stimulation; if the kitten is not exposed to normal light during this period, its vision will be permanently defective. The rat, on the other hand, seems remarkably capable of recovering from a period of visual deprivation that lasts at least as long. (However, an extended period of normal visual experience may be necessary before the rat recovers fully.) A useful way to view critical periods is as a time of *lowered threshold* for certain experiences. Following the critical lowest-threshold period, the threshold may remain sufficiently low that the same, or a more intense, experience will result in normal development; alternatively, the threshold may rise to such an extent that naturally occurring stimulation cannot have its developmental effect.

When we use the term "environment," we generally refer to the world external to the organism. For the developmental psychobiologist, however, the term can also refer to the environment of the brain, including the body and its hormonal and other chemical constituents. It is this aspect of the environment that is important in Seymour Levine's discussion of the way in which "Sex Differences in the Brain" are determined by the genetic potential of the organism. The research that Levine describes indicates that many of the male or female properties of the adult depend upon hormones acting upon the brain during a critical period early in development.

In the following selection, "Stimulation in Infancy," Seymour Levine describes a critical period in the early development of emotional responsiveness for which the external environment is important. During later maturation and adulthood, the organism will be exposed to a broad variety of experiences to which it must react. Some of these experiences will involve little or no stress upon the organism, but others, highly stressful, may threaten the animal's health or even its life. How is it that developing animals come to respond appropriately to novel environmental situations? Seymour Levine's findings indicate that the organism must be exposed to stressful experiences very shortly after its birth if it is to develop normal neural, hormonal, and behavioral stress response patterns.

For the typical animal raised in a laboratory, early stimulation is an experimental treatment, and its lack is the norm; in the natural environment, one might imagine that only the rare newborn litter fails to be stimulated. When early stimulation occurs in a similar form in the laboratory and in the natural environment, then experimental deprivation can help us to understand its role in the development of behavior. A deprivation experiment can tell us whether some particular aspect of the environment is essential to normal development; in fact, the bulk of the animal experimentation evaluating the role of environmental influences in development has used some form of this technique. Austin H. Riesen, in "Arrested Vision," describes the critical role of light and pattern in the development of the primate visual system. In contrast to the preceding two papers, in which the critical period for experience was relatively clearcut, visual input seems to be required for both the development and the maintenance of the visual system. That is, a prolonged period of visual deprivation has an effect on vision at any time in the chimpanzee's life, although the effects of deprivation in early life seem to be the most severe.

There are, of course, pitfalls in interpreting the results of deprivation experiments. One difficulty is that the deprivation generally affects other systems in addition to those under study. In Riesen's experiments, for example, the animals are also deprived of normal social experiences, and as L. I. Gardner points out in Section III of this volume, show evidence of "deprivation dwarfism." Another problem is that one cannot always be certain why development has been affected by deprivation. For example, Riesen points out that the retinas of the eyes were damaged by total light deprivation. If the retina could not operate in a normal manner, then, even if the visual centers of the brain were able to function properly, the animal would not be able to see his surroundings. Not only has the deprivation prevented normal maturation; it has actually caused the visual system to degenerate to a level below that of the newborn infant. Robert L. Fantz, in "The Origin of Form Perception," uses deprivation in some primate work but emphasizes the normal pattern of maturation of the human visual system. Fantz's data indicate that pattern vision exists in a meaningful way in the newborn human child, although maturation with visual experience is certainly required for its full development.

Beyond the ability to extract information from his world, the successful organism must also be able to act upon it. For this, the information sources (sensory systems) and the action sources (motor systems) must be in synchrony. As the organism grows, relationships between systems will change: limbs grow longer and extend farther from the eyes; distance between the eyes increases; more delicate movements may be performed. Coordination between systems must be maintained and improved while these physical changes are taking place. Richard Held, in "Plasticity in Sensory-Motor Systems," describes experiments on the establishment of visual-motor coordination in immature and adult organisms. Held's results indicate that this process remains "plastic," that is, capable of change or adaptation, even after the organism has reached maturity. In addition, the knowledge that some aspects of development appear to continue throughout life provides understanding and direction for those involved in the rehabilitation of patients suffering from neuromuscular disorders.

SUGGESTED READINGS

Blakemore, C., and Cooper, G. F. Development of the brain depends on the visual environment. *Nature,* Vol. 228, pages 477–478, 1970.

Coleman, P. D., and Riesen, A. H. Environmental effects on cortical dendritic fields. I. Rearing in the dark. *Journal of Anatomy,* Vol. 102, pages 363–374, 1968.

Landauer, T. E., and Whiting, J. W. M. Infantile stimulation and adult stature of human males. *American Anthropologist,* Vol. 66, pages 1007–1028, 1964.

Valverde, F. Apical dendritic spines of the visual cortex and light deprivation in the mouse. *Experimental Brain Research,* Vol. 3, pages 337–352, 1967.

Young, W. C., Goy, R. W., and Phoenix, C. H. Hormones and sexual behavior. *Science,* Vol. 143, pages 212–218, 1964.

Further Readings From *Scientific American*

Denenberg, V. H. Early experience and emotional development. *Scientific American,* June, 1963 (Offprint 478).

Levine, S. Stress and behavior. *Scientific American,* January, 1971 (Offprint 532).

Thompson, W. R., and Melzack, R. Early environment. *Scientific American,* January, 1956 (Offprint 469).

6

SEX DIFFERENCES IN THE BRAIN

SEYMOUR LEVINE
April 1966

*There is increasing evidence that mammalian behavior
patterns are basically female and that male patterns
are induced by the action of the sex hormone
testosterone on the brain of the newborn animal*

What makes a male mammal male and a female mammal female? We might sum up the answer in the word heredity, but this would evade the question. How is the genetic information translated into the differentiation of the sexes, as expressed in their physiology and behavior? Again we might summarize the answer in a single word: hormones. Recent investigations have revealed, however, that sexual differentiation in mammals cannot be explained solely in terms of hormones. There is now considerable evidence that the brain is also involved. According to this evidence there are distinct differences between the male brain and the female brain in a mammal, differences that determine not only sexual activity but also certain other forms of behavior.

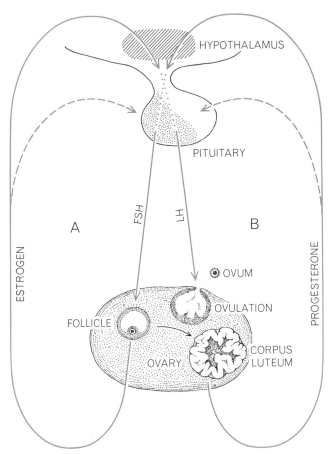

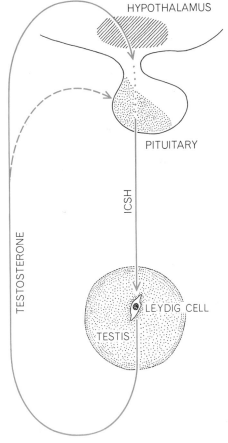

INTERPLAY OF SEX HORMONES differs in the female mammal (*left*) and the male (*right*). In the cyclic female system the pituitary initially releases a follicle-stimulating hormone (FSH) that makes the ovary produce estrogen (*colored arrows at A*): the estrogen then acts on the hypothalamus of the brain to inhibit the further release of FSH by the pituitary and to stimulate the release of a luteinizing hormone (LH) instead. This hormone both triggers ovulation and makes the ovary produce a second hormone, pro-gesterone (*colored arrows at B*). On reaching the hypothalamus the latter hormone inhibits further pituitary release of LH, thereby completing the cycle. In the noncyclic male system the pituitary continually releases an interstitial-cell-stimulating hormone (ICSH) that makes the testes produce testosterone; the latter hormone acts on the hypothalamus to stimulate further release of ICSH by the pituitary. Broken arrows represent the earlier theory that the sex hormones from ovaries and testes stimulated the pituitary directly.

Let us begin by examining one of the principal distinctions between males and females. In most species of mammals the female has a cyclic pattern of ovulation. The human female ovulates about every 28 days; the guinea pig, about every 15 days; the rat, every four to five days. The process is dominated by hormones of the pituitary gland. In cyclic fashion the anterior (front) part of the pituitary delivers to the ovary a follicle-stimulating hormone (FSH), which promotes the growth of Graafian follicles, and a luteinizing hormone (LH), which induces the formation of corpora lutea and triggers ovulation. The formation of corpora lutea is clear evidence that ovulation has occurred. The ovary in turn responds to FSH by releasing the female sex hormone estrogen and to LH by releasing the female sex hormone progesterone [*see illustration on preceding page*].

The male mammal shows no such cycle. Its testes continually receive from the pituitary the same hormone (LH) that stimulates formation of corpora lutea in the female's ovary; in the male, however, this hormone is known as the interstitial-cell-stimulating hormone (ICSH) because it causes the interstitial cells of the testes to secrete testosterone. Thus the patterns of pituitary effects on the sex organs are distinctly different in the two sexes: cyclic in the female, noncyclic in the male.

What might account for this difference? When the interaction of the pituitary and sex organs was discovered, it was natural to suppose that the sex hormones regulated the pituitary's secretions. In the female the pituitary hormones controlled the process that led to ovulation; the consequent output of estrogen and progesterone by the ovary caused the pituitary to cut down production of its stimulating hormones, and the cycle might therefore be described as a negative-feedback system.

Thirty years ago the endocrinologist Carroll A. Pfeiffer, then working at the Yale University School of Medicine, reported a series of studies unequivocally demonstrating that the process of sexual differentiation occurred very early in the course of a mammal's development. In these studies he undertook to exchange the sex organs in the formative period of early life. In newborn male rats he removed the testes and replaced them with transplanted ovaries; in newborn females he replaced the ovaries with testes; other animals in his experiments were provided with both organs—testes and ovaries. The

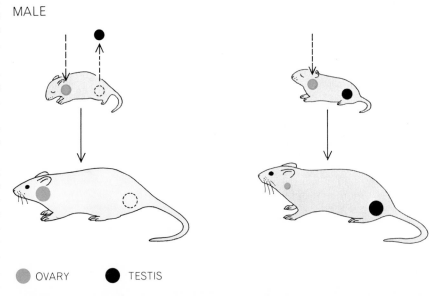

FEMALE

OVARY   TESTIS

REVERSAL OF SEX in young female rats was achieved experimentally by Carroll A. Pfeiffer of the Yale University School of Medicine 30 years ago in proof of the action of the male sex hormone testosterone. When the ovaries of a young female (*at top left in color*) were removed and testes were implanted, the animal in effect became male (*gray*) and showed no estrus at maturity. Even when a female's ovaries were left intact (*top right*), the output of testosterone from the implant prevented normal functioning of the ovaries.

MALE

OVARY   TESTIS

LACK OF TESTOSTERONE permitted a similar reversal of sex among young male rats in the Pfeiffer experiment. When the rat's testes were removed and an ovary was then implanted (*top left*), the ovary continued to function and the animal in effect became female (*color*). When an ovary was implanted in a normal male, however (*top right*), the male's output of testosterone kept the ovary from functioning and the rat remained male (*gray*).

main findings that emerged were these: Males with ovaries in place of testes showed the female capacity for producing corpora lutea in the ovarian tissues. Those that possessed testes as well as ovaries failed to form any corpora lutea in the implanted ovaries. Of the females that had testes implanted, many failed to show estrous cycles or any formation of corpora lutea in their ovaries if the ovaries were left intact.

From these results Pfeiffer deduced that, since the controlling factor seemed to be the presence or absence of testosterone, in the newborn rat testosterone acted to induce a permanent sexual differentiation of the pituitary. If testosterone was present during this critical early period, it would cause the pituitary to produce stimulating secretions thereafter in the noncyclic, male mode; if testosterone was absent, the pituitary would behave throughout life as if it belonged to a female.

Pfeiffer's hypothesis that the pituitary itself was sexually differentiated did not stand up, however. Direct evidence on this question was produced in the 1950's by Geoffrey W. Harris of the University of Oxford and investigators working with him at the Institute of Psychiatry in London. Harris and Dora Jacobsohn found that when the pituitary gland of a male rat was transplanted under the hypothalamus of a female, her reproductive functions and behavior remained entirely female and normal. The same absence of change was noted when pituitaries from female

rats were implanted in males. Meanwhile the late F. H. A. Marshall of the University of Cambridge was able to demonstrate that a close relation exists between the external environment and reproduction. In many species of mammals the female cycle of ovulation is affected by light, diet, temperature and emotional stress. Moreover, electrical stimulation of the hypothalamus could induce ovulation, and lesions of the hypothalamus could block ovulation.

Reviewing Pfeiffer's findings and the other experimental evidence, Harris and another investigator, the late William C. Young of the University of Kansas, suggested that it was the brain (not the

pituitary, as Pfeiffer had proposed) that was subject to differentiation by the action of hormones. According to this view, the brain of a mammal was essentially female until a certain stage of development (which in the rat came within a short time after birth). If testosterone was absent at this stage, the brain would remain female; if testosterone was present, the brain would develop male characteristics.

Under Harris' leadership the author and other investigators working in the department of neuroendocrinology at the Institute of Psychiatry started a systematic and extensive program of experiments to test this hypothesis. The

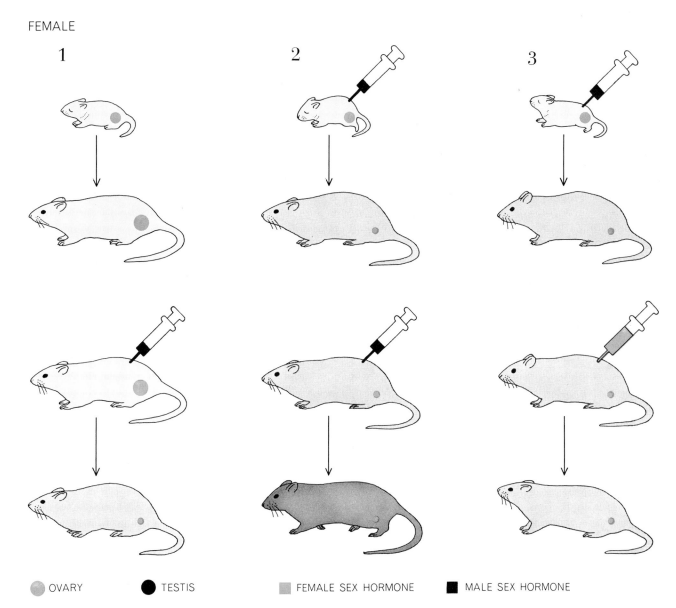

FEMALE

⬤ OVARY   ● TESTIS   ▢ FEMALE SEX HORMONE   ■ MALE SEX HORMONE

MASCULINIZED FEMALE RATS were produced by injections of testosterone (*black syringe*) at birth. In Column 1 a normal female (*color*) is injected with male hormone when mature; the animal exhibits some male sexual behavior (*gray*). In Column 2 the female is injected with male hormone in infancy; when reinjected at maturity, it exhibits full male sexual behavior. In Column 3, in spite of an injection of female hormone (*colored syringe*) at maturity, the masculinized female fails to exhibit female sexual behavior.

program has been continued at the Stanford University School of Medicine. We worked mainly with rats, and the basic procedure entailed alteration of the newborn animal's normal exposure to sex hormones within the first four days after birth. Instead of transplanting organs we simply injected the hormone whose effects we wished to test; it was already known that a single injection of testosterone (in the form of the long-acting compound testosterone propionate) in a newborn female rat could produce the same effects as the implantation of male testes.

We found that females injected with testosterone in this critical early period did not develop the normal female pattern of physiology when they became adults. Their ovaries were dwarfed and they failed to produce corpora lutea or show the usual cycle of ovulation. On the other hand, males that were castrated (and thus deprived of testosterone) within the first days after birth did show signs of female physiology; when ovaries were implanted in them as adults, they developed corpora lutea. It was clear that a permanent control over the activity of the pituitary in the rat was established by the absence or presence of testosterone in the critical first few days after birth. In the absence of testosterone a pattern

of cyclic release of FSH and LH by the pituitary was formed; if testosterone was present, it abolished the cycle.

Essentially the same effect has been demonstrated in guinea pigs and monkeys, but the critical period for these longer-gestating mammals occurs before birth. A series of injections of testosterone in the fetal stage of a female guinea pig or monkey produces permanent masculinizing effects such as we have observed in the female rat.

What are the effects of the early administration of testosterone on the rat's sexual behavior? In this area, as in physiology, there are measurable

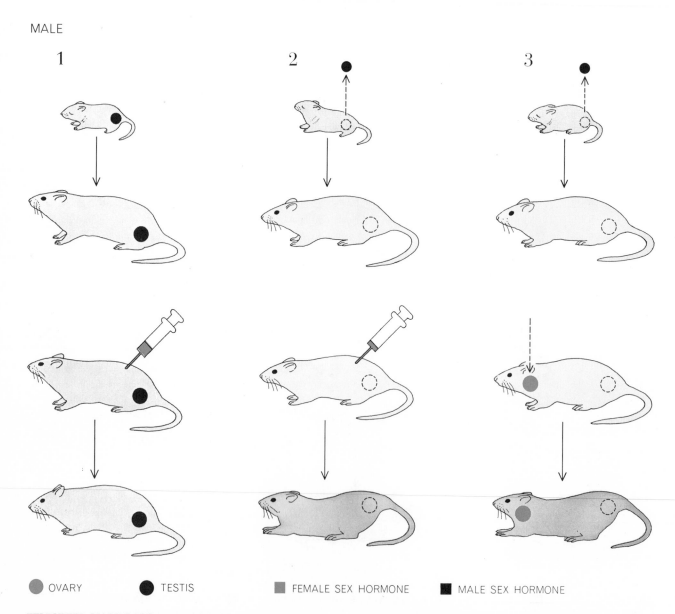

MALE

1   2   3

● OVARY   ● TESTIS   ■ FEMALE SEX HORMONE   ■ MALE SEX HORMONE

FEMINIZED MALE RATS were produced by injections of estrogen and progesterone or by ovary implants only when the males had been castrated at birth and thereby deprived of testosterone during the critical first days of life. In Column 1 a normal male (*gray*) is unaffected by the injection of female hormones (*colored syringe*) at maturity. In Column 2 a castrated male is similarly injected; it then assumes the female's permissive sexual posture. In Column 3 the same behavior is produced by implanting an ovary.

criteria for male and female behavior. The male goes through a complex pattern of behavior that begins with mounting of the female and proceeds through several stages to the final ejaculation. The female's display of sexual receptivity is marked by a "lordosis response" (which consists of arching the back and elevating the pelvis) ·when she is mounted by the male. Now, in most subprimate mammals, including the rat, the female's sexual behavior depends entirely on the hormones circulating in her bloodstream. Removal of the ovaries (and hence the elimination of estrogen and progesterone) will completely suppress her normal female sexual behavior, and conversely injections of estrogen and progesterone will restore it. Hence it was no surprise to find that the testosterone treatment of newborn female rats, which disrupted their normal secretion of sex hormones, affected their sexual behavior. The effects were marked, however, by several unusual features.

These masculinized females not only lost the usual female sexual receptivity, including the normal lordosis response to a male, but also failed to show the normal response even when they were given large replacement injections of estrogen and progesterone. Moreover, they showed male behavior that went beyond any previously observed. Male sex behavior is not uncommon even in normal female animals; they can often be observed going through the motions of mounting. A normal adult female rat, if injected with testosterone, will sometimes go so far as to mimic some components of the male's act of copulation. Some of our female rats that had been testosteronized at birth went further, however. Although such females lack any semblance of male genitalia, when they were given a new dose of testosterone as adults, they performed the entire male sexual ritual, including the motions that accompany ejaculation.

The male rats in our experiments showed a similarly striking change of sexual behavior as a result of hormonal alteration at birth. Normally it is extremely difficult to elicit female sexual behavior in an adult male merely by injecting him with female hormones. When, however, newborn male rats were castrated, so that they lacked testosterone at the critical stage of development occurring in the few days after birth, it was found that injection of very small doses of estrogen and progesterone in these males as adults caused them to display sexual behavior precisely like that of normal females. Clearly the

change in these animals involved the central.nervous system; the system's response to female hormones, as reflected in the animal's behavior, had been altered.

Thus all the experiments, both on males and on females, left little doubt that testosterone could determine the sexual differentiation of the brain in the first few days after birth. In some manner testosterone produced a profound and permanent change in the sensitivity of the brain to sex hormones. In the female it made the brain tissue much more sensitive to testosterone and insensitive to estrogen and progesterone, so that the animal did not display normal female behavior in response to these female hormones. In the male the absence of testosterone at the critical period caused the animal to be sensitive to estrogen and progesterone. To put it another way, the absence of testosterone at the differentiation stage would leave both males and females sensitive to the female hormones and capable of displaying female behavior; the presence of testosterone, on the other hand, would desensitize females as well as males, so that both sexes failed to display feminine behavior when they were challenged with female hormones.

That the sex hormones can act directly on the brain was clearly demonstrated in experiments by Harris and Richard Michael. They implanted a synthetic estrogen (stilbestrol) into the hypothalamus of female cats and found that the implant evoked full female sexual behavior although the cats did not show the usual physiological signs of estrus. In similar experiments with males Julian M. Davidson of Stanford University showed that implants of testosterone in the brain of a castrated male rat would elicit male sexual behavior, although again there was no sign of effects on the anatomy of the male reproductive system.

If the brain differentiates into male and female types, may not the difference be reflected in fields of behavior other than the sexual? A few experiments looking into this question have been conducted; they suggest that other forms of behavior can indeed be influenced by· hormonal treatment during the critical period of sexual differentiation.

One of these studies involved a difference between male and female behavior that Curt P. Richter of the Johns Hopkins School of Medicine observed many

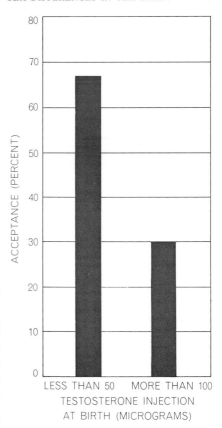

SEXUAL BEHAVIOR of female rats was substantially modified by the injection of male hormone at birth. Although dosed with female hormones at maturity, females that had received 100 micrograms or more of testosterone at birth were less than half as responsive to male sexual advances as rats that had received little or no male hormone.

years ago. He used an activity wheel that measured the amount of voluntary running activity an animal would perform each day. The activity of females, he found, went in cycles, rising to a peak at the time of ovulation; males, on the other hand, performed more uniformly from day to day. Harris recently applied this activity test to male rats that had been castrated shortly after birth and then implanted with an ovary as adults. They showed a cyclic pattern of running activity corresponding to the cycle of ovulation (covering four to five days) of the female rat.

Another test employed the open-field apparatus with which we have gauged animals' behavior in response to various emotion-evoking stimuli [see "Stimulation in Infancy," by Seymour Levine; SCIENTIFIC AMERICAN Offprint 436]. In this apparatus females tend to be more exploratory and to defecate less often than males. We found that female rats to which testosterone had been administered at birth displayed the male pattern of defecation behavior instead of the female pattern [*see illustration on this page*].

Analyzing the play of young monkeys before they reach sexual maturity, Young and his co-workers found that the juvenile male's behavior is distinctly different from the female's: the male is more inclined to rough-and-tumble play, more aggressive and more given to threatening facial expressions. Again experiments showed that injections of testosterone during the critical differentiation period (before birth in the monkey's case) caused females to display the male type of behavior in play.

Obviously the findings so far are only first steps in what promises to be an important new field of investigation. They invite a full exploration of the extent to which behavior, nonsexual as well as sexual, can be masculinized by testosterone treatment or feminized by castration at the critical stage of sexual differentiation. It presents a new biological mystery: If testosterone at the critical period does indeed produce sexual differentiation in the brain, by what mechanism does it do so? The studies on animals may well have clinical implications for human beings with respect to the problem of homosexuality. Human homosexual behavior undoubtedly involves many psychological factors that do not apply to the lower animals, but it may also depend in a fundamental sense on what the hormonal makeup of the individual happens to be during the development of the nervous system.

There are other questions of broader interest. Do the hormones of the thyroid

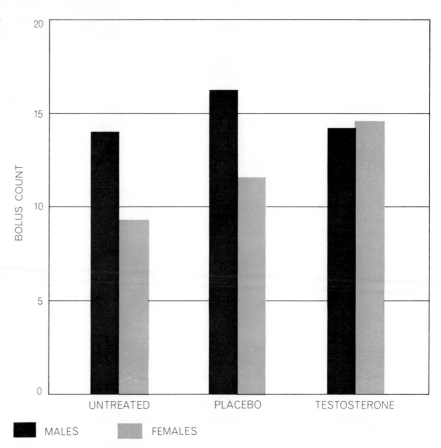

EXPLORATORY BEHAVIOR, more extensive among female rats than among males, was modified when the females were injected with male hormones at birth. The bar chart shows the frequency of defecation, which is inversely proportional to exploration, in three minutes' exposure in an open-field apparatus. When the females had not been injected at birth (*left and center*), their count was significantly lower than the males'. Females that had been masculinized (*right*), however, defecated at a rate insignificantly different from the males'.

gland, the adrenal cortex and other organs of the endocrine system exert differentiating effects on the developing brain? To what extent may the various hormones acting on the brain during infancy shape the future behavior of an individual? The artificially masculinized female rat and the feminized male have opened a wide field for speculation and research.

7

STIMULATION IN INFANCY

SEYMOUR LEVINE
May 1960

*Both painful shocks and gentle handling enhance
the development of normal stress responses in infant
animals. The absence of such treatment leads to
behavioral disorders when the animal matures*

When the Emperor of Lilliput accepted Lemuel Gulliver into favor, His Most Sublime Majesty first secured Gulliver's solemn oath upon an agreement to observe certain rules of etiquette. The fourth article of the agreement stipulated that Gulliver should not take any Lilliputian subjects into his hands without their consent. Gulliver learned later to appreciate the sentiments behind this article in an intensely subjective way. In the country of Brobdingnag he was himself picked up in the huge hand of a Brobdingnagian. He recalled his reactions: "All I ventured was to raise my eyes towards the sun, and place my hands together in a supplicating posture, and to speak some words in an humble melancholy tone, suitable to the condition I then was in."

What Jonathan Swift describes here is the essence of an experience that befalls children and small animals every day. It happens whenever a parent picks up a baby, or a child tussles with his puppy. Almost all experiences of infancy involve some handling by a parent or some other larger and supremely powerful figure. Even the tenderest handling must at times be the occasion of emotional stress. Perhaps the only children insulated from such experience are those reared in orphanages and other institutions, and the only animals those that live in laboratories. Certainly the laboratory animal must find a minimum of stress and little stimulation of any other kind in an environment controlled for temperature, humidity, light and so on. In the ordinary world the infant must grow under the changing pressures and sudden challenges of an inconstant environment. One may well wonder how the stressful experiences of infancy affect the behavior and physiology of the adult organism later on.

When in 1954 we began our investigations into the broad area defined by this question, we naturally turned first to the presumably more obvious effects of early painful or traumatic experience. We subjected a group of infant rats to mild electric shocks, scheduled at the same hour each day. For control purposes we routinely placed the members of another group in the shock cage for the same length of time each day but did not give them shocks. A third group of infant rats was left in the nest and not handled at all. We expected that the shocked rats would be affected by their experience, and we looked for signs of emotional disorder when they reached adulthood. To our surprise it was the second control group—the rats we had not handled at all—that behaved in a peculiar manner. The behavior of the shocked rats could not be distinguished from that of the control group which had experienced the same handling but no electric shock. Thus the results of our first experiment caused us to reframe our question. Our investigation at the Columbus Psychiatric Institute and Hospital of Ohio State University has since been concerned not so much with the effects of stressful experience—which after all is the more usual experience of infants—as with the effects of the absence of such experience in infancy.

We have repeated our original experiment many times, subjecting the infant animals to a variety of stresses and degrees of handling. Invariably it is the nonmanipulated "controls" that exhibit deviations of behavior and physiology when they are tested as adults. Significantly these deviations involve the organism's response to stress, and they show up in most of the diverse aspects of that response. In a standard behavioral test, for example, the animal is placed in the unfamiliar, but otherwise neutral, surroundings of a transparent plastic box. The nonmanipulated animals crouch in a corner of the box; animals that have been handled and subjected to stress in infancy freely explore the space. The same contrast in behavior may be observed and recorded quantitatively in the "open field": an area three feet square marked off into smaller squares. In terms of the number of squares crossed during a fixed time period, shocked and manipulated animals show a much greater willingness to run about and explore their surroundings. In both situations the nonmanipulated animals, cowering in a corner or creeping timidly about, tend to defecate and urinate frequently. Since these functions are largely controlled by the sympathetic nervous system, and since certain responses to stress are principally organized around the sympathetic nervous system, this behavior is a sure sign of reactivity to stress.

Another objective and quantitative index of stress response is provided by the hormones and glands of the endocrine system. Under stress, in response to prompting by the central nervous system, the pituitary releases larger quantities of various hormones, one of the principal ones being the adrenal-corticotrophic hormone (ACTH). Stimulation by ACTH causes the outer layer, or cortex, of the adrenal gland to step up the release of its several steroids; distributed by the bloodstream, these hormones accelerate the metabolism of the tissues in such a way as to maintain their integrity under stress. The activity of the endocrine system may be measured conveniently in a number of ways: by the enlargement of the adrenal glands, by the volume of adrenal steroids in circulation or by the depletion of ascorbic acid (vitamin C) in the adrenals. By some of these measurements the nonstimulated animals showed a markedly higher reactivity when subjected to a variety of stresses, including toxic injection of glucose, conditioning to avoid a painful stimulus and swimming in a water maze.

The conclusion that these animals are hyperreactive to stress is, however, an oversimplification that conceals an even more important difference in their stress response. Recently we measured the

steroids in circulation in both stimulated and nonstimulated animals during the period immediately following stress by electric shock. Whereas the two groups showed the same volume of steroids in circulation before shock, the animals that had been exposed to stress in infancy showed a much higher output of steroids in the first 15 minutes after shock. The nonstimulated animals achieve the same output but more slowly, and appear to maintain a high level of steroid secretion for a longer period of

time. There is thus a distinct difference in the pattern of the stress response in the two kinds of animal.

This observation acquires its full significance when it is considered in the light of the biological function of the stress response. The speed and short duration of the response in the stimulated animal obviously serve the useful purpose of mobilizing the resources of the organism at the moment when it is under stress. The delay in the endocrine response of the nonstimulated animal

MILD STIMULATION consisted of picking up the infant rats, removing them from their breeding cage and enclosing them in a small compartment for three minutes a day. The rats were then returned to their nests. The rats shown here are about 11 days old.

is thus, by contrast, maladaptive. Moreover, the prolongation of the stress response, as observed in these animals, can have severely damaging consequences: stomach ulcers, increased susceptibility to infection and eventually death due to adrenal exhaustion.

The maladaptive nature of the stress response in the nonmanipulated animal is further manifested in the fact that it may be elicited in such a neutral situation as the open-field test. The animal that has been manipulated in infancy shows no physiological stress response in this situation although it exhibits a vigorous and immediate endocrine response when challenged by the pain and threat of an electric shock.

In this connection we have made the interesting discovery that stimulation by handling and stress hastens the maturation of the stress response in the infant animal. Although the adrenal glands begin to function shortly after birth and the pituitary appears to contain ACTH early in the course of development, the nerve mechanism that controls the release of ACTH does not seem to come into operation until the rat is about 16 days of age. When we exposed infant rats that had been handled from birth to severe cold stress, however, they showed a significant ACTH response as early as 12 days of age. This four days' difference represents a considerable acceleration of development in the rat, equivalent to several months in the growth of a human infant. The manipulated animals, more-

PAINFUL STIMULATION consisted of subjecting the infant rats to an electric shock lasting from several seconds to several minutes. The effects on the rat's behavior as an adult were indistinguishable from those produced by the routine shown on the opposite page.

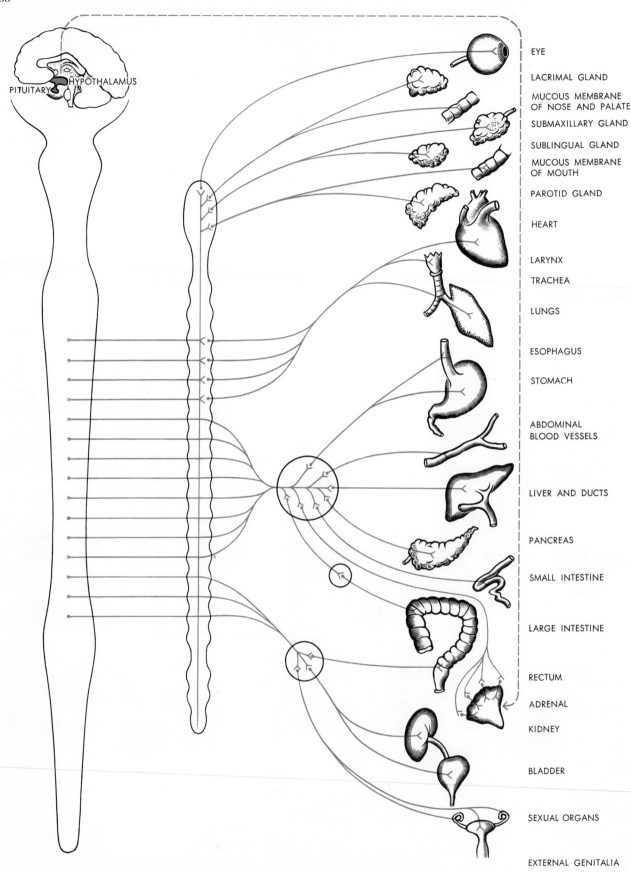

PITUITARY HYPOTHALAMUS

EYE

LACRIMAL GLAND

MUCOUS MEMBRANE
OF NOSE AND PALATE

SUBMAXILLARY GLAND

SUBLINGUAL GLAND

MUCOUS MEMBRANE
OF MOUTH

PAROTID GLAND

HEART

LARYNX

TRACHEA

LUNGS

ESOPHAGUS

STOMACH

ABDOMINAL
BLOOD VESSELS

LIVER AND DUCTS

PANCREAS

SMALL INTESTINE

LARGE INTESTINE

RECTUM

ADRENAL

KIDNEY

BLADDER

SEXUAL ORGANS

EXTERNAL GENITALIA

RESPONSES TO STRESS are partly controlled by the pathways shown in this diagram of the human sympathetic nervous system. Sympathetic fibers (*solid colored lines*) originating in the spinal cord (*far left*) innervate the internal organs via the chain ganglia (*left center*) and the ganglia of the celiac plexus (*right center*).

Extreme stress upsets the normal rhythm of this system, causing disturbances such as loss of bladder control and increased pulse rate. Stress also stimulates the hypothalamus and the pituitary to produce ACTH, which reaches the adrenals via the bloodstream (*broken line*) and stimulates them to produce steroid hormones.

over, reached an adult level of response considerably earlier than their untreated litter mates.

From the evidence it may be inferred that stimulation must have accelerated the maturation of the central nervous system in these animals. We have direct evidence that this is so from analysis of the brain tissue of our subjects. The brains of infant rats that have been handled from birth show a distinctly higher cholesterol content. Since the cholesterol content of the brain is related principally to the brain's white matter, this is evidence that in these animals the maturation of structure parallels the maturation of function.

In all respects, in fact, the manipulated infants exhibit a more rapid rate of development. They open their eyes earlier and achieve motor coordination sooner. Their body hair grows faster, and they tend to be significantly heavier at weaning. They continue to gain weight more rapidly than the nonstimulated animals even after the course of stimulation has been completed at three weeks of age. Their more vigorous growth does not seem to be related to food intake but to better utilization of the food consumed and probably to a higher output of the somatotrophic (growth) hormone from the pituitary. These animals may also possess a higher resistance to pathogenic agents; they survive an injection of leukemia cells for a considerably longer time.

Another contrast between the stimulated and unstimulated animals developed when we electrically destroyed the septal region of their brains, the region between and under the hemispheres of the midbrain. Such damage makes an animal hyperexcitable, vicious and flighty. It will attack a pencil extended to it, react with extreme startle to a tap on the back, is exceedingly difficult to capture and upon capture will bite wildly and squeal loudly. In systematic observation of these responses we found that manipulated animals are far tamer postoperatively than nonmanipulated ones. The latter rank as the most excitable and vicious rats we have ever observed in the laboratory; it was not unusual for one of these animals to pursue us around the room, squealing and attacking our shoes and pants legs.

At the very least our experiments yield an additional explanation for the variability among laboratory animals that so often confuses results in experimental biology. This has been attributed to genetic differences, unknown factors and sometimes to experimental error. It

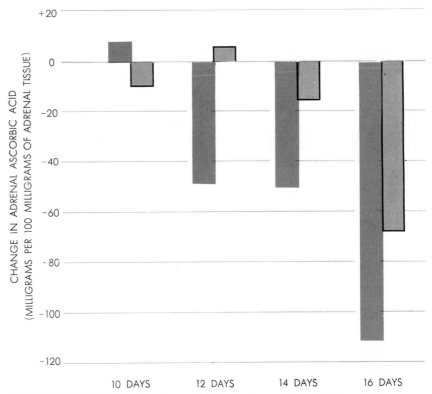

EXPOSURE TO COLD produced a marked drop in the ascorbic acid (vitamin C) concentration in the adrenal glands of stimulated rats more than 10 days old (*colored bars*), but produced no significant effect on the nonstimulated rats until they were 16 days old.

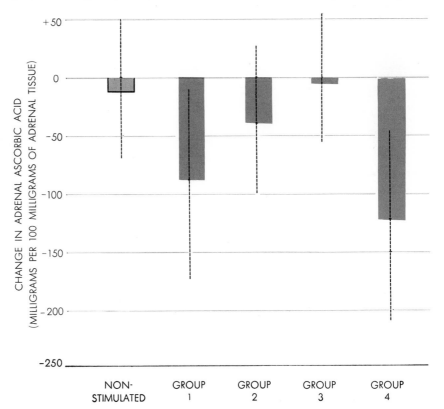

CRITICAL PERIOD in the development of the stress response was determined by stimulating infant rats at different stages of life. They were then exposed to cold and the drop in their adrenal ascorbic acid level was analyzed. Rats in Group 1 (stimulated from the second to the fifth days of life) and in Group 4 (stimulated from the second to the 13th days) responded better than both the nonstimulated rats and those in Groups 2 and 3 (stimulated from the sixth to the ninth and from the 10th to the 13th days, respectively). The bars show the average drop in the concentration and the broken lines the range.

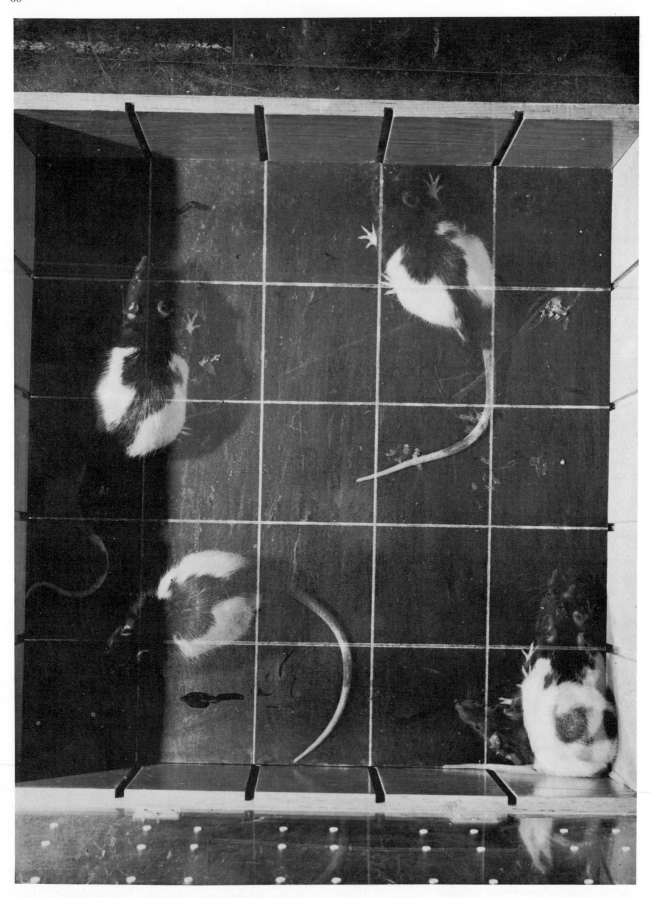

OPEN-FIELD EXPERIMENT illustrates how the behavior of a full-grown rat stimulated during infancy differs from that of a previously nonstimulated one. This multiple-exposure photograph shows how a nonstimulated rat (*lower right*) cowers in a corner when placed in an unfamiliar environment; the stimulated animal is much more willing to run about and explore his surroundings.

is apparent that the character of early infant experience is another important determinant of individual differences in animals.

The same consideration leads to the broader question of "nature v. nurture," that is, the contribution of genetic factors as opposed to the influence of the environment. Both sets of factors are essential and they interact to give rise to the individual organism. The basic patterns of development are most likely determined by heredity. But the genetic determinants do not find expression except in interaction with various aspects of the environment. In the normal course of events the environment provides the substance, energy and milieu for the unfolding of the organism's potentialities; in the extreme, environmental influences can determine whether the process of development will continue and produce an organism. In other words, organisms do not grow in a vacuum. This is true even of our nontreated animals. litter mates and the routine laboratory procedures furnish stimulation of all kinds. Such stimulation does not compare, however, with that provided by our experimental treatments. We have dealt with only a limited range of effects, and have focused primarily on the physiological and behavioral responses to stress. But our results clearly indicate that stimulation of the infant organism has quite universal consequences upon the behavior and physiology of the adult.

One must be careful in attempting to bridge the gap between animal experimentation and human biology. The effects of early experience have proved to be significant, however, in many species of mammal, including the monkey, dog, cat, guinea pig and mouse, and in such nonmammals as fish and fowl. It cannot be said that the phenomenon is species-limited. A great deal of clinical evidence, moreover, clearly indicates that infant experience in humans has a profound effect in shaping the character and constitution of the adult. Investigators concerned with maternal deprivation report that children raised in foundling homes develop at a retarded rate and are more susceptible to disease. These observations are similar to those we have made in our animal experiments. It may be that the detrimental effects of the foundling home have less to do with maternal deprivation than with the simple lack of stimulation that is inevitable in most such environments. The character of early experience may thus also underlie many problems in psychosomatic medicine and may explain in part why one

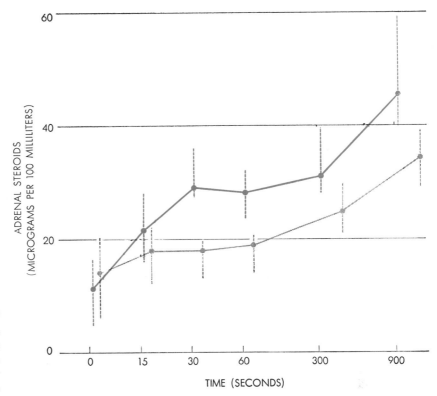

SLUGGISH RESPONSE to an electric shock is indicated by the slow rise in the concentration of circulating steroid hormones in previously nonstimulated rats (*gray curve*). In the stimulated animals (*colored curve*) the level increases rapidly for about 15 minutes. The points on the curve indicate the average level and the broken lines the range of values.

individual develops ulcers, another migraine headaches and yet another shows little or no psychosomatic involvement under the same pressures of living.

One of the most encouraging aspects of our research is that it has raised more questions than it has answered. We have not yet, for example, identified the critical element in our stimulation procedures that leads to such predictable and profound effects. Painful and extreme forms of stimulation seem to have effects indistinguishable from those produced by merely picking up an animal and placing it in another location for a brief period of time. Is picking up an infant organism as casual and insignificant a procedure as it appears? Or is the experience of the infant closer to that of Gulliver in Brobdingnag? Mere handling may, in fact, constitute a stimulation as compelling and severe as the more obviously traumatic forms of stimulation. It may be that some degree of stressful experience in infancy is necessary for successful adaptation of the organism to the environment it encounters in later life.

Another important question is whether there is a critical infantile period (or periods) during which stimulation is

most effective. The evidence so far points to a period following immediately after birth. In one study we handled the animals in three separate groups for four days each, from the second through the fifth day, from the sixth through the ninth day and from the 10th through the 13th day. When we tested them for stress response on the 14th day, only the first group showed any evidence that they were capable of an endocrine response. Other investigators have had similar results. This should not be taken to mean, however, that stimulation has no effect after the critical period is past or that one critical period sets all responses.

Still other questions have not yet been satisfied by even partial answers. There is, for example, the question of therapy: Can the effects of lack of stimulation in the critical period be counteracted by stimulation of any sort after the critical period has passed? The most pressing question—the most "stimulating" question—is how stimulation causes change in the infant organism. The answer to this question should lead to a fuller understanding of the differences between individual constitutions and of the physiological mechanisms that are involved in behavior.

8

ARRESTED VISION

AUSTIN H. RIESEN
July 1950

In which chimpanzees raised in the dark shed light on the relationship between visual experience and visual development

MANY primitive organisms show immediate and highly uniform reactions to light from the moment of birth. In man vision is a much more complex skill that develops gradually through the years of infancy and childhood. How much of this capacity is innate and how much is acquired by learning or through the natural maturation of the eyes during the child's early years? What are the factors that determine visual perception? If we knew the answers to these questions we could do a great deal more than we can now to improve defective vision.

The task of separating the hereditary factors from the effects of experience in human vision obviously is not easy. For example, a newborn infant at first shows no clear indication of any response to a bright disk presented before its eyes. Only after several weeks does the growing infant begin to look at the disk. Is this the result of growth, of experience or of both? Does the change in response come about through practice in the use of the eyes, or through a natural maturation that occurs, quite independently of use, in the retina of the eye, in the eye or neck muscles, in fiber tracts of the central nervous system or in several of these parts combined?

Scientific studies of the growth of behavior have shown that certain abilities do develop without use as animals mature. Thus tadpoles raised under anesthesia to prevent swimming movements nevertheless improve in swimming ability. Chicks and rats kept in darkness for a time show some progress in vision-controlled behavior. Children also demonstrate a basic rate of maturation in some capacities: there is a limit to the degree of retardation or acceleration of these abilities that can be effected by restricting or expanding their training.

But some of these studies have revealed curious contradictions. Wendell Cruze at North Carolina State College found that after newly hatched chicks had been kept in darkness for five days, they were generally able to peck at and hit 24 of the first 25 grains presented to them; this score was 12 per cent better than the average of hits by chicks immediately after hatching. On the other hand, S. G. Padilla at the University of Michigan showed that if the period of darkness was extended to 14 days, the pecking response failed to appear, presumably because the instinct to peck at spots on the ground died out through disuse. The chicks began to starve in the midst of plenty. So it appears that lack of practice, at least if sufficiently prolonged, can interfere with the development of behavior which is basically instinctive or reflex in nature.

In human beings the most nearly pertinent evidence on this problem has come from studies of patients operated upon at advanced ages for congenital cata-

CHIMPANZEES WERE BLINDFOLDED when they were not kept in a darkroom (*left*). When the chimpanzees were brought into the light at the age of 16 months (*right*), they exhibited a serious retardation of vision.

racts. These patients, who have passed all their lives in near-blindness, ranging from the bare ability to tell day from night to some ability to distinguish colors and localize light, invariably report an immediate awareness of a change after a successful operation. They begin at once to distinguish differences in the parts of the visual field, although they cannot identify an object or describe its shape. After a few days' practice they can name colors. From this point on progress is slow, often highly discouraging, and some patients never get beyond the ability to distinguish brightness and color. Others, over a period of months and even years, develop the ability to identify simple geometric figures, read letters and numbers and, in rare cases, to identify complex patterns such as words, outline drawings and faces. During their efforts to improve their visual skill the patients go through a long period of picking out elements in an object and inferring the nature of the object from these elements—often erroneously. For example, a child of 12, some months after her operation, is reported by her doctor to have pointed to a picture and called it "a camel, because it has a hump." What she identified as a hump was the dorsal fin of a fish.

But such cases of congenital cataract do not give us very satisfactory evidence on the elementary problem of how disuse affects the development of visual behavior. There are too many other variables; we must take into account (1) the degree of the patient's previous blindness, since he was not in total darkness, (2) the limit that is imposed on his potentialities for improvement by the

fact that the eye operated on lacks a lens, and (3) the circumstance that in all these cases there appears to be another visual handicap—jerky movements of the eyeballs known as spontaneous nystagmus. The effects of these combined difficulties are not readily calculable. For a more meaningful study it is highly desirable to eliminate these variables by setting up a controlled experiment that will determine the effects of disuse on normal eyes. Obviously such an experiment cannot be risked in human beings; no one would wish to impose permanent reading difficulties on any person having to adjust himself to a civilized society. The most logical subject for the experiment is another higher primate. The chimpanzee was chosen, because its behavior, like man's, is dominated by vision, and because it is intelligent and tractable.

In 1942 at the Yerkes Laboratories of Primate Biology in Orange Park, Fla., an infant male chimpanzee was separated from its mother on the day of birth and blindfolded with a gauze bandage and adhesive tape. This animal defeated the experimenters by loosening the tape at the side of his left nostril and habitually peeking down his nose with his left eye. By the age of 16 weeks he gained full freedom from facial bandages. Although he did not recognize his feeding bottle at this time, nor show fixation of persons or objects, he developed fairly adequate visual behavior within a few weeks.

In 1945 the experimenters tried again. This time two newborn chimpanzee infants, a male and a female respectively named Snark and Alfalfa, were housed

in a completely darkened room. During the first 16 months the only light these infants experienced was an electric lamp turned on for intervals of 45 seconds several times daily for their routine care and feeding. When they were first tested for visual perception at the age of 16 months, both chimpanzees showed extreme incompetence. Their reflex responses indicated that their eyes were sensitive to light—the pupils constricted; sudden changes of illumination startled the animals; they responded to a slowly waving flashlight with jerky pursuit movements of the eyes and side to side following motions of the head. But both chimpanzees failed to show any visual responses to complex patterns of light until after they had spent many hours in illuminated surroundings. They did not respond to play objects or their feeding bottles unless these touched some part of the body. They did not blink at a threatening motion toward the face. When an object was advanced slowly toward the face, there was no reaction until the object actually touched the face, and then the animal gave a startled jump.

After the 16-month period of darkness, Alfalfa was placed on a limited light schedule until the age of 21 months and Snark until 33 months. When Alfalfa was later moved into a normal daylight environment, in the course of many months she developed normal recognition of objects, began to blink in response to threats and ceased to be startled by a touch. Snark was much more retarded. Between the ages of 20 and 27 months, while he was still on rationed light, he learned after many hundreds of trials to

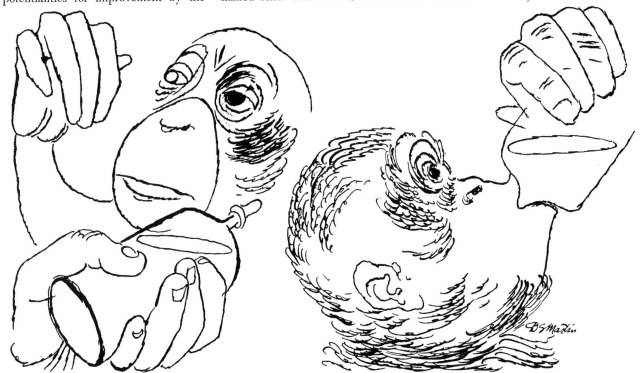

CHIMPANZEES WERE FED during tests of their visual development. Chimpanzee raised in the dark (*left*) was unable to grasp a bottle, even after several trials. Normal chimpanzee grasped it after one trial.

tell the difference between contrasting signs, differing in color or pattern, which indicated either food or a mild electric shock. His visual acuity, as measured by ability to discriminate between horizontal and vertical lines, was well below that of normally raised animals. At the end of 33 months he began to live in the normally lighted chimpanzee nursery and later out of doors with chimpanzees of his own age. It was expected that he would rapidly acquire normal visual behavior. He did improve slightly at first, but after this small initial improvement he actually lost ground in visual responsiveness, until even reflex activity began to die away.

What is the explanation of this deterioration? Had the development of his eyes been permanently arrested by the absence of light? There had been no previous evidence that stimulation by light is essential for the normal growth of the primate retina or optic nerve. It was a surprise to find that, while the eyes of these chimpanzees remained sensitive to light after 16 months in darkness, the retina and optic disk in both animals did not reflect as much light as normal chimpanzee eyes do. Snark later developed a marked pallor of the optic disk in both eyes. There is other evidence suggesting that fish and amphibians, at least, need light-stimulation for normal eye development. So the physiological effects of the lack of light may be part of the explanation for Snark's loss of visual function. But it is not the whole explanation for all the visual abnormalities in these two chimpanzees, nor does it explain the

visual difficulties of the cataract patients. These patients have excellent color discrimination, and, incidentally, do not show pallor of the optic disk. Moreover, we now have clear evidence from further experiments with chimpanzees that not merely light itself but stimulation by visual patterns is essential to normal visual development.

In these experiments three other newborn chimpanzees, two females and a male, were put into the darkroom. Debi was raised for seven months in complete darkness, even during her feedings and other care. Kora was raised for the same period on a ration of an average of one and a half hours of light daily, but the light, admitted through a white Plexiglas mask, was diffuse and unpatterned. Lad was given one and a half hours of patterned light daily: he could observe the edges of his crib, the variations in pattern introduced by movements of his own body and appendages, and all the accompaniments of bottle-feeding, including the moving about of persons in the moderately lighted room.

At seven months, when the three subjects were removed to normal daylight surroundings, Lad's visual performance was indistinguishable from that of chimpanzees raised normally. Kora and Debi, however, showed the same kinds of retardation as had Snark and Alfalfa, with some minor exceptions. Kora did not develop the blink response to a moving object until six days after her removal from darkness, and Debi not until 15 days. It took Kora 13 days and Debi 30 days to acquire the ability to pursue a

moving person with the eyes, and they did this by a series of refixations instead of following smoothly as normal animals of comparable age do; it took Kora 20 days and Debi 16 days to pursue visually a moving feeding bottle; Kora 13 days and Debi 30 days to fixate the image of a stationary person.

These differences between Debi and Kora may lie within the range of variation that would occur in a group of animals treated exactly the same as either Debi or Kora. This question could be checked only by repeating the experiment many times.

Between seven and 10 months of age Debi and Kora both showed a moderate and intermittent outward (wall-eyed) deviation of the eyes. This gradually was overcome. Both infants also showed an initial spontaneous nystagmus, i.e., jerky eye movements. It appeared only sporadically, and was more pronounced under general excitement than when the animals were well relaxed.

Normal animals of seven months learn to avoid a large yellow and black striped disk after receiving one or two mild electric shocks from it. Debi and Kora, however, were shocked by the disk twice a day for six and nine days, respectively, before they so much as whimpered when it was shown. Only after 13 days in Kora's case and 15 days in Debi's did they consistently indicate by some sort of avoidance response that they saw the disk within five seconds of the time that it was raised in front of their eyes.

In still another study an infant chimpanzee named Kandy was put in the

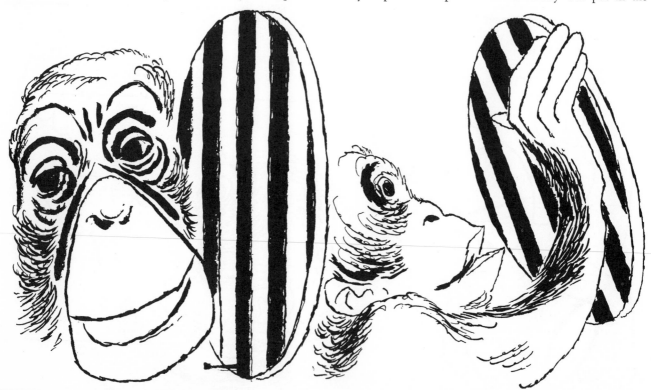

NORMAL AND ABNORMAL ANIMALS were subjected to the same stimuli. At the left an abnormal chimpanzee is given a mild electric shock by a disk with a contact at bottom. At right normal chimpanzee is shocked.

darkroom for only the first three months of life. After she was removed to daylight surroundings, her progress on the same tests was approximately parallel to that of Debi and Kora. There were three interesting differences: 1) Kandy showed a convergent squint (cross-eyes), which cleared up in a little less than two months; 2) she did not have spontaneous nystagmus; 3) she required 24 days, as compared with 13 or 15, to develop consistent avoidance of the black and yellow shock-disk. The last difference suggests that Kandy learned more slowly because of her younger age; in other words, that the development of visual discrimination was a matter of maturity as well as learning. This conclusion was strongly supported by the finding that an infant chimpanzee started through the same training at the age of two days failed to show avoidance in a month's time.

All these observations demonstrate that vision must be put to use if it is to develop normally, but they also indicate that during the first few months of an infant's life visual development is advanced by growth factors which are entirely independent of practice. Normally reared animals, for example, do not blink in response to the movement of objects across the visual field until they have reached the age of two months; the older darkroom animals, despite previous lack of experience, began to show this response within about two weeks after they were transferred to daylight surroundings.

The development and maintenance of normal visual functions in higher primates depends on a whole complex of interrelated factors, hereditary and environmental, and it can readily be disturbed at any stage of the individual's growth. This was shown in an experiment with a chimpanzee named Faik. Faik was raised in the normal light of the laboratory's nursery until the age of seven months. At that time the standard series of tests described above showed that he had excellent use of vision. Then from the age of eight to 24 months he was kept in the darkroom. He lived an active life filled with tactile, auditory, olfactory, gustatory and kinesthetic stimulation. He invited rough-house play from his caretakers at feeding times, and his general state of health remained entirely satisfactory.

When Faik was returned to daylight living quarters at 24 months, he had lost all ability to utilize vision in his interplay with the environment. He no longer recognized the feeding bottle, and failed to look at objects or persons, either stationary or moving. More than this, he possessed a strong spontaneous nystagmus and was even unable to follow a moving light in a darkroom until the fifth day after he was put back into a lighted environment. His first visual following movements, like those of all the darkroom-raised subjects, were not smooth but a series of jerky refixations, made even more jerky by the pronounced spontaneous nystagmus.

Even in direct sunlight Faik failed to grimace or close his eyelids; he gave no indication of the slightest discomfort when the sun shone in his eyes. (The chimpanzees raised in the darkroom from birth did close their lids in intense light.) Faik showed pallor similar to that of Snark and Alfalfa in his optic disks. His recovery of vision has been slow and is still only partial. Explanation of his case, and that of Snark, remains a challenge to further research.

These chimpanzee studies have established several fundamental points. They show that newborn animals, and older infants that have been kept in darkness for a time, exhibit visual reflexes when they are first subjected to light. Some responses that bear a close resemblance to reflex behavior, such as blinking at something rapidly approaching the face, become automatic only after considerable practice. Visual pursuit of moving objects, the coordination of the two eyes and convergent fixation, and the first recognition of objects come only after many hours or weeks of experience in use of the eyes. It takes the chimpanzee hundreds of hours of active utilization of the eyes to develop its vision to the stage where it can adequately guide locomotion and complex manipulations. The findings in the cases of two subjects that were kept in darkness for long periods indicate that the postponement of light exposure for too long can result in making the development of normal visual mechanisms extremely difficult if not impossible.

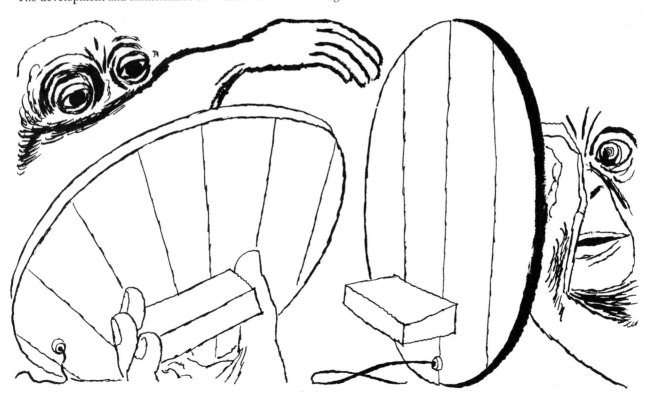

NORMAL AND ABNORMAL RESPONSE to shocking-disk was exhibited by animals. At left a normal chimpanzee responds violently after one shock. At right abnormal chimpanzee fails to avoid disk after many shocks.

9

THE ORIGIN OF FORM PERCEPTION

ROBERT L. FANTZ
May 1961

*Is man's ability to perceive the form of objects inborn
or must it be learned? Experiments indicate that it is
innate but that maturation and learning play important
roles in its development*

Long before an infant can explore his surroundings with hands and feet he is busy exploring it with his eyes. What goes on in the infant's mind as he stares, blinks, looks this way and that? Does he sense only a chaotic patchwork of color and brightness or does he perceive and differentiate among distinctive forms? The question has always fascinated philosophers and scientists, for it bears on the nature and origin of knowledge. At issue is the perennial question of nature *v.* nurture. On one side is the nativist, who believes that the infant has a wide range of innate visual capacities and predilections, which have evolved in animals over millions of years, and that these give a primitive order and meaning to the world from the "first look." On the other side is the extreme empiricist, who holds that the infant learns to see and to use what he sees only by trial and error or association, starting, as John Locke put it, with a mind like a blank slate.

It has long been known that very young infants can see light, color and movement. But it is often argued that they cannot respond to such stimuli as shape, pattern, size or solidity; in short, that they cannot perceive form. This position is the last stronghold of the empiricist, and it has been a hard one to attack. How is one to know what an infant sees? My colleagues and I have recently developed an experimental method of finding out. We have already disposed of the basic question, that of whether babies can perceive form at all. They can, at least to some degree, although it appears that neither the view of the simple nativist nor that of the simple empiricist tells the whole story. Now we are investigating the further question of how and when infants use their capacity to perceive form to confer order and meaning on their environment.

The technique grew out of studies with lower animals, which are of importance in themselves. They were undertaken in 1951 at the University of Chicago with newly hatched chicks. Paradoxically, chicks can "tell" more directly what they see than higher animals can. Soon after they break out of the shell they go about the business of finding things to peck at and eat. Their purposeful, visually dominated behavior is ideally suited for observation and experiment.

We presented the chicks with a number of small objects of different shapes.

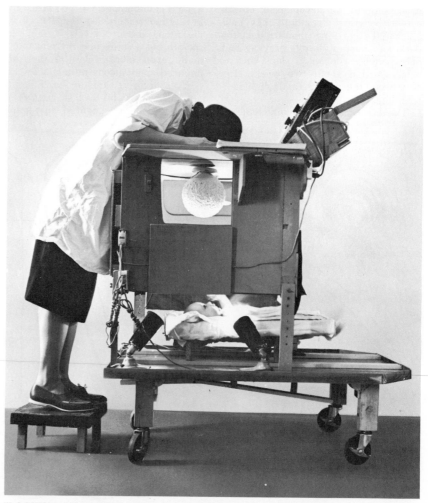

"LOOKING CHAMBER" was used to test the visual interests of chimpanzee and human infants. Here a human infant lies on a crib in the chamber, looking at objects hung from the ceiling. The observer, watching through a peephole, records the attention given each object.

Each object was enclosed in a clear plastic container to eliminate the possible influence of touch, smell or taste, but this did not prevent the chicks from pecking at preferred forms for hours on end. An electrical circuit attached to each container recorded the number of pecks at it.

More than 1,000 chicks were tested on some 100 objects. To exclude any opportunity for learning, the chicks were hatched in darkness and tested on their first exposure to light, before they had had any experience with real food. Presented with eight objects of graded angularity, from a sphere to a pyramid, the subjects pecked 10 times oftener at the sphere than they did at the pyramid. Among the flat forms, circles were preferred to triangles regardless of comparative size; among circles, those of ⅛-inch diameter drew the most attention. In a test of the effect of three-dimensionality the chicks consistently selected a sphere over a flat disk.

The results provided conclusive evidence that the chick has an innate ability to perceive shape, three-dimensionality and size. Furthermore, the chick uses the ability in a "meaningful" way by selecting, without learning, those objects most likely to be edible: round, three-dimensional shapes about the size of grain or seeds. Other birds exhibit similar visual capacity. For example, N. Tinbergen of the University of Oxford found selective pecking by newly hatched herring gulls. These chicks prefer shapes resembling that of the bill of the parent bird, from which they are fed [see "The Evolution of Behavior in Gulls," by N. Tinbergen; SCIENTIFIC AMERICAN Offprint 456].

Of course, what holds true for birds does not necessarily apply to human beings. The inherent capacity for form perception that has developed in birds may have been lost somewhere along the evolutionary branch leading to the primates, unlikely as it seems. Or, more plausibly, the primate infant may require a period of postnatal development to reach the level of function of the comparatively precocious chick.

When we set out to determine the visual abilities of helpless infants, the only indicator we could find was the activity of the eyes themselves. If an infant consistently turns its gaze toward some forms more often than toward others, it must be able to perceive form. Working on this premise, we developed a visual-interest test, using as our first subjects infant chimpanzees at the Yerkes Laboratories of Primate Biology in Orange Park, Fla.

A young chimpanzee lay on its back in a comfortable crib inside a "looking chamber" of uniform color and illumination. We attached to the ceiling of the chamber pairs of test objects, slightly separated from each other. They were exposed to view, alternately at right and left, in a series of short periods. Through a peephole in the ceiling we could see tiny images of the objects mirrored in the subjects' eyes. When the image of

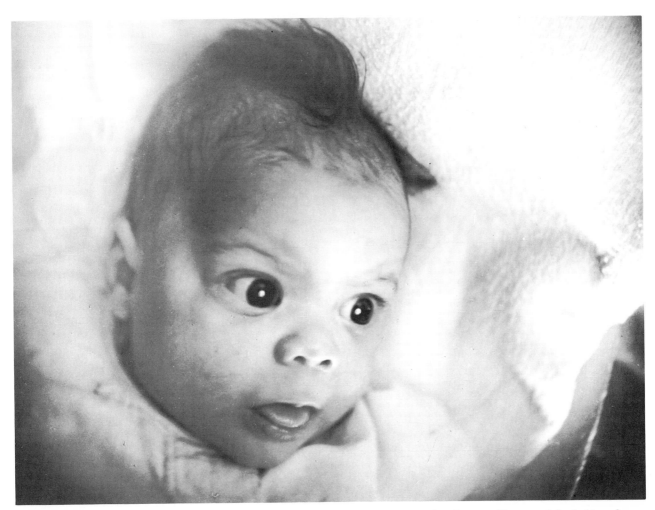

VISUAL INTEREST in various shapes was determined by noting reflections in the subject's eyes. In this case, with the reflection over the center of the infant's eye, the reflected object is being fixated, or looked at directly. (Because this young infant's binocular coordination is poor, only the right eye is fixating the object.) The length of each such fixation was recorded electrically.

PATTERN PREFERENCE of newly hatched chicks is studied by recording their pecks at each of a number of different shapes in plastic containers set into the wall of a test box.

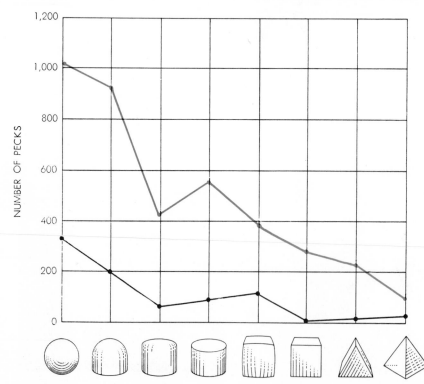

PREFERENCE FOR ROUNDNESS is shown by this record of total pecks by 112 chicks at the eight test objects shown across the bottom of the chart. The results are for the chicks' first 10 minutes (*black line*) and first 40 minutes (*colored line*) of visual experience.

one of the objects was at the center of the eye, over the pupil, we knew the chimpanzee was looking directly at it. The experimenter recorded on an electric timer the amount of attention given each target. The results were then analyzed to determine their statistical significance. Our first subject was a five-month-old chimpanzee. Later we followed a chimpanzee from birth, keeping it in darkness except during the tests. In both cases we found a definite preference for certain objects, indicating an inborn ability to distinguish among them.

Turning to human infants, we made no major change in our procedure except that we did not tamper with their everyday environment. The experiments did not disturb the infants but they did demand great patience of the investigators. Human infants are more rapidly bored than chimpanzees and they tend to go to sleep.

In the first experiment we tested 30 infants, aged one to 15 weeks, at weekly intervals. Four pairs of test patterns were presented in random sequence. In decreasing order of complexity they were: horizontal stripes and a bull's-eye design, a checkerboard and two sizes of plain square, a cross and a circle, and two identical triangles. The total time spent looking at the various pairs differed sharply, the more complex pairs drawing the greater attention. Moreover, the relative attractiveness of the two members of a pair depended on the presence of a pattern difference. There were strong preferences between stripes and bull's-eye and between checkerboard and square. Neither the cross and circle nor the two triangles aroused a significant differential interest. The differential response to pattern was shown at all ages tested, indicating that it was not the result of a learning process. The direction of preference between stripes and bull's-eye, on the other hand, changed at two months of age, due either to learning or to maturation.

Later we learned that a Swiss pediatrician, F. Stirnimann, had obtained similar results with still younger infants. He held cards up to the eyes of infants one to 14 days old and found that patterned cards were of more interest than those with plain colors.

Clearly some degree of form perception is innate. This, however, does not dispose of the role of physiological growth or of learning in the further development of visual behavior. Accordingly we turned our attention to the influence of these factors.

By demonstrating the existence of form perception in very young infants we had already disproved the widely held notion that they are anatomically incapable of seeing anything but blobs of light and dark. Nevertheless, it seems to be true that the eye, the visual nerve-pathways and the visual part of the brain are poorly developed at birth. If this is so, then the acuteness of vision—the ability to distinguish detail in patterns—should increase as the infant matures.

To measure the change in visual acuity we presented infants in the looking chamber with a series of patterns composed of black and white stripes, each pattern paired with a gray square of equal brightness. The width of the stripes was decreased in graded steps from one pattern to the next. Since we already knew that infants tend to look longer and more frequently at a patterned object than at a plain one, the width of the stripes of the finest pattern that was preferred to gray would provide an index to visual acuity. In this modified version the visual-interest test again solved the difficulties involved in getting infants to reveal what they see.

The width of the finest stripes that could be distinguished turned out to decrease steadily with increasing age during the first half-year of life. By six months babies could see stripes 1/64 inch wide at a distance of 10 inches—a visual angle of five minutes of arc, or 1/12 degree. (The adult standard is one minute of arc.) Even when still less than a month old, infants were able to perceive ⅛-inch stripes at 10 inches, corresponding to a visual angle of a little less than one degree. This is poor performance compared to that of an adult, but it is a far cry from a complete lack of ability to perceive pattern.

The effects of maturation on visual acuity are relatively clear and not too hard to measure. The problem of learning is more subtle. Other investigators have shown that depriving animals of patterned visual stimuli for a period after birth impairs their later visual performance, especially in form perception [see "Arrested Vision," by Austin H. Riesen; SCIENTIFIC AMERICAN Offprint 408]. Learned behavior is particularly vulnerable, but even innate responses are affected. For example, chicks kept in darkness for several weeks after hatching lose the ability to peck at food.

Research is now under way at Western Reserve University on this perplexing problem. We have raised monkeys in darkness for periods varying from one to 11 weeks. In general, the longer the period of deprivation, the poorer the performance when the animals were finally exposed to light and the more time they required to achieve normal responses. When first brought into the light, the older infant monkeys bumped into things, fell off tables, could not locate objects visually—for all practical purposes they were blind. It sometimes took weeks for them to "learn to see."

Monkeys kept a shorter time in the dark usually showed good spatial orientation in a few hours or days. Moreover, they showed normal interest in patterned objects, whereas the animals deprived of light for longer periods seemed more interested in color, brightness and size.

These results cannot be explained by innate capacity, maturation or learning alone. If form perception were wholly innate, it would be evident without experience at any age, and visual deprivation would have no effect. If maturation were the controlling factor, younger infant animals would be inferior rather than superior to older ones with or without visual experience. If form perception were entirely learned, the same period of experience would be required regardless of age and length of deprivation.

Instead there appears to be a complex interplay of innate ability, maturation

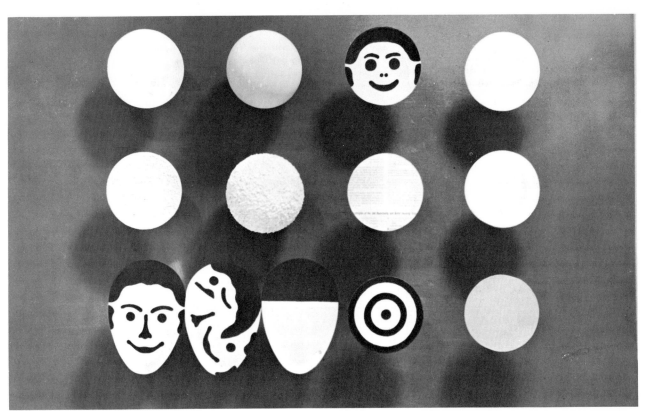

TEST OBJECTS included smooth and textured disks and spheres (*upper left*) to check interest in solidity. Attention to faces was tested with three patterns at lower left. The six round patterns at the right included (*top to bottom, left to right*) a face, a piece of printed matter, a bull's-eye, yellow, white and red disks. Round objects are six inches in diameter; "faces," nine inches long.

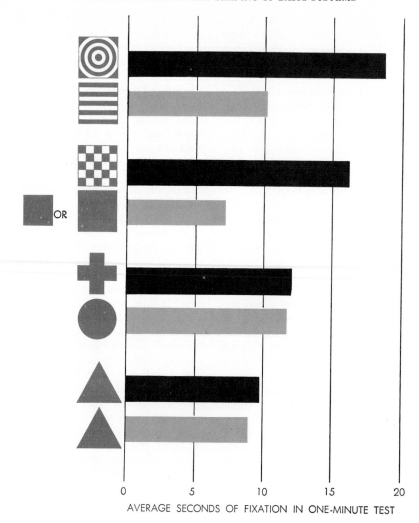

AVERAGE SECONDS OF FIXATION IN ONE-MINUTE TEST

INTEREST IN FORM was proved by infants' reactions to various pairs of patterns (*left*) presented together. (The small and large plain squares were used alternately.) The more complex pairs received the most attention, and within each of these pairs differential interest was based on pattern differences. These results are for 22 infants in 10 weekly tests.

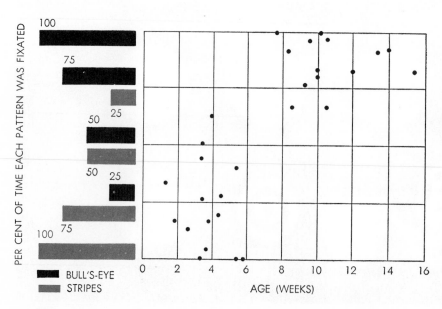

REVERSAL OF INTEREST from the striped pattern to the bull's-eye was apparent at two months of age. Each dot is for a single infant's first test session. It shows the time spent looking at the bull's-eye and at the stripes as a per cent of the time spent looking at both.

and learning in the molding of visual behavior, operating in this manner: there is a critical age for the development of a given visual response when the visual, mental and motor capacities are ready to be used and under normal circumstances will be used together. At that time the animal will either show the response without experience or will learn it readily. If the response is not "imprinted" at the critical age for want of visual stimulus, development proceeds abnormally, without the visual component. Presented with the stimulus later on, the animal learns to respond, if it responds at all, only with extensive experience and training. This explanation, if verified by further studies, would help to reconcile the conflicting claims of the nativist and the empiricist on the origin of visual perception.

To return to human infants, the work described so far does not answer the second question posed earlier in this article: whether or not the infant's innate capacity for form perception introduces a measure of order and meaning into what would otherwise be a chaotic jumble of sensations. An active selection process is necessary to sort out these sensations and make use of them in behavior. In the case of chicks such a process is apparent in the selection of forms likely to be edible.

In the world of the infant, people have an importance that is perhaps comparable to the importance of grain in the chick's world. Facial pattern is the most distinctive aspect of a person, the most reliable for distinguishing a human being from other objects and for identifying him. So a facelike pattern might be expected to bring out selective perception in an infant if anything could.

We tested infants with three flat objects the size and shape of a head. On one we painted a stylized face in black on a pink background, on the second we rearranged the features in a scrambled pattern, and on the third we painted a solid patch of black at one end with an area equal to that covered by all the features. We made the features large enough to be perceived by the youngest baby, so acuity of vision was not a factor. The three objects, paired in all possible combinations, were shown to 49 infants from four days to six months old.

The results were about the same for all age levels: the infants looked mostly at the "real" face, somewhat less often at the scrambled face, and largely ignored the control pattern. The degree of preference for the "real" face to the other one was not large, but it was

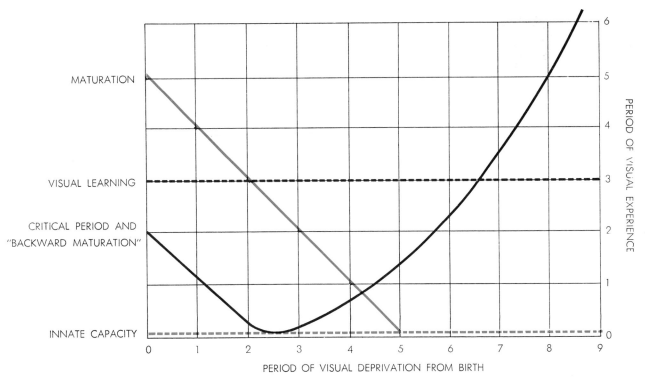

HYPOTHETICAL RESULTS that might be expected if any one developmental factor operated alone are plotted. The horizontal axis shows the period of rearing without visual experience; the vertical axis, the time subsequently required in the light until a given response is shown. Units of time are arbitrary. If innate capacity alone were effective, the response would always come without any experience (*broken colored line*). If maturation were necessary, the response would not be shown before a certain age, in this case five units, regardless of deprivation (*solid colored line*). If learning alone were operative, the required amount of experience would be constant (*broken black line*). Actually tests with chicks and monkey infants suggest the result shown by the solid black curve: after a short period of maturation, a "critical period" is reached when innate capacity can be manifested; more deprivation brings on "backward maturation," in which more and more experience is required before a response is shown.

consistent among individual infants, especially the younger ones. The experiment suggested that there is an unlearned, primitive meaning in the form perception of infants as well as of chicks.

Further support for the idea was obtained when we offered our infant subjects a choice between a solid sphere and a flat circle of the same diameter. When the texture and shading clearly differentiated the sphere from the circle —in other words, when there was a noticeable difference in pattern—the solid form was the more interesting to infants from one to six months old. This unlearned selection of a pattern associated with a solid object gives the infant a basis for perceiving depth.

The last experiment to be considered is a dramatic demonstration of the interest in pattern in comparison to color and brightness. This time there were six test objects: flat disks six inches in diameter. Three were patterned—a face, a bull's-eye and a patch of printed matter. Three were plain—red, fluorescent yellow and white. We presented them, against a blue background, one at a time in varied sequence and timed the length of the first glance at each.

The face pattern was overwhelmingly the most interesting, followed by the printing and the bull's-eye. The three brightly colored plain circles trailed far behind and received no first choices. There was no indication that the interest in pattern was secondary or acquired.

What makes pattern so intrinsically interesting to young infants? It seems to me that the answer must lie in the uses of vision for the child and adult.

One of these functions is the recognition of objects under various conditions. The color and brightness of objects

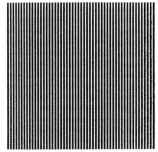

VISUAL ACUITY was tested with these stripes: 1/8, 1/16, 1/32 and 1/64 inch wide. Each pattern was displayed with a gray square of equal brightness 10 inches from the infants' eyes. The finest pattern consistently preferred to gray showed how narrow a stripe the infant could perceive. Infants under a month old could see the 1/8-inch stripes and the six-month-olds could see 1/64-inch stripes.

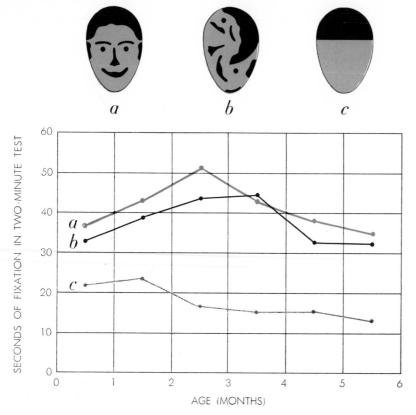

ADAPTIVE SIGNIFICANCE of form perception was indicated by the preference that infants showed for a "real" face (a) over a scrambled face (b), and for both over a control (c). The results charted here show the average time scores for infants at various ages when presented with the three face-shaped objects paired in all the possible combinations.

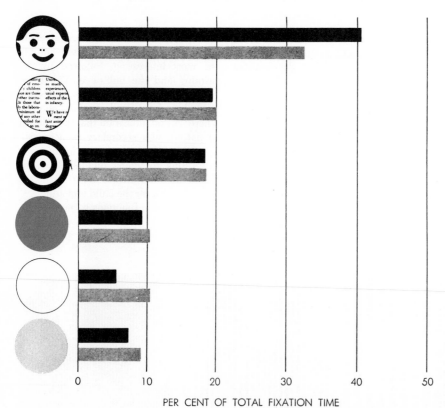

IMPORTANCE OF PATTERN rather than color or brightness was illustrated by the response of infants to a face, a piece of printed matter, a bull's-eye and plain red, white and yellow disks. Even the youngest infants preferred patterns. Black bars show the results for infants from two to three months old; gray bars, for infants more than three months old.

change with illumination; apparent size changes with distance; outline changes with point of view; binocular depth perception is helpful only at short range. But the pattern of an object—the texture, the arrangement of details, the complexity of contours—can be relied on for identification under diverse conditions.

A good example is social perception. As noted earlier, the general configuration of a face identifies a human being to an infant. At a later age a specific person is recognized primarily by more precise perception of facial pattern. Still later, subtle details of facial expression tell the child whether a person is happy or sad, pleased or displeased, friendly or unfriendly.

Another important function of vision is to provide orientation in space. For this purpose James J. Gibson of Cornell University has shown clearly the importance of a specific type of pattern: surface texture. For example, texture indicates a solid surface, whereas untextured light usually indicates air or water. Gradual changes in texture show whether a surface is vertical or horizontal or oblique, flat or curved or angular—and therefore indicate whether it can be walked on, walked around or climbed over. Discontinuities in texture mark the edges of objects and abrupt changes in surfaces.

From these few examples there can be no question of the importance of visual pattern in everyday life. It is therefore reasonable to suppose that the early interest of infants in form and pattern in general, as well as in particular kinds of pattern, play an important role in the development of behavior by focusing attention on stimuli that will later have adaptive significance.

Further research is necessary to pin down this and other implications more concretely, but the results to date do require the rejection of the view that the newborn infant or animal must start from scratch to learn to see and to organize patterned stimulation. Lowly chicks as well as lofty primates perceive and respond to form without experience if given the opportunity at the appropriate stage of development. Innate knowledge of the environment is demonstrated by the preference of newly hatched chicks for forms likely to be edible and by the interest of young infants in kinds of form that will later aid in object recognition, social responsiveness and spatial orientation. This primitive knowledge provides a foundation for the vast accumulation of knowledge through experience.

10

PLASTICITY IN SENSORY-MOTOR SYSTEMS

RICHARD HELD
November 1965

An animal's own movements change what it sees and hears. Laboratory experiments that tamper with this feedback loop show that it is a key to developing and maintaining spatial orientation in advanced mammals

Anyone who has worn eyeglasses is likely to have experienced distorted vision the first time he put them on. The distortion may have been severe enough to cause him trouble in motor coordination, as in reaching out to touch something or in being sure of where he stepped. Such a person will also recall, however, that in a day or two the distortion disappeared. Evidently his central nervous system had made some adjustment so that the things he saw through the glasses looked normal again and he could have renewed confidence in his touch and step.

This process of adjustment, particularly as it operates in recovery from radical transformations of vision (as when the world is made to appear upside down or greatly shifted to one side by special goggles), has attracted the attention of scientists at least since the time of the great 19th-century investigator Hermann von Helmholtz. What has intrigued us all is the finding that correct perception of space and accurate visually guided action in space are in the long run not dependent on unique and permanently fixed optical properties of the paths taken by light rays traveling from object to eye. This finding, however, must be squared with the normally high order of precision in spatial vision and its stability over a period of time. How can the visual control of spatially coordinated action be stable under normal circumstances and yet sufficiently modifiable to allow recovery from transformation? Recovery takes time and renewed contact with the environment. Adaptation must result from information drawn from this contact with the environment. If the end product of adaptation is recovery of the former stability of perception, then the information on which that recovery is

based must be as reliable and unvarying as its end product. The investigations my colleagues and I have undertaken (first at Brandeis University and more recently at the Massachusetts Institute of Technology) have been directed toward discovering this source of information and elucidating the mechanism of its use by the perceiving organism. A useful tool in our work has been deliberate distortion of visual and auditory signals, a technique we call rearrangement.

Visual rearrangement can be produced experimentally with prisms [see "Experiments with Goggles," by Ivo Kohler; SCIENTIFIC AMERICAN Offprint 465]. Similarly, the apparent direction of sounds can be distorted in the laboratory by suitable apparatus. We have used such devices to show that in many cases the viewer or the listener subjected to these distortions soon adapts to them, provided that during the experiment he has been allowed to make voluntary use of his muscles in a more or less normal way.

The proviso suggests that there is more to the mechanism of perceptual adaptation than a change in the way the sensory parts of the central nervous system process data from the eyes and ears. The muscles and motor parts of the nervous system are evidently involved in the adaptation too—a revelation that has been very important in our efforts to discover the responsible source of information. The concept of a relation between sensory and motor activities in the adaptive process is reinforced by what happens when humans and certain other mammals undergo sensory deprivation through prolonged isolation in monotonous environments, or motor deprivation through prolonged immobilization. Their performance on perceptual

and motor tasks declines. By the same token, the young of higher mammals fail to develop normal behavior if they undergo sensory or motor deprivation.

Taken together, these findings by various experimenters suggested to us that a single mechanism is involved in three processes: (1) the development of normal sensory-motor control in the young, (2) the maintenance of that control once it has developed and (3) the adaptation to changes or apparent changes in the data reported by the senses of sight and hearing. A demonstration that such a mechanism exists would be of value in understanding these processes. Moreover, it would help to explain a phenomenon that otherwise could be accounted for only by the existence of enormous amounts of genetically coded information. That phenomenon is the adjustment of the central nervous system to the growth of the body—on the sensory side to the fact that the afferent, or input, signals must change with the increasing separation between the eyes and between the ears, and on the motor side to the fact that the growth of bone and muscle must call for a gradual modification of the efferent, or output, signals required to accomplish a particular movement. This problem is especially critical for animals that grow slowly and have many jointed bones. The possibility that the need for genetically coded information has been reduced by some such mechanism is of course contingent on the assumption that the animal's environment is fairly stable. For these reasons it is not surprising that clear evidence for adaptation to rearrangement and for dependence of the young on environmental contact in developing coordination has been found only in primates and in cats.

Such, in brief, is the background of

our effort to discover the operating conditions of the suspected mechanism. Our conclusion has been that a key to its operation is the availability of "reafference." This word was coined by the German physiologists Erich von Holst and Horst Mittelstädt to describe neural excitation following sensory stimulation that is systematically dependent on movements initiated by the sensing animal; von Holst and Mittelstädt also used the word "exafference" to describe the result of stimulation that is inde-

pendent of self-produced movement. "Afference" alone refers to any excitation of afferent nerves. These concepts should become clearer to the reader from the remainder of this article.

Among the contributions von Helmholtz made to science were many that were later incorporated into psychology. His experiments included work on the displacement of visual images by prisms. He was the first to report that the misreaching caused by such a dis-

placement is progressively reduced during repeated efforts and that on removal of the prism the subject who has succeeded in adapting to this displacement will at first misreach in the opposite direction.

Helmholtz' findings and those of similar experiments by many other workers have often been interpreted as resulting from recognition of error and consequent correction. We doubted this interpretation because of our conviction that a single mechanism underlies both

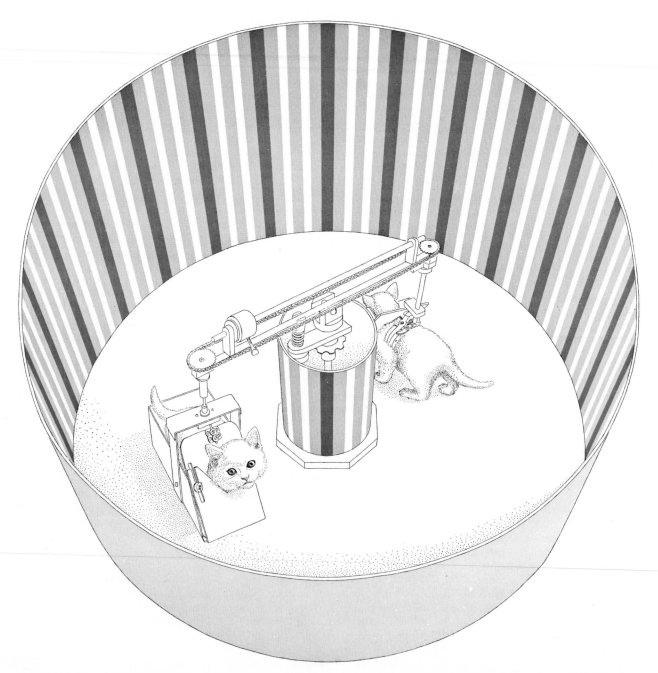

ACTIVE AND PASSIVE MOVEMENTS of kittens were compared in this apparatus. The active kitten walked about more or less freely; its gross movements were transmitted to the passive kitten by the chain and bar. The passive kitten, carried in a gondola, received essentially the same visual stimulation as the active kitten because of the unvarying pattern on the wall and on the center post. Active kittens developed normal sensory-motor coordination; passive kittens failed to do so until after being freed for several days.

adaptation to rearrangement in the adult and the development of the young. An error-correcting process could hardly explain the original acquisition of co-ordination. If an infant initially has no sense of the spatial relation between his efforts to move his hand and their visual consequences, he cannot recognize a visible error in reaching. Yet infants do acquire eye-hand coordination in their earliest months. Hence we suspected that error recognition was no more necessary for adaptation in the adult than it was in the development of the infant's coordination. To test this assumption we designed an experiment that prevented the subject from recognizing his error. If he still managed to correct his reach to allow for a displaced image, it would be evident that there was more to the matter of adaptation than the simple fact that the subject could see his error directly.

With this objective in mind we designed the apparatus shown in the top illustration at the left. In this apparatus the subject saw the image of a square target reflected by a mirror and was asked to mark on a piece of paper under the mirror the apparent position of the corners of the square. Because of the mirror, he could see neither the marks nor his hand. After he had marked each point 10 times, withdrawing his hand between markings so that he would have to position it anew each time, the mirror and marking sheet were removed and a prism was substituted. Looking through the prism, the subject then spent several minutes moving his hand in various ways, none of which involved deliberate reaching for a target. Thereafter the original situation was restored and the subject made more marks under the mirror. These marks revealed that each of the subjects was making some correction for the displacement of image that had been caused by the prism.

Having thus established that at least partial adaptation can occur in the absence of direct recognition of error, we used the apparatus to test the role of motor-sensory feedback in adaptation. Our main purpose was to see what degree of adaptation would occur under the respective conditions of active and passive movement—in other words, under conditions of reafference and exafference in which the afference was equivalent. In these experiments the subject's writing arm was strapped to a board pivoted at his elbow to allow left and right movement. He then looked at his hand through a prism under three

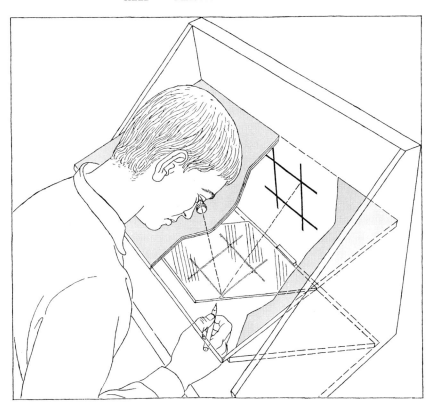

MIRROR APPARATUS tests subject's ability to guide his unseen hand to a visible target. Subject first marks under the mirror the apparent location of the corners of the square as he sees them in the mirror. He then looks through a prism, as depicted in the illustration below, after which he makes more marks. They show his adaptation to the prism effect.

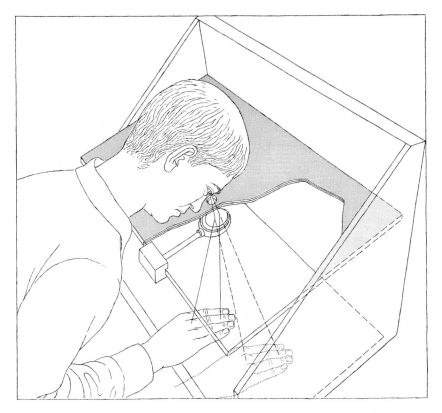

VIEW THROUGH PRISM displaces a visual image. Some subjects looked at their motionless hand, some moved the arm back and forth in a left-right arc, and some had the arm moved passively in a similar arc. They then made marks under the mirror as shown in the illustration at the top of the page. Typical results appear in illustrations on following page.

BEFORE   AFTER

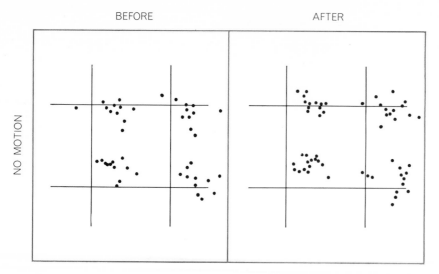

NO MOTION

MARKINGS made by a subject before and after looking through a prism as described in illustrations on preceding page are shown. He kept hand still while viewing it through prism.

BEFORE   AFTER

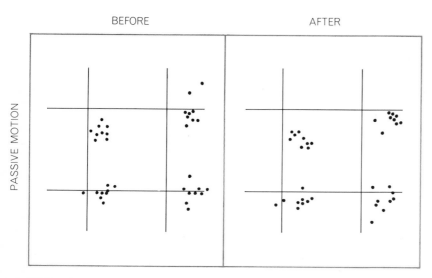

PASSIVE MOTION

PASSIVE MOVEMENT of subject's hand as he viewed it through prism produced these marks. They show no adaptation to horizontal displacement of images caused by the prism.

BEFORE   AFTER

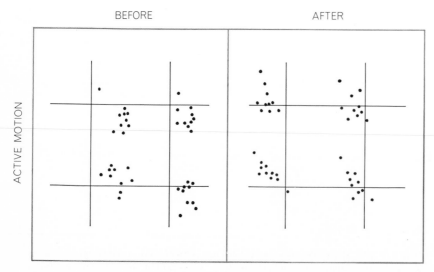

ACTIVE MOTION

ACTIVE MOVEMENT of subject's hand produced a clear adaptation to displacement of images by prism. Tests showed importance of such movement in sensorimotor coordination.

conditions: (1) no movement, (2) active movement, in which he moved the arm back and forth himself, and (3) passive movement, in which he kept his arm limp and it was moved back and forth by the experimenter. In each case he marked the apparent location of points under the mirror before and after looking through the prism.

Comparison of these marks showed that a few minutes of active movement produced substantial compensatory shifts [*see illustrations at left*]. Indeed, many of the subjects showed full adaptation, meaning exact compensation for the displacement caused by the prism, within half an hour. In contrast, the subjects in the condition of passive movement showed no adaptation. Even though the eye received the same information from both active and passive conditions, the evidently crucial connection between motor output and sensory input was lacking in the passive condition. These experiments showed that movement alone, in the absence of the opportunity for recognition of error, does not suffice to produce adaptation; it must be self-produced movement. From the point of view of our approach this kind of movement, with its contingent reafferent stimulation, is the critical factor in compensating for displaced visual images.

What about an adaptive situation involving movements of the entire body rather than just the arm and hand? We explored this situation in two ways, using an apparatus in which the subject judged the direction of a target only in reference to himself and not to other visible objects [*see top illustration on opposite page*]. This kind of direction-finding is sometimes called egocentric localization.

The apparatus consisted initially of a drum that could be rotated by the experimenter, after which the subject, sitting in a chair that he could rotate, was asked to position himself so that a target appeared directly in front of him. Later we dispensed with the drum and merely put the subject in a rotatable chair in a small room. After the experimenter had randomly positioned the target, which was a dimly illuminated slit, the subject rotated himself to find the target.

The first of the two ways in which we tested the role of reafferent stimulation involving movement of the whole body was an experiment in adaptation to short-term exposure to prisms. After several trials at locating the target, the subject put on prism goggles. He then walked for an hour along an outdoor path or sat in a wheelchair that was pushed along the same path for the same length of time. Thereupon he removed the goggles and went back to the target-finding apparatus for more tests. Any error in target-finding after wearing the prism goggles would be a measure of the adaptation the subject had made to the visual displacements produced by the prisms.

Again the degree of adaptation achieved by the subjects who had been involved in active movement was far greater than that of the subjects who had been carried in the wheelchair. This was true both when one subject had been exposed to the active condition and another to the passive and when a single subject had been exposed successively to each condition. Even more striking contrasts appeared in our second test, which involved wearing prisms for several hours at a time under conditions of active and passive movement. In these circumstances several of the subjects who were able to move voluntarily achieved full adaptation, whereas subjects whose movements were passive achieved virtually no adaptation.

In this connection it will be useful to mention an experiment we conducted on directional hearing. The sound emanating from a localized source reaches the listener's nearer ear a fraction of a second sooner than it reaches his farther ear. This small difference in the time of arrival of the sound at the two ears is the first stage in ascertaining the direction from which the sound comes. If, then, a subject's ears could be in effect displaced around the vertical axis of his head by a small angle, he would err by an equivalent angle in his location of the sound. This effect can be produced artificially by a device called the pseudophone, in which microphones substitute for the external ears. Subjects who have worn a pseudophone for several hours in a normally noisy environment show compensatory shifts in locating sounds, provided that they have been able to move voluntarily. In addition they occasionally report that they hear two sources of sound when only one is present. When measurements are made of the two apparent directions of the source, they differ by approximately the angle at which the ears were displaced around the center of the head during the exposure period. I have called the effect diplophonia.

The reports of doubled localization

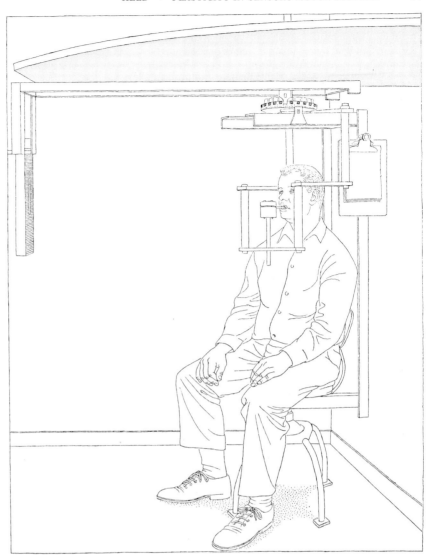

DIRECTION-FINDING by egocentric localization, in which a subject judges the direction of a target only in relation to himself and not to other visual cues, uses this apparatus. Target is randomly positioned at subject's eye level; he then rotates himself so that the target is directly in front of him. He does this before and after wearing prism goggles with which he either walks on an outdoor path or is pushed along the same path in a wheelchair. Change in direction-finding after wearing prisms measures adaptation to the prisms.

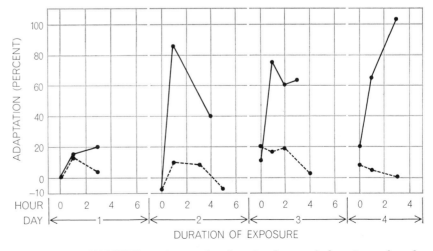

PROLONGED EXPOSURE to prisms produced varying degrees of adaptation to them depending on whether a subject's movement was active (*solid lines*) or passive (*broken lines*).

following adaptation suggest that compensation for rearrangement consists in the acquisition of a new mode of coordination that is objectively accurate for the condition of rearrangement but that coexists along with the older and more habitual mode. If this is true, the gradual and progressive course of adaptation usually found in experiments must be considered the result of a slow shift by the subject from the older direction of localization to the newer direction.

All these experiments strongly suggested the role in adaptation of the close correlation between signals from the motor nervous system, producing active physical movement, and the consequent sensory feedback. This correlation results from the fact that the feedback signals are causally related to movement and that in a stable environ-

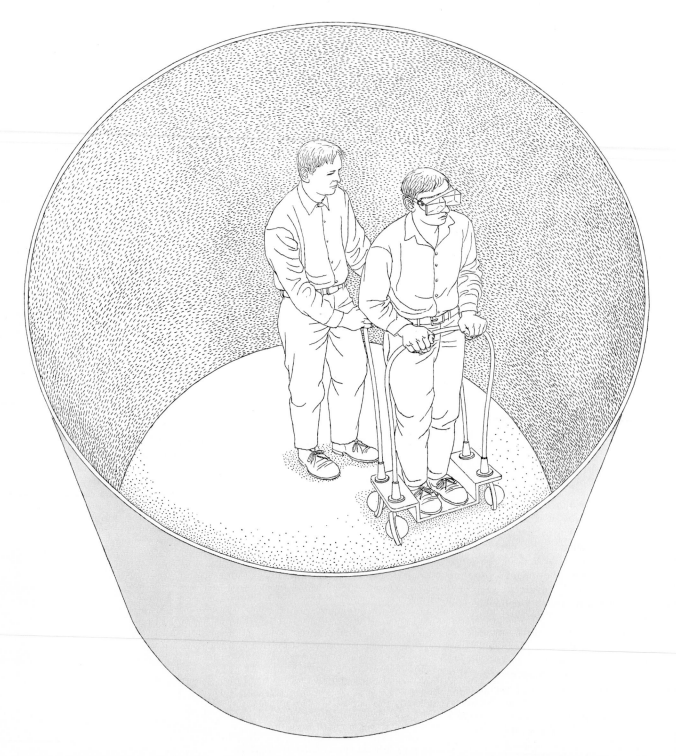

PASSIVE TRANSPORT of a subject wearing prism goggles while viewing a random scene is depicted. Purpose of the apparatus was to test the hypothesis that subjects moving actively through such a scene, which looks the same with or without prisms, would show a degree of adaptation to the prisms whereas subjects moved passively would not. That is what happened. Tests showed a link between visual and motor processes in the central nervous system by altering the correlation between motor outflow and visual feedback.

ment there is a unique feedback signal for any particular movement. The correlation is reduced by environmental instability: the presence either of objects that themselves move or of passive movements of the body that are produced by external forces. Under these conditions more than one feedback signal may accompany any particular movement.

From a theoretical point of view the importance of body movement and particularly of self-produced movement derives from the fact that only an organism that can take account of the output signals to its own musculature is in a position to detect and factor out the decorrelating effects of both moving objects and externally imposed body movement. One way to verify the importance of the correlation would be to set up an experimental situation in which the correlation was impaired or deliberately decorrelated. If the consequence was a loss of coordination, evidence for the role of normally correlated reafference in maintaining normal coordination would be strengthened.

We conducted such an experiment in visual perception by means of an apparatus that provided a prism effect of continually varying power [*see top illustration at right*]. In such an apparatus an object such as the hand seems to move constantly, and the movement perceived is wholly independent of whatever actual motion may be taking place. The same arm movement made at different times will produce different retinal feedbacks. Since the subject does not control the continual changes in his visual input that are produced by the prism, his nervous system has no means of distinguishing these changes in the input from those that are self-initiated.

With this apparatus we conducted various experiments, again including active and passive arm movements of the type described previously. We found that the coordination between eye and hand was significantly degraded under conditions of active movement but not under conditions of passive movement. Similar results appeared in tests made by Sanford Freedman of Tufts University of the effect of decorrelation on hearing. Again the performance of subjects who were allowed to move actively during decorrelation deteriorated badly, whereas the performance of subjects whose bodily movements were restricted did not deteriorate. Both the visual and the auditory experiments confirmed the importance of the correlation between

VERIFICATION EXPERIMENT sought to show role of correlation of sensory feedback and active physical movement by impairing it. Means of decorrelation was the rotating-prism apparatus shown here. It produces apparently continuous movement of subject's hand in one dimension, thus breaking the link between actual movement and visual feedback.

	VERTICAL DISPLACEMENT		HORIZONTAL DISPLACEMENT	
BEFORE EXPOSURE				
AFTER EXPOSURE				

RESULTS OF DECORRELATION are shown in markings made by a subject before and after looking through rotating prism. In one condition (*left*) prisms displaced images vertically; in another (*right*), horizontally. Markings after long exposure are spread out in the direction of displacement, showing a loss of precision in visual-motor coordination.

movement and sensory feedback in maintaining accurate coordination.

In another test of our hypothesis about reafference we undertook to see what would happen when subjects looked through prisms at a random scene, lacking in the lines and curves that provide normal visual cues. The straight lines characteristic of normal scenes look curved when viewed through a prism. When the prism is removed, such lines seem to curve in the opposite direction. What if straight lines looked curved after a subject had removed prism goggles through which he had viewed a random scene?

Our hypothesis was that such an effect would be produced in subjects who moved actively while viewing the random field but not in those whose movements were passive. If such a result occurred, we would have shown that the subjective geometry of the visual field can be altered by reafference. This finding would have the surprising implication that a motor factor is involved in a process traditionally regarded as purely visual. We would have demonstrated in another way the close, one-to-one correlation between movement and visual feedback and would have further evidence of a link between motor and visual mechanisms in the central nervous system.

Our apparatus for testing this hypothesis consisted of a large drum that had on its inside surface an irregular array of small spots [see illustration on page 78]. These spots looked the same whether viewed with a prism or not. Each subject, before putting on prism goggles and entering the drum, was tested for his perception of a vertical line; we did this by having him indicate when a grating of bars given varying curvatures by prisms appeared straight. Thereafter, entering the drum with the goggles on, the subject either walked around in the drum or was transported on a cart. He stayed in the drum for half an hour and then, after removing the goggles, again took the test with the grating of bars. Without exception the active subjects perceived curvature when looking at lines that were actually straight, whereas the passive subjects perceived little or none.

Having established by these various means the role of reafference in adaptation to changed sensory inputs, we decided to examine its role in the development of visually controlled coordination in the newborn. The contribution of experience to the development

of perceived space and of spatially oriented behavior has been debated for some centuries. During the past few decades a number of experimental approaches to the issue have been made. The technique most often used involves depriving very young animals of sensory contact with the environment. It has been hoped that the procedure would decide whether or not sensory experience, as opposed to maturation alone in the absence of such experience, is required for the development of spatial discrimination.

In certain species of higher mammals, including man, various forms of visual deprivation ranging from total absence of light to mere absence of gross movement in a normally illuminated environment have all resulted in deficiencies in visually guided behavior. Unfortunately these deficiencies are not easily interpreted. They can be attributed, at least in part, to several alternative causes, including pathological changes in the anatomy of the retina and its projections to the brain. Since our findings implicated movement-produced stimulation, they enabled us to test this factor without depriving animals of normal visual stimulation.

The experiments my colleague Alan Hein and I have performed to study the earliest development of vision originated from observations made by Austin H. Riesen of the University of California at Riverside and his collaborators. Riesen's research demonstrated that kittens restrained from walking from the time of their earliest exposure to light develop marked deficiencies in the visual control of behavior compared with unrestrained animals reared normally. The deficiencies of Riesen's animals may have resulted either from the lack of variation in visual stimulation, which was the explanation he preferred, or from the lack of visual stimulation correlated with movement, which was our own hypothesis.

To decide between these alternatives we devised an apparatus in which the gross movements of a kitten moving more or less normally were transmitted to a second kitten that was carried in a gondola [see illustation on page 74]. These gross movements included turns to left and right, circular progress around the center post of the apparatus and any up-and-down motions made by the first kitten. The second kitten was allowed to move its head, since prior experimenters had reported that head movement alone was not sufficient to

produce normal behavior in kittens, and it could also move its legs inside the gondola. Both kittens received essentially the same visual stimulation because the pattern on the walls and the center post of the apparatus was unvarying.

Eight pairs of kittens were reared in darkness until the active member of each pair had enough strength and coordination to move the other kitten in the apparatus; the ages at which that state was attained ranged from eight to 12 weeks. Two other pairs were exposed to patterned light for three hours a day between the ages of two and 10 weeks; during exposure they were in a holder that prevented locomotion. Thereafter all 10 pairs spent three hours a day in the apparatus under the experimental condition; when they were not in the apparatus, they were kept with their mothers and littermates in unlighted cages.

After an average of about 30 hours in the apparatus the active member of each pair showed normal behavior in several visually guided tasks. It blinked at an approaching object; it put out its forepaws as if to ward off collision when gently carried downward toward a surface, and it avoided the deep side of a visual cliff—an apparatus in which two depths, one shallow and the other a sharp drop, appear beneath a sheet of glass [see the article "The Visual Cliff,'" by Eleanor J. Gibson and Richard D. Walk, beginning on page 19]. After the same period of exposure each of the passive kittens failed to show these types of behavior. The passive kittens did, however, develop such types of behavior within days after they were allowed to run about in a normal environment.

In sum, the experiments I have described have led us to conclude that the correlation entailed in the sensory feedback accompanying movement—reafference—plays a vital role in perceptual adaptation. It helps the newborn to develop motor coordination; it figures in the adjustment to the changed relation between afferent and efferent signals resulting from growth; it operates in the maintenance of normal coordination, and it is of major importance in coping with altered visual and auditory inputs. The importance of the correlation in all these functions has been revealed by experiments that tamper with its normal operation. In the process these experiments have uncovered a fundamental role of the motor-sensory feedback loop.

III

ENVIRONMENTAL DETERMINANTS OF COMPLEX BEHAVIOR

III

ENVIRONMENTAL DETERMINANTS OF COMPLEX BEHAVIOR

INTRODUCTION

It is obvious that the organism with fully developed and integrated sensory and motor capacities is better prepared to deal with its environment than is one who is lacking in development of these abilities. Beyond the coordination of input and output, however, additional skills are necessary for the higher organism to be successful in its world. The animal must be able to recognize other members of its species, often as individuals, and it must know how to interact with them. It must understand the contingencies that apply to its social and individual behavioral choices. These basic concepts of action and reaction, cause and effect, behavior and its consequences— which must be acquired through experience with the environment —are the building blocks upon which the organism's continuing understanding of his world will depend.

The complex behavior of an organism is shaped and modified throughout its life. Everything it learns becomes available to guide its future behavioral choices. As with the development of basic systems, however, there are periods of development during which the organism is uniquely suited to certain types of interaction with its environment, and a deficiency in certain types of experience may be difficult or impossible to overcome later. In "'Imprinting' in a Natural Laboratory," Eckhard H. Hess discusses one of the classic examples of the critical-period phenomenon. Earlier work by Hess and others (see "'Imprinting' in Animals," by Eckhard H. Hess, *Scientific American*, March, 1958 Offprint 416) had indicated that the newly hatched precocial bird, during a period lasting only a few hours after hatching, formed a social bond that profoundly affected his later social and reproductive choices. Earlier laboratory studies, however, had failed to detect the role of vocal interactions between the mother and the young prior to hatching. Hess describes how these signals may serve both to synchronize the time of hatching in a clutch of eggs and to predispose the young to follow their natural parent during the critical post-hatching period. Thus the "following response" is not an all-or-none behavioral act that forever determines social choices; rather, it appears to be a critical stage in the over-all development of social behavior.

That the social development of advanced mammals requires even more extensive parent-infant interaction over a prolonged period is seen in "Love in Infant Monkeys," by Harry F. Harlow. Many traditional theories of child development had held that the child's love for its mother came about because the mother was associated with rewards such as food and warmth. Harlow chose to examine such assumptions in a species relatively closely related to man, the Rhesus monkey. His data indicate that the infant is born with a need for contact with a soft object, and that the fulfillment of this need is more important to the formation of an emotional attachment than is fulfillment of biological needs such as hunger and thirst.

The need for warmth and affection during early development is at least as great in the human child. Lytt I. Gardner in "Deprivation Dwarfism," reports that early emotional deprivation can lead to profound biological defects as well as psychological inadequacies. Although the physiological sources of the phenomenon are only beginning to be understood, it seems clear from the data Gardner presents that the ultimate cause of the retardation of biological development is the lack of a normal mother-child relationship. Resulting emotional disturbances may indirectly influence hormones involved in growth by affecting patterns of sleep.

In "Social Deprivation in Monkeys," Harry F. Harlow and Margaret Kuenne Harlow again experimentally challenge traditional theories of development, which had neglected the role of interaction with other children in psychological development. The Harlows, working with young Rhesus monkeys, find that the development of normal social behavior is critically dependent upon social experience with peers during early life. As the Harlows point out, such findings cannot be directly generalized to humans. Consider, for example, the complexities introduced by language, most of which is generally learned from the parents. On the other hand, the findings leave little doubt as to the importance of interaction among children on the development of personality and make it clear that this is an area that can no longer be overlooked. One should be careful not to view this research as support for the beneficial effects of overly large family size. Certainly there is little support for the notion that children from large families are more successful in our society, although factors of economics, nutrition, religion, and health care, among others, make clear interpretations of such work difficult. For an interesting sidelight on this problem, the reader may wish to consult John B. Calhoun's article, "Population Density and Social Pathology" (*Scientific American*, February, 1962, Offprint 506).

Just as the development of normal social behavior depends upon appropriate social experience, the ability to deal effectively with a constantly changing world seems to depend upon experience with such an environment. Mark R. Rosenzweig, Edward L. Bennett, and Marian Cleeves Diamond, in "Brain Changes in Response to Experience," describe some effects they have seen in the brain and behavior of rats that have been exposed to a complex environment. These "enriched" animals are superior to siblings reared in impoverished surroundings on several measures of learning ability. Correlated with the behavioral differences are differences in the chemistry and anatomy of the brain. Many of the differences that these investigators discuss indicate that experience with a complex environment affects the size and number of synapses — the basic links through which nerve cells of the brain communicate with one another. A particularly interesting feature of the Rosenzweig, Bennett, and Diamond research is that many effects of a complex environment are not dependent on age. Adults show many (but almost certainly not all) of the brain changes that are seen in young animals. This again emphasizes that many of the processes that begin in development continue throughout life as the everyday experience of the organism continues to modify its behavior. The findings also raise an interesting question: to what extent can the effects of a deprived environment during human childhood be reversed in later life?

Slightly rephrased, one might ask to what extent differences in behavior or intelligence in later life reflect differences in early environment and, conversely, to what extend do they represent differences in the genetic complement? Walter F. Bodmer and Luigi Luca Cavalli-Sforza, in "Intelligence and Race," discuss the complexities involved in trying to answer such a question. The extent to which intelligence is genetically determined has become a question of social, as well as scientific, importance. (It should be noted that Rosenzweig, Bennett, and Diamond use siblings in their experiments in an attempt to reduce genetic differences between the environmental groups). Bodmer and Cavalli-Sforza conclude that, although both genetic and environmental factors are important in the determination of intelligence, the relative contributions of these sources cannot be determined, and the distinction is essentially useless at an individual level. With intelligence as with behavior in general, those who wish to specify quantitatively the genetic and environmental contribution appear doomed to failure, although as the readings in this book show, important advances have been made in understanding nature and nurture, and their interaction, in the development of mature organisms.

SUGGESTED READINGS

Cooper, R. M., and Zubek, J. P. Effects of enriched and restricted early environments on the learning ability of bright and dull rats. *Canadian Journal of Psychology*, Vol. 12, 159–164, 1958.

Madsen, M. C. Cooperative and competitive motivation of children in three mexican subcultures. *Psychological Reports*, Vol. 20, pages 1307–1320, 1967.

Paraskevopoulos, J., and Hunt, J. McV. Object construction and imitation under different conditions of rearing. *Journal of Genetic Psychology*, Vol. 119, pages 301–321, 1971.

Volkmar, F. R., and Greenough, W. T. Rearing complexity affects branching of dendrites in the visual cortex of the rat. *Science*, Vol. 176, pages 1445–1447, 1972.

Further Readings From *Scientific American*

Kagan, J. Do infants think? *Scientific American*, March, 1972 (Offprint 542).

Piaget, J. How children form mathematical concepts. *Scientific American*, November, 1953 (Offprint 420).

Rosenthal, R., and Jacobson, L. F. Teacher expectations for the disadvantaged. *Scientific American*, April, 1968 (Offprint 514).

11

"IMPRINTING" IN A NATURAL LABORATORY

ECKHARD H. HESS
August 1972

*A synthesis of laboratory and field techniques has led
to some interesting discoveries about imprinting,
the process by which newly hatched birds rapidly form
a permanent bond to the parent*

In a marsh on the Eastern Shore of Maryland, a few hundred feet from my laboratory building, a female wild mallard sits on a dozen infertile eggs. She has been incubating the eggs for almost four weeks. Periodically she hears the faint peeping sounds that are emitted by hatching mallard eggs, and she clucks softly in response. Since these eggs are infertile, however, they are not about to hatch and they do not emit peeping sounds. The sounds come from a small loudspeaker hidden in the nest under the eggs. The loudspeaker is connected to a microphone next to some hatching mallard eggs inside an incubator in my laboratory. The female mallard can hear any sounds coming from the laboratory eggs, and a microphone beside her relays the sounds she makes to a loudspeaker next to those eggs.

The reason for complicating the life of an expectant duck in such a way is to further our understanding of the phenomenon known as imprinting. It was through the work of the Austrian zoologist Konrad Z. Lorenz that imprinting became widely known. In the 1930's Lorenz observed that newly hatched goslings would follow him rather than their mother if the goslings saw him before they saw her. Since naturally reared geese show a strong attachment for their parent, Lorenz concluded that some animals have the capacity to learn rapidly and permanently at a very early age, and in particular to learn the characteristics of the parent. He called this process of acquiring an attachment to the parent *Prägung*, which in German means "stamping" or "coinage" but in English has been rendered as "imprinting." Lorenz regarded the phenomenon as being different from the usual kind of learning because of its rapidity and apparent permanence. In fact, he was hesitant at first to regard imprinting as a form of learn-

ing at all. Some child psychologists and some psychiatrists nevertheless perceived a similarity between the evidence of imprinting in animals and the early behavior of the human infant, and it is not surprising that interest in imprinting spread quickly.

From about the beginning of the 1950's many investigators have intensively studied imprinting in the laboratory. Unlike Lorenz, the majority of them have regarded imprinting as a form of learning and have used methods much the same as those followed in the study of associative learning processes. In every case efforts were made to manipulate or stringently control the imprinting process. Usually the subjects are incuba-

CLUCKS emitted by a female wild mallard in the fourth week of incubating eggs are shown in the sound spectrogram (*upper illustration*). Each cluck lasts for about 150 milliseconds

tor-hatched birds that are reared in the laboratory. The birds are typically kept isolated until the time of the laboratory imprinting experience to prevent interaction of early social experience and the imprinting experience. Various objects have been used as artificial parents: duck decoys, stuffed hens, dolls, milk bottles, toilet floats, boxes, balls, flashing lights and rotating disks. Several investigators have constructed an automatic imprinting apparatus into which the newly hatched bird can be put. In this kind of work the investigator does not observe the young bird directly; all the bird's movements with respect to the imprinting object are recorded automatically.

Much of my own research during the past two decades has not differed substantially from this approach. The birds I have used for laboratory imprinting studies have all been incubated, hatched and reared without the normal social and environmental conditions and have then been tested in an artificial situation. It is therefore possible that the behavior observed under such conditions is not relevant to what actually happens in nature.

It is perhaps not surprising that studies of "unnatural" imprinting have produced conflicting results. Lorenz' original statements on the permanence of natural imprinting have been disputed. In many instances laboratory imprinting experiences do not produce permanent and exclusive attachment to the object selected as an artificial parent. For example, a duckling can spend a considerable amount of time following the object to which it is to be imprinted, and immediately after the experience it will follow a completely different object.

In one experiment in our laboratory we attempted to imprint ducklings to ourselves, as Lorenz did. For 20 continuous hours newly hatched ducklings were exposed to us. Before long they followed us whenever we moved about. Then they were given to a female mallard that had hatched a clutch of ducklings several hours before. After only an hour and a half of exposure to the female mallard and other ducklings the human-imprinted ducklings followed the female on the first exodus from the nest. Weeks later the behavior of the human-imprinted ducks was no different from the behavior of the ducks that had been hatched in the nest. Clearly laboratory imprinting is reversible.

We also took wild ducklings from their natural mother 16 hours after hatching and tried to imprint them to humans. On the first day we spent many hours with the ducklings, and during the next two months we made lengthy attempts every day to overcome the ducklings' fear of us. We finally gave up. From the beginning to the end the ducks remained wild and afraid. They were released, and when they had matured, they were observed to be as wary of humans as normal wild ducks are. This result suggests that natural imprinting, unlike artificial laboratory imprinting, is permanent and irreversible. I have had to conclude that the usual laboratory imprinting has only a limited resemblance to natural imprinting.

It seems obvious that if the effects of natural imprinting are to be understood, the phenomenon must be studied as it

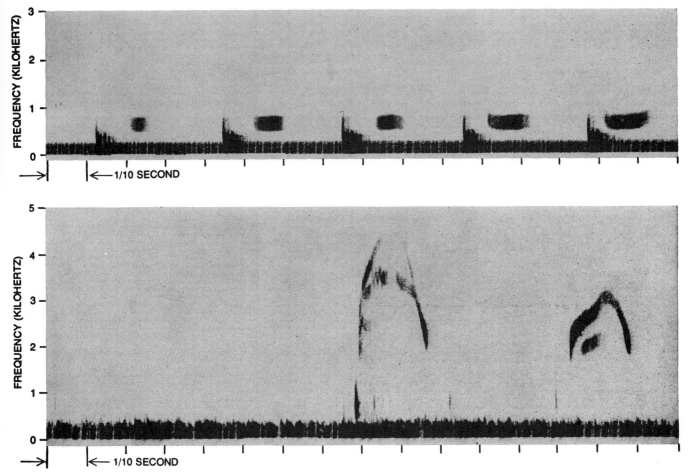

and is low in pitch: about one kilohertz or less. Sounds emitted by ducklings inside the eggs are high-pitched, rising to about four kilohertz (*lower illustration*). Records of natural, undisturbed imprinting events in the nest provide a control for later experiments.

operates in nature. The value of such studies was stressed as long ago as 1914 by the pioneer American psychologist John B. Watson. He emphasized that field observations must always be made to test whether or not conclusions drawn from laboratory studies conform to what actually happens in nature. The disparity between laboratory results and what happens in nature often arises from the failure of the investigator to really look at the animal's behavior. For years I have cautioned my students against shutting their experimental animals in "black boxes" with automatic recording devices and never directly observing how the animals behave.

This does not mean that objective laboratory methods for studying the behavior of animals must be abandoned. With laboratory investigations large strides have been made in the development of instruments for the recording of behavior. In the study of imprinting it is not necessary to revert to imprecise naturalistic observations in the field. We can now go far beyond the limitations of traditional field studies. It is possible to set up modern laboratory equipment in actual field conditions and in ways that do not disturb or interact with the behavior being studied, in other words, to achieve a synthesis of laboratory and field techniques.

The first step in the field-laboratory method is to observe and record the undisturbed natural behavior of the animal in the situation being studied. In our work on imprinting we photographed the behavior of the female mallard during incubation and hatching. We photographed the behavior of the ducklings

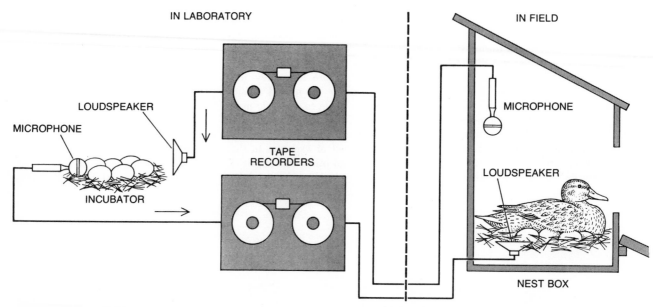

FEMALE MALLARD sitting on infertile eggs hears sounds transmitted from mallard eggs in a laboratory incubator. Any sounds she makes are transmitted to a loudspeaker beside the eggs in the laboratory. Such a combination of field and laboratory techniques permits recording of events without disturbing the nesting mallard and provides the hatching eggs with nearly natural conditions.

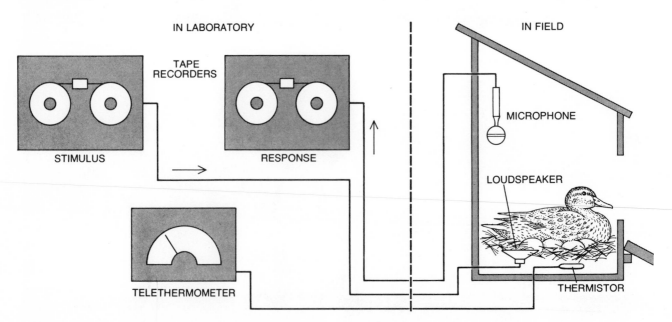

REMOTE MANIPULATION of prehatching sounds is accomplished by placing a sensitive microphone and a loudspeaker in the nest of a female wild mallard who is sitting on her own eggs. Prerecorded hatching-duckling sounds are played at specified times through the loudspeaker and the female mallard's responses to this stimulus are recorded. A thermistor probe transmits the temperature in the nest to a telethermometer and chart recorder. The thermistor records provide data about when females are on nest.

during and after hatching. We recorded all sounds from the nest before and after hatching. Other factors, such as air temperature and nest temperature, were also recorded.

A detailed inventory of the actual events in natural imprinting is essential for providing a reference point in the assessment of experimental manipulations of the imprinting process. That is, the undisturbed natural imprinting events form the control situation for assessing the effects of the experimental manipulations. This is quite different from the "controlled" laboratory setting, in which the ducklings are reared in isolation and then tested in unnatural conditions. The controlled laboratory study not only introduces new variables (environmental and social deprivation) into the imprinting situation but also it can prevent the investigator from observing factors that are relevant in wild conditions.

My Maryland research station is well suited for the study of natural imprinting in ducks. The station, near a national game refuge, has 250 acres of marsh and forest on a peninsula on which there are many wild and semiwild mallards. Through the sharp eyes of my technical assistant Elihu Abbott, a native of the Eastern Shore, I have learned to see much I might otherwise have missed. Initially we looked at and listened to the undisturbed parent-offspring interaction of female mallards that hatched their own eggs both in nests on the ground and in specially constructed nest boxes. From our records we noticed that the incubation time required for different clutches of eggs decreased progressively between March and June. Both the average air temperature and the number of daylight hours increase during those months; both are correlated with the incubation time of mallard eggs. It is likely, however, that temperature rather than photoperiod directly influences the duration of incubation. In one experiment mallard eggs from an incubator were slowly cooled for two hours a day in a room with a temperature of seven degrees Celsius, and another set of eggs was cooled in a room at 27 degrees C. These temperatures respectively correspond to the mean noon temperatures at the research station in March and in June. The eggs that were placed in the cooler room took longer to hatch, indicating that temperature affects the incubation time directly. Factors such as humidity and barometric pressure may also play a role.

We noticed that all the eggs in a wild

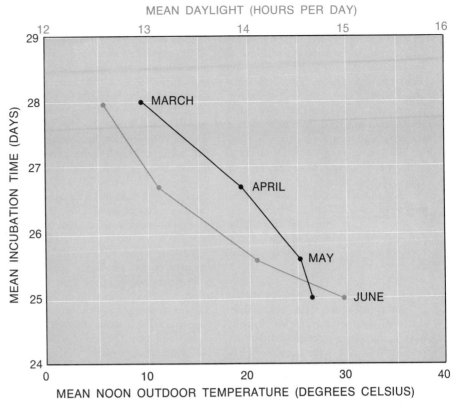

INCUBATION TIME of mallard eggs hatched naturally in a feral setting at Lake Cove, Md., decreased steadily from March to June. The incubation period correlated with both the outdoor temperature (*black curve*) and the daily photoperiod (*colored curve*).

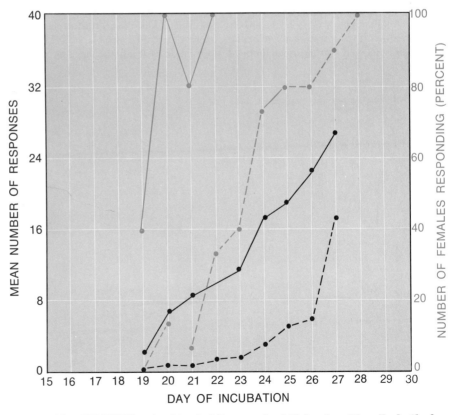

VOCAL RESPONSES to hatching-duckling sounds of 15 female wild mallards (*broken curves*) and five human-imprinted mallards (*solid curves*), which were later released to the wild, followed the same pattern, although the human-imprinted mallards began responding sooner and more frequently. A tape recording of the sounds of a hatching duckling was played daily throughout the incubation period to each female mallard while she was on her nest. Responses began on the 19th day of incubation and rose steadily until hatching.

nest usually hatch between three and eight hours of one another. As a result all the ducklings in the same clutch are approximately the same age in terms of the number of hours since hatching. Yet when mallard eggs are placed in a mechanical incubator, they will hatch over a two- or three-day period even when precautions are taken to ensure that all the eggs begin developing simultaneously. The synchronous hatching observed in nature obviously has some survival value. At the time of the exodus from the nest, which usually takes place between 16 and 32 hours after hatching, all the ducklings would be of a similar age and thus would have equal motor capabilities and similar social experiences.

Over the years our laboratory studies and actual observations of how a female mallard interacts with her offspring have pointed to the conclusion that imprinting is related to the age after hatching rather than the age from the beginning of incubation. Many other workers, however, have accepted the claim that age from the beginning of incubation determines the critical period for maximum effectiveness of imprinting. They base their belief on the findings of Gilbert Gottlieb of the Dorothea Dix Hospital in Raleigh, N.C., who in a 1961 paper described experiments that apparently showed that maximum imprint-

ing in ducklings occurs in the period between 27 and 27½ days after the beginning of incubation. To make sure that all the eggs he was working with started incubation at the same time he first chilled the eggs so that any partially developed embryos would be killed. Yet the 27th day after the beginning of incubation can hardly be the period of maximum imprinting for wild ducklings that hatch in March under natural conditions, because such ducklings take on the average 28 days to hatch. Moreover, if the age of a duckling is measured from the beginning of incubation, it is hard to explain why eggs laid at different times in a hot month in the same nest will hatch within six to eight hours of one another under natural conditions.

Periodic cooling of the eggs seems to affect the synchronization of hatching. The mallard eggs from an incubator that were placed in a room at seven degrees C. hatched over a period of a day and a half, whereas eggs placed in the room at 27 degrees hatched over a period of two and a half days (which is about normal for artificially incubated eggs). Cooling cannot, however, play a major role. In June the temperature in the outdoor nest boxes averages close to the normal brooding temperature while the female mallard is absent. Therefore an egg laid on June 1 has a head start in incubation over those laid a week later. Yet we have observed that all the eggs in clutches

laid in June hatch in a period lasting between six and eight hours.

We found another clue to how the synchronization of hatching may be achieved in the vocalization pattern of the brooding female mallard. As many others have noted, the female mallard vocalizes regularly as she sits on her eggs during the latter part of the incubation period. It seemed possible that she was vocalizing to the eggs, perhaps in response to sounds from the eggs themselves. Other workers had observed that ducklings make sounds before they hatch, and the prehatching behavior of ducklings in response to maternal calls has been extensively reported by Gottlieb.

We placed a highly sensitive microphone next to some mallard eggs that were nearly ready to hatch. We found that the ducklings indeed make sounds while they are still inside the egg. We made a one-minute tape recording of the sounds emitted by a duckling that had pipped its shell and was going to hatch within the next few hours. Then we made a seven-minute recording that would enable us to play the duckling sounds three times for one minute interspersed with one-minute silences. We played the recording once each to 37 female mallards at various stages of incubation. There were no positive responses from the female mallards during

NEST EXODUS takes place about 16 to 32 hours after hatching. The female mallard begins to make about 40 to 65 calls per minute and continues while the ducklings leave the nest to follow her. The ducklings are capable of walking and swimming from hatching.

the first and second week of incubation. In fact, during the first days of incubation some female mallards responded with threat behavior: a fluffing of the feathers and a panting sound. In the third week some females responded to the recorded duckling sounds with a few clucks. In the fourth week maternal clucks were frequent and were observed in all ducks tested.

We found the same general pattern of response whether the female mallards were tested once or, as in a subsequent experiment, tested daily during incubation. Mallards sitting on infertile eggs responded just as much to the recorded duckling sounds as mallards sitting on fertile eggs did. Apparently after sitting on a clutch of eggs for two or three weeks a female mallard becomes ready to respond to the sounds of a hatching duckling.. There is some evidence that the parental behavior of the female mallard is primed by certain neuroendocrine mechanisms. We have begun a study of the neuroendocrine changes that might accompany imprinting and filial behavior in mallards.

To what extent do unhatched ducklings respond to the vocalization of the female mallard? In order to find out we played a recording of a female mallard's vocalizations to ducklings in eggs that had just been pipped and were scheduled to hatch within the next 24 hours. As before, the sounds were interspersed with periods of silence. We then recorded all the sounds made by the ducklings during the recorded female mallard vocalizations and also during the silent periods on the tape. Twenty-four hours before the scheduled hatching the ducklings emitted 34 percent of their sounds during the silent periods, which suggests that at this stage they initiate most of the auditory interaction. As hatching time approaches the ducklings emit fewer and fewer sounds during the silent periods. The total number of sounds they make, however, increases steadily. At the time of hatching only 9 percent of the sounds they make are emitted during the silent periods. One hour after hatching, in response to the same type of recording, the ducklings gave 37 percent of their vocalizations during the silent periods, a level similar to the level at 24 hours before hatching.

During the hatching period, which lasts about an hour, the female mallard generally vocalizes at the rate of from zero to four calls per one-minute interval. Occasionally there is an interval in which she emits as many as 10 calls. When the duckling actually hatches, the female mallard's vocalization increases

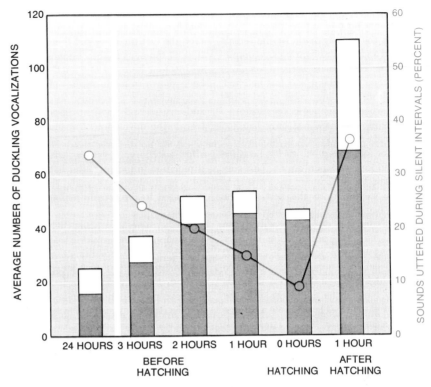

NUMBER OF SOUNDS from ducklings before and after hatching are shown. The ducklings heard a recording consisting of five one-minute segments of a female mallard's clucking sounds interspersed with five one-minute segments of silence. The recording was played to six mallard eggs and the number of vocal responses by the ducklings to the clucking segments (*gray bars*) and to the silent segments (*white bars*) were counted. Twenty-four hours before hatching 34 percent of the duckling sounds were made during the silent interval, indicating the ducklings initiated a substantial portion of the early auditory interaction. As hatching time approached the ducklings initiated fewer and fewer of the sounds and at hatching vocalized most in response to the clucks of the female mallard.

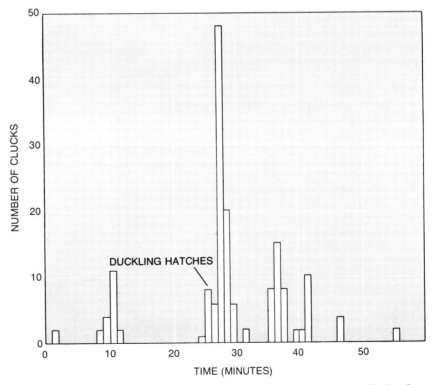

CLUCKING RATE of a wild, ground-nesting female mallard rose dramatically for about two minutes while a duckling hatched and then slowly declined to the prehatching rate. Each bar depicts the number of clucks emitted by the female during a one-minute period.

dramatically to between 45 and 68 calls per minute for one or two minutes.

Thus the sounds made by the female mallard and by her offspring are complementary. The female mallard vocalizes most when a duckling has just hatched. A hatching duckling emits its cries primarily when the female is vocalizing.

After all the ducklings have hatched the female mallard tends to be relatively quiet for long intervals, giving between zero and four calls per minute. This continues for 16 to 32 hours until it is time for the exodus from the nest. As the exodus begins the female mallard quickly builds up to a crescendo of between 40 and 65 calls per minute; on rare occasions we have observed between 70 and 95 calls per minute. The duration of the high-calling-rate period depends on how quickly the ducklings leave the nest to follow her. There is now a change in the sounds made by the female mallard. Up to this point she has been making clucking sounds. By the time the exodus from the nest takes place some of her sounds are more like quacks.

The auditory interaction of the female mallard and the duckling can begin well before the hatching period. As I have indicated, the female mallard responds to unhatched-duckling sounds during the third and fourth week of incubation. Normally ducklings penetrate a membrane to reach an air space inside the eggshell two days before hatching. We have not found any female mallard that vocalized to her clutch before the duckling in the egg reached the air space. We have found that as soon as the duckling penetrates the air space the female begins to cluck at a rate of between zero and four times per minute. Typically she continues to vocalize at this rate until the ducklings begin to pip their eggs (which is about 24 hours after they have entered the air space). As the eggs are being pipped the female clucks at the rate of between 10 ·and 15 times per minute. When the pipping is completed, she drops back to between zero and four calls per minute. In the next 24 hours there is a great deal of auditory interaction between the female and her unhatched offspring; this intense interaction may facilitate the rapid formation of the filial bond after hatching, although it is quite possible that synchrony of hatching is the main effect. Already we have found that a combination of cooling the eggs daily, placing them together so that they touch one another and transmitting parent-young vocal responses through the microphone-loudspeaker hookup between the female's nest and the laboratory incubator causes the eggs in the incubator to hatch as synchronously as eggs in nature do. In fact, the two times we did this we found that all the eggs in the clutches hatched within four hours of one another. It has been shown in many studies of imprinting, including laboratory studies, that auditory stimuli have an important effect on the development of filial attachment. Auditory stimulation, before and after hatching, together with tactile stimulation in the nest after hatching results in ducklings that are thoroughly imprinted to the female mallard that is present.

Furthermore, it appears that auditory interaction before hatching may play an important role in promoting the synchronization of hatching. As our experiments showed, not only does the female mallard respond to sounds from her eggs but also the ducklings respond to her clucks. Perhaps the daily cooling of the eggs when the female mallard leaves the nest to feed serves to broadly synchronize embryonic and behavioral development, whereas the auditory interaction of the mother with the ducklings and of one duckling with another serves to provide finer synchronization. Margaret Vince of the University of Cambridge has shown that the synchronization of hatching in quail is promoted by the mutual auditory interaction of the young birds in the eggs.

Listening to the female mallards vocalize to their eggs or to their newly hatched offspring, we were struck by the fact that we could tell which mallard was vocalizing, even when we could not see her. Some female mallards regularly emit single clucks at one-second intervals, some cluck in triple or quadruple clusters and others cluck in clusters of different lengths. The individual differences in the vocalization styles of female mallards may enable young ducklings to identify their mother. We can also speculate that the characteristics of a female mallard's voice are learned by her female offspring, which may then adopt a similar style when they are hatching eggs of their own.

The female mallards not only differ from one another in vocalization styles but also emit different calls in different situations. We have recorded variations in pitch and duration from the same mallard in various nesting situations. It

SOUND SPECTROGRAM of the calls of newly hatched ducklings in the nest and the mother's responses is shown at right. The high-pitched peeps of the ducklings are in the

DISTRESS CALLS of ducklings in the nest evoke a quacklike response from the female mallard. The cessation of the distress calls and the onset of normal duckling peeping sounds

seems likely that such variations in the female mallard call are an important factor in the imprinting process.

Studies of imprinting in the laboratory have shown that the more effort a duckling has to expend in following the imprinting object, the more strongly it prefers that object in later testing. At first it would seem that this is not the case in natural imprinting; young ducklings raised by their mother have little difficulty following her during the exodus from the nest. Closer observation of many nests over several seasons showed, however, that ducklings make a considerable effort to be near their parent. They may suffer for such efforts, since they can be accidentally stepped on, squeezed or scratched by the female adult. The combination of effort and punishment may actually strengthen imprinting. Work in my laboratory showed that chicks given an electric shock while they were following the imprinting object later showed stronger attachment to the object than unshocked chicks did. It is reasonable to expect similar results with ducklings.

Slobodan Petrovich of the University of Maryland (Baltimore County) and I have begun a study to determine the relative contributions of prehatching and posthatching auditory experience on imprinting and filial attachment. The auditory stimuli consist of either natural mallard maternal clucks or a human voice saying "Come, come, come." Our results indicate that prehatching stimulation by natural maternal clucks may to a degree facilitate the later recognition of the characteristic call of the mallard. Ducklings lacking any experience with a maternal call imprint as well to a duck decoy that utters "Come, come, come" as to a decoy that emits normal mallard clucks. Ducklings that had been exposed to a maternal call before hatching imprinted better to decoys that emitted the mallard clucks. We found, however, that the immediate posthatching experiences, in this case with a female mallard on the nest, can highly determine the degree of filial attachment and make imprinting to a human sound virtually impossible.

It is important to recognize that almost all laboratory imprinting experiments, including my own, have been deprivation experiments. The justification for such experiments has been the ostensible need for controlling the variables of the phenomenon, but the deprivation may have interfered with the normal behavioral development of the young ducklings. Whatever imprinting experiences the experimenter allows therefore do not produce the maximum effect.

Although our findings are far from complete, we have already determined enough to demonstrate the great value of studying imprinting under natural conditions. The natural laboratory can be profitably used to study questions about imprinting that have been raised but not answered by traditional laboratory experiments. We must move away from the in vitro, or test-tube, approach to the study of behavior and move toward the in vivo method that allows interaction with normal environmental factors. Some of the questions are: What is the optimal age for imprinting? How long must the imprinting experience last for it to have the maximum effect? Which has the greater effect on behavior: first experience or the most recent experience? Whatever kind of behavior is being studied, the most fruitful approach may well be to study the behavior in its natural context.

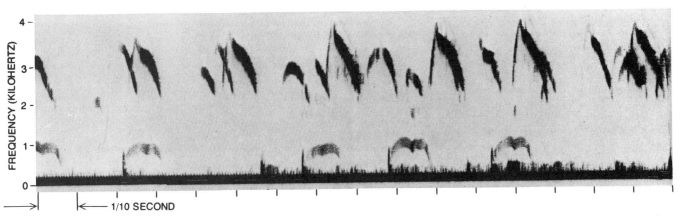

two-to-four-kilohertz range. They normally have the shape of an inverted *V*. The female mallard's clucks are about one kilohertz and last about 130 milliseconds. After the eggs hatch the vocalization of the female changes both in quantity and in quality of sound.

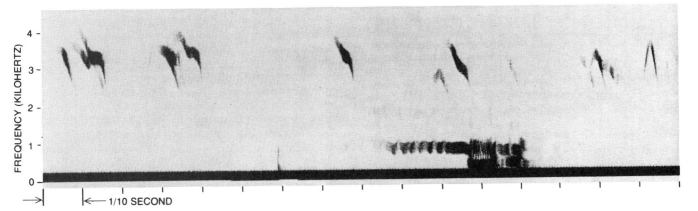

is almost immediate, as can be seen in this sound spectrogram. The female mallard's quacklike call is about one kilohertz in pitch and has a duration of approximately 450 milliseconds. The call is emitted about once every two seconds in response to distress cries.

12

LOVE IN INFANT MONKEYS

HARRY F. HARLOW
July 1959

*Affection in infants was long thought to be generated
by the satisfactions of feeding. Studies of young rhesus
monkeys now indicate that love derives mainly from
close bodily contact*

The first love of the human infant is for his mother. The tender intimacy of this attachment is such that it is sometimes regarded as a sacred or mystical force, an instinct incapable of analysis. No doubt such compunctions, along with the obvious obstacles in the way of objective study, have hampered experimental observation of the bonds between child and mother.

Though the data are thin, the theoretical literature on the subject is rich. Psychologists, sociologists and anthropologists commonly hold that the infant's love is learned through the association of the mother's face, body and other physical characteristics with the alleviation of internal biological tensions, particularly hunger and thirst. Traditional psychoanalysts have tended to emphasize the role of attaining and sucking at the breast as the basis for affectional development. Recently a number of child psychiatrists have questioned such simple explanations. Some argue that affectionate handling in the act of nursing is a variable of importance, whereas a few workers suggest that the composite activities of nursing, contact, clinging and even seeing and hearing work together to elicit the infant's love for his mother.

Now it is difficult, if not impossible, to use human infants as subjects for the studies necessary to break through the present speculative impasse. At birth the infant is so immature that he has little or no control over any motor system other than that involved in sucking. Furthermore, his physical maturation is so slow that by the time he can achieve precise, coordinated, measurable responses of his head, hands, feet and body, the nature and sequence of development have been hopelessly confounded and obscured. Clearly research into

the infant-mother relationship has need of a more suitable laboratory animal. We believe we have found it in the infant monkey. For the past several years our group at the Primate Laboratory of the University of Wisconsin has been employing baby rhesus monkeys in a study that we believe has begun to yield significant insights into the origin of the infant's love for his mother.

Baby monkeys are far better coordinated at birth than human infants. Their responses can be observed and evaluated with confidence at an age of 10 days or even earlier. Though they mature much more rapidly than their human contemporaries, infants of both species follow much the same general pattern of development.

Our interest in infant-monkey love grew out of a research program that involved the separation of monkeys from their mothers a few hours after birth. Employing techniques developed by Gertrude van Wagenen of Yale University, we had been rearing infant monkeys on the bottle with a mortality far less than that among monkeys nursed by their mothers. We were particularly careful to provide the infant monkeys with a folded gauze diaper on the floor of their cages, in accord with Dr. van Wagenen's observation that they would tend to maintain intimate contact with such soft, pliant surfaces, especially during nursing. We were impressed by the deep personal attachments that the monkeys formed for these diaper pads, and by the distress that they exhibited when the pads were briefly removed once a day for purposes of sanitation. The behavior of the infant monkeys was reminiscent of the human infant's attachment to its blankets, pillows, rag dolls or cuddly teddy bears.

These observations suggested the series of experiments in which we have sought to compare the importance of nursing and all associated activities with that of simple bodily contact in engendering the infant monkey's attachment to its mother. For this purpose we contrived two surrogate mother monkeys. One is a bare welded-wire cylindrical form surmounted by a wooden head with a crude face. In the other the welded wire is cushioned by a sheathing of terry cloth. We placed eight newborn monkeys in individual cages, each with equal access to a cloth and a wire mother [*see illustration on opposite page*]. Four of the infants received their milk from one mother and four from the other, the milk being furnished in each case by a nursing bottle, with its nipple protruding from the mother's "breast."

The two mothers quickly proved to be physiologically equivalent. The monkeys in the two groups drank the same amount of milk and gained weight at the same rate. But the two mothers proved to be by no means psychologically equivalent. Records made automatically showed that both groups of infants spent far more time climbing and clinging on their cloth-covered mothers than they did on their wire mothers. During the infants' first 14 days of life the floors of the cages were warmed by an electric heating pad, but most of the infants left the pad as soon as they could climb on the unheated cloth mother. Moreover, as the monkeys grew older, they tended to spend an increasing amount of time clinging and cuddling on her pliant terry-cloth surface. Those that secured their nourishment from the wire mother showed no tendency to spend more time on her than feeding required, contradicting the idea that affection is a response that is learned or derived in asso-

CLOTH AND WIRE MOTHER-SURROGATES were used to test the preferences of infant monkeys. The infants spent most of their time clinging to the soft cloth "mother," (*foreground*) even when nursing bottles were attached to the wire mother (*background*).

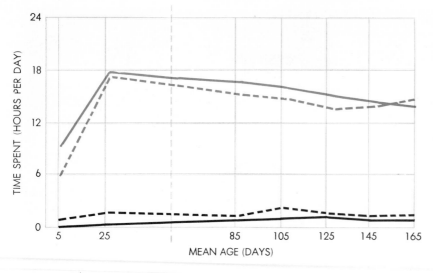

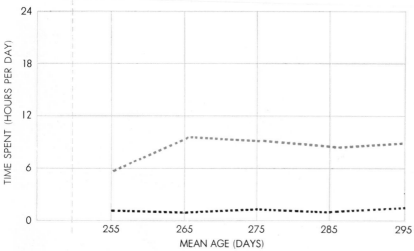

STRONG PREFERENCE FOR CLOTH MOTHER was shown by all infant monkeys.
Infants reared with access to both mothers from birth (*top chart*) spent far more time on the cloth mother (*colored curves*) than on the wire mother (*black curves*). This was true regardless of whether they had been fed on the cloth (*solid lines*) or on the wire mother (*broken lines*). Infants that had known no mother during their first eight months (*bottom chart*) soon came to prefer cloth mother, but spent less time on her than the other infants.

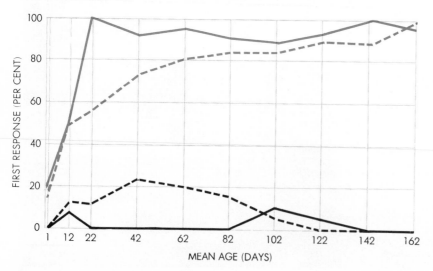

RESULTS OF "FEAR TEST" (*see photographs on opposite page*) showed that infants confronted by a strange object quickly learned to seek reassurance from the cloth mother (*colored curves*) rather than from the wire mother (*black curves*). Again infants fed on the wire mother (*broken lines*) behaved much like those fed on cloth mother (*solid lines*)

ciation with the reduction of hunger or thirst.

These results attest the importance—possibly the overwhelming importance—of bodily contact and the immediate comfort it supplies in forming the infant's attachment for its mother. All our experience, in fact, indicates that our cloth-covered mother surrogate is an eminently satisfactory mother. She is available 24 hours a day to satisfy her infant's overwhelming compulsion to seek bodily contact; she possesses infinite patience, never scolding her baby or biting it in anger. In these respects we regard her as superior to a living monkey mother, though monkey fathers would probably not endorse this opinion.

Of course this does not mean that nursing has no psychological importance. No act so effectively guarantees intimate bodily contact between mother and child. Furthermore, the mother who finds nursing a pleasant experience will probably be temperamentally inclined to give her infant plenty of handling and fondling. The real-life attachment of the infant to its mother is doubtless influenced by subtle multiple variables, contributed in part by the mother and in part by the child. We make no claim to having unraveled these in only two years of investigation. But no matter what evidence the future may disclose, our first experiments have shown that contact comfort is a decisive variable in this relationship.

Such generalization is powerfully supported by the results of the next phase of our investigation. The time that the infant monkeys spent cuddling on their surrogate mothers was a strong but perhaps not conclusive index of emotional attachment. Would they also seek the inanimate mother for comfort and security when they were subjected to emotional stress? With this question in mind we exposed our monkey infants to the stress of fear by presenting them with strange objects, for example a mechanical teddy bear which moved forward, beating a drum. Whether the infants had nursed from the wire or the cloth mother, they overwhelmingly sought succor from the cloth one; this differential in behavior was enhanced with the passage of time and the accrual of experience. Early in this series of experiments the terrified infant might rush blindly to the wire mother, but even if it did so it would soon abandon her for the cloth mother. The infant would cling to its cloth mother, rubbing its body against hers. Then, with its fears assuaged through intimate contact with the moth-

FRIGHTENING OBJECTS such as a mechanical teddy bear caused almost all infant monkeys to flee blindly to the cloth mother, as in the top photograph. Once reassured by pressing and rubbing against her, they would then look at the strange object (*bottom*).

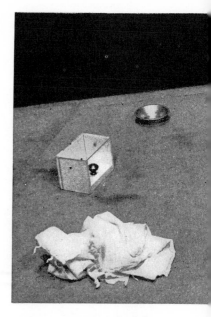

"OPEN FIELD TEST" involved placing a monkey in a room far larger than its accustomed cage; unfamiliar objects added an addi-tional disturbing element. If no mother was present, the infant would typically huddle in a corner (*left*). The wire mother did

er, it would turn to look at the previously terrifying bear without the slightest sign of alarm. Indeed, the infant would some-times even leave the protection of the mother and approach the object that a few minutes before had reduced it to abject terror.

The analogy with the behavior of hu-man infants requires no elaboration. We found that the analogy extends even to less obviously stressful situations. When a child is taken to a strange place, he usually remains composed and happy so long as his mother is nearby. If the moth-er gets out of sight, however, the child is often seized with fear and distress. We developed the same response in our infant monkeys when we exposed them to a room that was far larger than the cages to which they were accustomed. In the room we had placed a number of unfamiliar objects such as a small arti-ficial tree, a crumpled piece of paper, a folded gauze diaper, a wooden block and a doorknob [*a similar experiment is depicted in the illustrations on these two pages*]. If the cloth mother was in the room, the infant would rush wildly to her, climb upon her, rub against her and cling to her tightly. As in the previous experiment, its fear then sharply di-minished or vanished. The infant would begin to climb over the mother's body and to explore and manipulate her face. Soon it would leave the mother to inves-tigate the new world, and the unfamiliar objects would become playthings. In a typical behavior sequence, the infant might manipulate the tree, return to the mother, crumple the wad of paper, bring it to the mother, explore the block, ex-

plore the doorknob, play with the paper and return to the mother. So long as the mother provided a psychological "base of operations" the infants were unafraid and their behavior remained positive, exploratory and playful.

If the cloth mother was absent, how-ever, the infants would rush across the test room and throw themselves face-down on the floor, clutching their heads and bodies and screaming their distress. Records kept by two independent ob-servers—scoring for such "fear indices" as crying, crouching, rocking and thumb-and toe-sucking—showed that the emo-tionality scores of the infants nearly tripled. But no quantitative measure-ment can convey the contrast between the positive, outgoing activities in the presence of the cloth mother and the stereotyped withdrawn and disturbed behavior in the motherless situation.

The bare wire mother provided no more reassurance in this "open field" test than no mother at all. Control tests on monkeys that from birth had known only the wire mother revealed that even these infants showed no affection for her and obtained no comfort from her presence. Indeed, this group of animals exhibited the highest emotionality scores of all. Typically they would run to some wall or corner of the room, clasp their heads and bodies and rock convulsively back and forth. Such activities closely re-semble the autistic behavior seen fre-quently among neglected children in and out of institutions.

In a final comparison of the cloth and wire mothers, we adapted an experiment originally devised by Robert A. Butler

at the Primate Laboratory. Butler had found that monkeys enclosed in a dimly lighted box would press a lever to open and reopen a window for hours on end for no reward other than the chance to look out. The rate of lever-pressing de-pended on what the monkeys saw through the opened window; the sight of another monkey elicited far more activi-ty than that of a bowl of fruit or an emp-ty room [see "Curiosity in Monkeys," by Robert A. Butler; SCIENTIFIC AMERICAN Offprint 426]. We now know that this "curiosity response" is innate. Three-day-old monkeys, barely able to walk, will crawl across the floor of the box to reach a lever which briefly opens the window; some press the lever hundreds of times within a few hours.

When we tested our monkey infants in the "Butler box," we found that those reared with both cloth and wire mothers showed as high a response to the cloth mother as to another monkey, but dis-played no more interest in the wire mother than in an empty room. In this test, as in all the others, the monkeys fed on the wire mother behaved the same as those fed on the cloth mother. A con-trol group raised with no mothers at all found the cloth mother no more inter-esting than the wire mother and neither as interesting as another monkey.

Thus all the objective tests we have been able to devise agree in showing that the infant monkey's relationship to its surrogate mother is a full one. Com-parison with the behavior of infant mon-keys raised by their real mothers con-firms this view. Like our experimental monkeys, these infants spend many

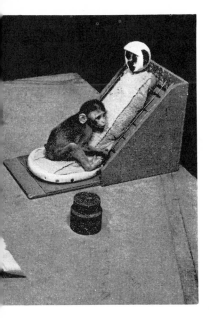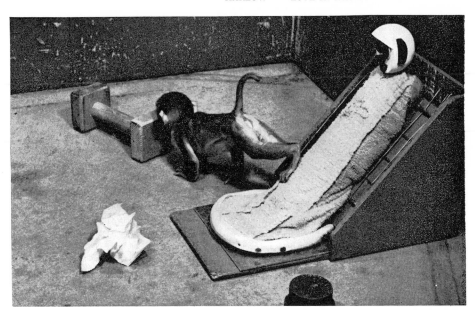

not alter this pattern of fearful behavior, but the cloth mother provided quick reassurance. The infant would first cling to her (*center*) and then set out to explore the room and play with the objects (*right*), returning from time to time for more reassurance.

hours a day clinging to their mothers, and run to them for comfort or reassurance when they are frightened. The deep and abiding bond between mother and child appears to be essentially the same, whether the mother is real or a cloth surrogate.

While bodily contact clearly plays the prime role in developing infantile affection, other types of stimulation presumably supplement its effects. We have therefore embarked on a search for these other factors. The activity of a live monkey mother, for example, provides her infant with frequent motion stimulation. In many human cultures mothers bind their babies to them when they go about their daily chores; in our own culture parents know very well that rocking a baby or walking with him somehow promotes his psychological and physiological well-being. Accordingly we compared the responsiveness of infant monkeys to two cloth mothers, one stationary and one rocking. All of them preferred the rocking mother, though the degree of preference varied considerably from day to day and from monkey to monkey. An experiment with a rocking crib and a stationary one gave similar results. Motion does appear to enhance affection, albeit far less significantly than simple contact.

The act of clinging, in itself, also seems to have a role in promoting psychological and physiological well-being. Even before we began our studies of affection, we noticed that a newborn monkey raised in a bare wire cage survived with difficulty unless we provided it with a cone to which it could cling. Re-

cently we have raised two groups of monkeys, one with a padded crib instead of a mother and the other with a cloth mother as well as a crib. Infants in the latter group actually spend more time on the crib than on the mother, probably because the steep incline of the mother's cloth surface makes her a less satisfactory sleeping platform. In the open-field test, the infants raised with a crib but no mother clearly derived some emotional support from the presence of the crib. But those raised with both showed an unequivocal preference for the mother they could cling to, and they evidenced the benefit of the superior emotional succor they gained from her.

Still other elements in the relationship remain to be investigated systematically. Common sense would suggest that the warmth of the mother's body plays its part in strengthening the infant's ties to her. Our own observations have not yet confirmed this hypothesis. Heating a cloth mother does not seem to increase her attractiveness to the infant monkey, and infants readily abandon a heating pad for an unheated mother surrogate. However, our laboratory is kept comfortably warm at all times; experiments in a chilly environment might well yield quite different results.

Visual stimulation may forge an additional link. When they are about three months old, the monkeys begin to observe and manipulate the head, face and eyes of their mother surrogates; human infants show the same sort of delayed responsiveness to visual stimuli. Such stimuli are known to have marked ef-

fects on the behavior of many young animals. The Austrian zoologist Konrad Lorenz has demonstrated a process called "imprinting"; he has shown that the young of some species of birds become attached to the first moving object they perceive, normally their mothers [see "'Imprinting' in Animals," by Eckhard H. Hess; SCIENTIFIC AMERICAN Offprint 416]. It is also possible that particular sounds and even odors may play some role in the normal development of responses or attention.

The depth and persistence of attachment to the mother depend not only on the kind of stimuli that the young animal receives but also on when it receives them. Experiments with ducks show that imprinting is most effective during a critical period soon after hatching; beyond a certain age it cannot take place at all. Clinical experience with human beings indicates that people who have been deprived of affection in infancy may have difficulty forming affectional ties in later life. From preliminary experiments with our monkeys we have found that their affectional responses develop, or fail to develop, according to a similar pattern.

Early in our investigation we had segregated four infant monkeys as a general control group, denying them physical contact either with a mother surrogate or with other monkeys. After about eight months we placed them in cages with access to both cloth and wire mothers. At first they were afraid of both surrogates, but within a few days they began to respond in much the same way as the other infants. Soon they were

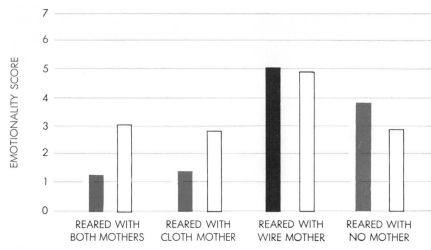

SCORES IN OPEN FIELD TEST show that all infant monkeys familiar with the cloth mother were much less disturbed when she was present (*color*) than when no mother was present (*white*); scores under 2 indicate unfrightened behavior. Infants that had known only the wire mother were greatly disturbed whether she was present (*black*) or not (*white*).

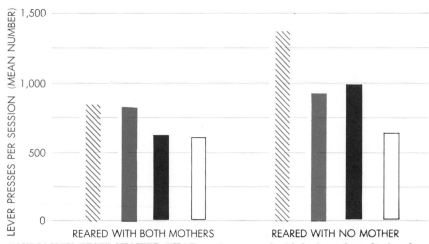

"CURIOSITY TEST" SHOWED THAT monkeys reared with both mothers displayed as much interest in the cloth mother (*solid color*) as in another monkey (*hatched color*); the wire mother (*black*) was no more interesting than an empty chamber (*white*). Monkeys reared with no mother found cloth and wire mother less interesting than another monkey.

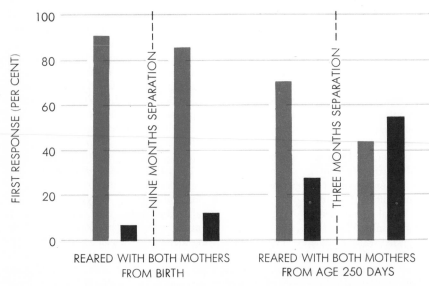

EARLY "MOTHERING" produced a strong and unchanging preference for the cloth mother (*color*) over the wire mother (*black*). Monkeys deprived of early mothering showed less marked preferences before separation and no significant preference subsequently.

spending less than an hour a day with the wire mother and eight to 10 hours with the cloth mother. Significantly, however, they spent little more than half as much time with the cloth mother as did infants raised with her from birth.

In the open-field test these "orphan" monkeys derived far less reassurance from the cloth mothers than did the other infants. The deprivation of physical contact during their first eight months had plainly affected the capacity of these infants to develop the full and normal pattern of affection. We found a further indication of the psychological damage wrought by early lack of mothering when we tested the degree to which infant monkeys retained their attachments to their mothers. Infants raised with a cloth mother from birth and separated from her at about five and a half months showed little or no loss of responsiveness even after 18 months of separation. In some cases it seemed that absence had made the heart grow fonder. The monkeys that had known a mother surrogate only after the age of eight months, however, rapidly lost whatever responsiveness they had acquired. The long period of maternal deprivation had evidently left them incapable of forming a lasting affectional tie.

The effects of maternal separation and deprivation in the human infant have scarcely been investigated, in spite of their implications concerning child-rearing practices. The long period of infant-maternal dependency in the monkey provides a real opportunity for investigating persisting disturbances produced by inconsistent or punishing mother surrogates.

Above and beyond demonstration of the surprising importance of contact comfort as a prime requisite in the formation of an infant's love for its mother —and the discovery of the unimportant or nonexistent role of the breast and act of nursing—our investigations have established a secure experimental approach to this realm of dramatic and subtle emotional relationships. The further exploitation of the broad field of research that now opens up depends merely upon the availability of infant monkeys. We expect to extend our researches by undertaking the study of the mother's (and even the father's!) love for the infant, using real monkey infants or infant surrogates. Finally, with such techniques established, there appears to be no reason why we cannot at some future time investigate the fundamental neurophysiological and biochemical variables underlying affection and love.

13

DEPRIVATION DWARFISM

LYTT I. GARDNER
July 1972

*Children raised in an emotionally deprived environment
can become stunted. The reason may be that abnormal
patterns of sleep inhibit the secretion of pituitary
hormones, including the growth hormone*

It has long been known that infants will not thrive if their mothers are hostile to them or even merely indifferent. This knowledge is the grain of truth in a tale, which otherwise is surely apocryphal, told about Frederick II, the 13th-century ruler of Sicily. It is said that Frederick, himself the master of six languages, believed that all men were born with an innate language, and he wondered what particular ancient tongue—perhaps Hebrew—the language was. He sought the answer through an experiment. A group of foster-mothers was gathered and given charge of certain newborn infants. Frederick ordered the children raised in silence, so that they would not hear one spoken word. He reasoned that their first words, owing nothing to their upbringing, would reveal the natural language of man. "But he labored in vain," the chronicler declares, "because the children all died. For they could not live without the petting and the joyful faces and loving words of their foster mothers."

Similar emotional deprivation in infancy is probably the underlying cause of the spectacularly high mortality rates in 18th- and 19th-century foundling homes [see "Checks on Population Growth: 1750–1850," by William L. Langer; SCIENTIFIC AMERICAN, February, 1972]. This, at least, was the verdict of one Spanish churchman, who wrote in 1760: "In the foundling home the child becomes sad, and many of them die of sorrow." Disease and undernourishment certainly contributed to the foundlings' poor rate of survival, but as recently as 1915 James H. M. Knox, Jr., of the Johns Hopkins Hospital noted that, in spite of adequate physical care, 90 percent of the infants in Baltimore orphanages and foundling homes died within a year of admission.

Only in the past 30 years or so have the consequences of emotional deprivation in childhood been investigated in ways that give some hope of understanding the causative mechanisms. One pioneer in the field, Harry Bakwin of New York University, began in 1942 to record the physiological changes apparent in infants removed from the home environment for hospital care. These children, he noted, soon became listless, apathetic and depressed. Their bowel movements were more frequent, and even though their nutritional intake was adequate, they failed to gain weight at the normal rate. Respiratory infections and fevers of unknown origin persisted. All such abnormalities, however, quickly disappeared when the infants were returned to their home and mother.

Another early worker, Margaret A. Ribble, studied infants at three New York maternity hospitals over a period of eight years; in several instances she was able to follow the same child from birth to preadolescence. When normal contact between mother and infant was disrupted, she noted, diarrhea was more prevalent and muscle tone decreased. The infants would frequently spit up their food and then swallow it again. This action is called "rumination" by pediatricians. Largely as the result of studies by Renata and Eugenio Gaddini of the University of Rome, it is recognized today as a symptom of psychic disturbance. Ribble concluded that alarm over a lack of adequate "mothering" was not mere sentimentality. The absence of normal mother-infant interaction was "an actual privation which may result in biological, as well as psychological, damage to the infant."

Two other psychiatrically oriented investigators of this period, René Spitz of the New York Psychoanalytic Institute and his colleague Katherine Wolf, took histories of 91 foundling-home infants in the eastern U.S. and Canada. They found that the infants consistently showed evidence of anxiety and sadness. Their physical development was retarded and they failed to gain weight normally or even lost weight. Periods of protracted insomnia alternated with periods of stupor. Of the 91, Spitz and Wolf reported, 34 died "in spite of good food and meticulous medical care." The period between the seventh and the 12th month of life was the time of the highest fatalities. Infants who managed to survive their first year uniformly showed severe physical retardation.

The comparative irrelevance of good diet, as contrasted with a hostile environment, was documented with startling clarity in Germany after World War II. In 1948 the British nutritionist Elsie M. Widdowson was stationed with an army medical unit in a town in the British Zone of Occupation where two small municipal orphanages were located. Each housed 50-odd boys and girls between four and 14 years of age; the children's average age was 8½. They had nothing except official rations to eat and were below normal in height and weight. The medical unit instituted a program of physical examinations of the orphans every two weeks and continued these observations for 12 months. During the first six months the orphanages continued to receive only the official rations. During the last six months the children in what I shall call Orphanage *A* received in addition unlimited amounts of bread, an extra ration of jam and a supply of concentrated orange juice.

The matron in charge of Orphanage *A* at the start of this study was a cheerful young woman who was fond of the children in her care. The woman in charge of Orphanage *B* was older, stern and a strict disciplinarian toward all the children in her care except a small group of favorites. It so happened that at the end of the first six months the cheerful matron left Orphanage A for other employment and the disciplinarian was transferred from Orphanage B to Orphanage A, bringing her eight favorites.

The examinations revealed that during the first six months the weight gained by the children in the "cheerful" orphanage was substantially more than the weight gained by the children in the "strict" orphanage. The strict matron's favorites of course did much better than the rest of her charges. The shift in matrons then occurred, coinciding with the provision of extra food for Orphanage A.

During the next six months the children of Orphanage B, whose food supply was not increased but who no longer had the stern matron, showed a rapid rise in weight. In spite of orange juice, jam and unlimited bread the disciplinarian's new charges in Orphanage A only gained weight at about the same rate as before; indeed, the figures showed that their average weight gain was slightly

less. The matron's favorites were an exception; their weight gain exceeded all the other children's [see illustration, page 107]. An identical trend was recorded with respect to increases in height.

It seems clear that the reaction of the orphans to an adverse emotional environment was a reduction in the normal growth rate. Although the operative mechanism is not easily identified from observations such as these, a unique opportunity arose recently in the U.S. to study in detail the effect of emotional deprivation on an infant's digestive apparatus. In 1965 a mother in upper New York state gave birth to a daughter with an underdeveloped esophagus. A surgical opening was made into the infant's stomach, a feeding tube was inserted and the mother was instructed in its use.

The mother and daughter soon left the hospital for home, where over the next 15 months the mother meticulously fed her child a standard daily dosage of nutrient formula, using a syringe to push the food through the feeding tube. The

mother was fearful, however, of dislodging the feeding tube, and she did not play with the child or cuddle her for the entire period. At the end of 15 months the child had become extremely depressed. She showed evidence of motor retardation, and her physical development was that of an eight-month-old. The child was brought to the University of Rochester Medical Center, where George L. Engel, Franz K. Reichsman and Harry L. Segal conducted extensive observations.

Engel and his associates described the child at the time of admission as exhibiting a "depression withdrawal" reaction. Her facial expression was sad and her muscles flaccid. She was inactive and withdrawn; the withdrawal frequently led to abnormally long periods of sleep. Her stomach secretions were deficient in pepsin and hydrochloric acid. Doses of histamine, which ordinarily stimulate a profuse outpouring of acid by the stomach lining, failed to elicit the normal response.

The investigators began to monitor

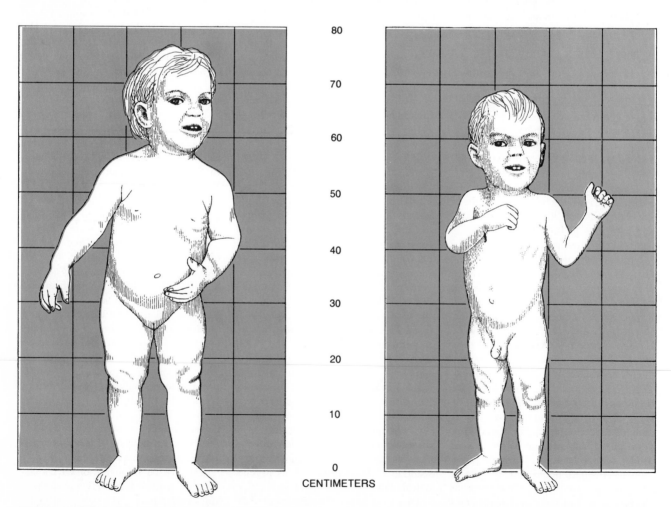

80

70

60

50

40

30

20

10

0

CENTIMETERS

TWINS, NORMAL AND DWARFED, offer evidence of the effect of emotional deprivation on infants. This drawing is based on photographs made when the children were almost 13 months old. The girl was near normal in weight and stature but her twin brother was the size of a seven-month-old. Some four months after the twins were born a period of stress began between the parents; the father then lost his job and left home. It appears that the mother's hostility toward her husband included the son but not the daughter.

the child's activities and keep a record of her emotional state as reflected in facial expressions, at the same time analyzing her gastric secretions. They found that the condition of the stomach was intimately linked with her behavior and emotions. When she was depressed and withdrawn, her production of hydrochloric acid was markedly reduced. When she was angry, talking or eating or otherwise actively relating to external objects, acid production increased.

The child quickly responded to the attention she received from the hospital staff. She gained weight and made up for lost growth; her emotional state improved strikingly. Moreover, these changes were demonstrably unrelated to any change in food intake. During her stay in the hospital she received the same standard nutrient dosage she had received at home. It appears to have been the enrichment of her environment, not of her diet, that was responsible for the normalization of her growth.

A relation between such a physiological deficiency and deprivation dwarfism had been observed in Boston nearly 20 years earlier. On that occasion the abnormality documented was endocrine imbalance. In 1947 Nathan B. Talbot, Edna H. Sobel and their co-workers at the Massachusetts General Hospital were reviewing the clinical findings with respect to some 100 children who were abnormally short for their age. In about half of the cases they found that physiological causes, including lesions of the pituitary gland, were responsible for the stunted growth. In 51 other cases, however, they could find no organic abnormalities. Within this group were 21 children who were not only dwarfed in stature but also abnormally thin. All 21 proved to have a history of emotional disturbance and disordered family environment; the most common finding was

rejection of the child by one parent or both. The investigators concluded that the children's poor condition was the result of an emotionally induced pituitary deficiency.

Some years after this initial observation of psychologically induced endocrine imbalance, Robert Gray Patton and I, working at the State University of New York's Upstate Medical Center in Syracuse, undertook the study of six such "thin dwarfs." We were able to continue observations of two of the children from infancy to late childhood. As we expected, all six were not only short but also far underweight for their age. They were also retarded in skeletal maturation: their "bone age" was substantially less than their actual age in years. In this connection the findings of Austin H. Riesen and Henry W. Nissen are of interest. Working at the Yerkes Laboratory of Primate Biology in the late 1940's, they subjected young chimpanzees to environmental deprivation by keeping them in the dark for long periods. The chimpanzees' "bone age" was considerably retarded as a result.

Our six patients all came from disordered family environments. For example, one of them, a girl 15 months old, was kept in a dark room, isolated and unattended; she was removed from this setting only at feeding times. The child was lethargic and slept as much as 16 or 18 hours a day. Following the children's hospital admission and the provision of a normal emotional environment, all six of them showed a rapid gain in weight, improvement in motor abilities and increased social responsiveness. Indeed, the changes were so consistently dramatic that we believe their presence or absence can serve as a diagnostic test for deprivation dwarfism.

In spite of these short-term gains few

of the children recovered entirely from their experience of deprivation dwarfism. They tended to remain below average in height, weight and skeletal maturation. Furthermore, the two we were able to follow until late childhood gave evidence of residual damage to personality structure and to intellect.

A remarkably vivid example of deprivation dwarfism, affecting one of a pair of twins, came to the attention of Joseph G. Hollowell and myself in 1964. The mother had given birth to a boy and a girl. Some four months later she found herself unwelcomely pregnant. A few weeks later her husband lost his job and after a few more weeks he left home.

Almost up to the time of the mother's new pregnancy the twins had been growing at the normal rate. Indeed, the boy, although he had begun to ruminate early in infancy, was progressing somewhat more rapidly than the girl. The mother's hostility toward the father, however, evidently became directed, consciously or unconsciously, toward her son as well. From the 15th week onward the boy's growth rate fell progressively behind his sister's. By the time he was a little over a year of age his height was only that of a seven-month-old.

The boy was then hospitalized. He began to recover lost ground and his rumination gradually subsided. Before the child was released from the hospital the father had returned to the mother. The boy's progress continued in the improved home environment; by his second birthday he had caught up to his sister.

Patton and I have postulated a physiological pathway whereby environmental deprivation and emotional disturbance might affect the endocrine apparatus and thereby have an impact on a child's growth. Impulses from the higher brain centers, in our view, travel along neu-

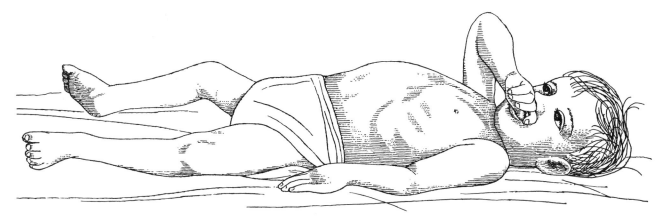

THREE-YEAR-OLD, treated for deprivation dwarfism 18 months earlier, actually lost weight on return to the care of a mother who appeared detached and unemotional in her relationship with the boy. His skeletal maturity on return to the hospital was at the level of a 15-month-old's; he was listless and lay on his back most of the time, his legs spraddled in a characteristic "frog" position.

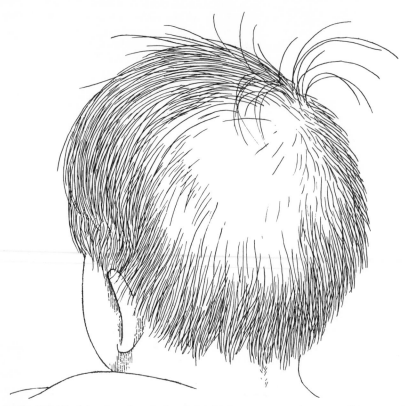

BALD SPOT had developed on the head of child shown on preceding page. This occurs frequently among emotionally deprived children, who will lie in one position for long periods.

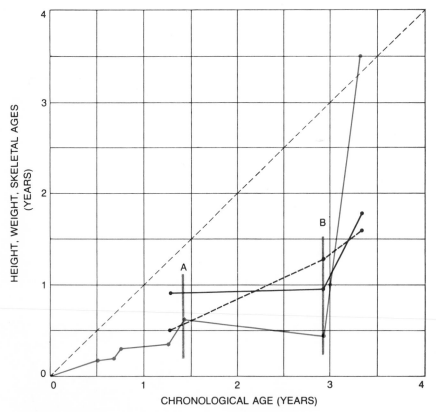

GROWTH RECORD of the boy shown on the preceding page traces his slow decline in weight *(color)* following his release from the hospital at about 18 months of age *(A)*. By the age of three he weighed no more than the average six-month-old and was also severely retarded in height *(black curve)* and in bone maturation *(broken curve)*. Reentering the hospital *(B)*, the child gained weight at a dramatic rate. Placed in a foster home thereafter, he reached a weight above average for his age. Height, weight and skeletal ages of the vertical scale refer to the height, weight or skeletal development of an average child of that age.

ral pathways to the hypothalamus and thence, by neurohumoral mechanisms, exert influence on the pituitary gland. Research on "releasing factors" secreted by the hypothalamus, which in turn are responsible for the secretion of various trophic hormones by the anterior pituitary, has shown that hypothalamic centers exercise a major influence over this neighboring gland. Moreover, it is now known that virtually all the blood reaching the pituitary has first bathed the hypothalamic median eminence. Apparently the releasing factors are transported to the pituitary in the blood flowing from the median eminence through the pituitary portal veins.

Evidence of pituitary involvement in deprivation dwarfism is now becoming increasingly abundant. For example, one of the six children that Patton and I had studied came to the attention of my colleague Mary Voorhess in 1963. Following the child's earlier discharge from the hospital, he had spent two years in his disordered home environment and once again exhibited deprivation dwarfism. He was depressed and in an advanced state of malnutrition. An X-ray examination showed that in terms of maturation his bone age was three years less than his chronological age.

A determination was made of the boy's reserve of one important hormone secreted by the anterior pituitary: the adrenocorticotrophic hormone (ACTH). This hormone stimulates the secretion of the steroid hydrocortisone by the adrenal cortex. The steroid is an important regulator of carbohydrate metabolism; it promotes the conversion of protein into sugar, thereby raising the level of blood sugar. The examination showed that the child's reserve of ACTH was abnormally low.

The child entered the hospital, and following his recovery he was placed in a foster home with a favorable emotional environment. Eighteen months after the first measurement of his ACTH reserve the examination was repeated. The child's pituitary function was normal with respect to ACTH reserve. Furthermore, his formerly lagging bone age had almost caught up with his age in years. Both observations provide support for the working hypothesis that the chain of events leading to the clinical manifestations of deprivation dwarfism involves disturbances in pituitary trophic hormone secretion.

Another important pituitary hormone is somatotrophin, the growth hormone. Like most chemical messengers, the growth hormone is present in the bloodstream in very small quantities; the normal adult on waking will have less than three micrograms of growth hormone in each liter of blood plasma. Even with refined assay techniques measurements at this low level of concentration are difficult. As a result ways have been sought to briefly stimulate the production of growth hormone. Such stimulation not only makes measurement easier but also, if there is little or no response to the stimulus, provides direct evidence for a pituitary deficiency.

Bernardo A. Houssay of Argentina was the first investigator to point to the metabolic antagonism between insulin and the growth hormone. Subsequent research showed that an injection of insulin lowers the recipient's blood-sugar level, and the reaction is normally followed by an increased output of growth hormone. Jesse Roth and his colleagues at the Veterans Administration Hospital in the Bronx perfected an insulin-stimulation test for growth-hormone concentration in the blood in 1963.

Several quantitative assessments of the relation between emotional deprivation and abnormalities in growth-hormone concentration have been made in recent years. For example, in 1967 George Powell and his colleagues at the Johns Hopkins Hospital worked with a group of children over three years old suffering from deprivation dwarfism. They found that the children's growth-hormone response to insulin stimulation was subnormal. After the children had been transferred to an adequate emotional environment insulin stimulation was followed by the normal increase in growth-hormone concentration. At the Children's Hospital of Michigan patients over the age of three with deprivation dwarfism showed a similar picture. Working there in 1971, Ingeborg Krieger and Raymond Mellinger found that the response to insulin stimulation in these children was subnormal. When they repeated the test with deprived children below the age of three, however, they were surprised to find that the concentration of growth hormone under fasting conditions was abnormally high, and that after insulin stimulation the concentration was normal. It is likely that the difference in the responses of the two age groups is related to maturation, perhaps the maturation of the cerebral cortex. In any event both the Johns Hopkins and the Michigan studies are further evidence of the connection between deprivation dwarfism and impaired pituitary function.

Loss of appetite is a well-known com-

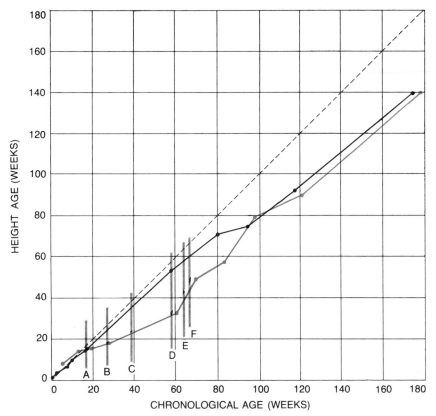

TWINS' INCREASE IN HEIGHT over a 3½-year period is plotted on this graph in terms of normal children's average growth. (The diagonal line marks the 50th percentile.) The boy who developed deprivation dwarfism also exhibited "rumination," that is, he spat up his food and swallowed it again. Nevertheless, his increase in height (color) was equal to or better than his sister's until his mother became pregnant (A). From that time on he fell steadily behind his sister as his father first lost his job (B) and then left home (C). Recovery of lost growth, begun when the boy was admitted to the hospital (D), continued on his return home (F), an event that followed his father's return (E). Before his second birthday the boy once more equaled his sister in height; both, however, were below normal.

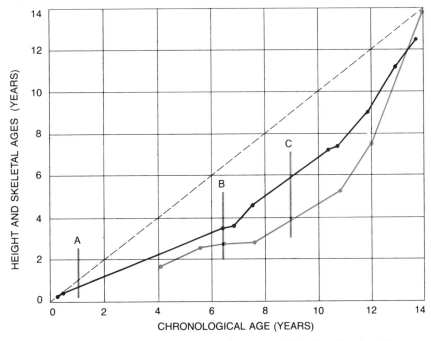

THIRTEEN YEARS of subnormal growth are shown in a child with a disordered home environment. Deserted by her husband (A), the mother worked full time. Six years later (B) the parents were divorced; then (C) the mother remarried and resumed keeping house. The child's bone development (color) but not his stature (black) finally became average.

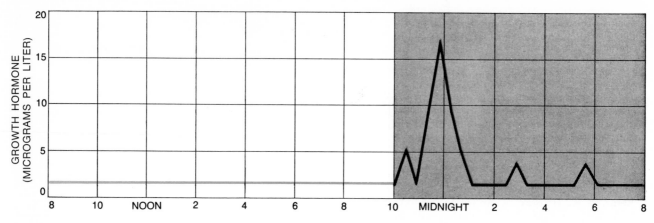

RELEASE OF GROWTH HORMONE increases during early hours of sleep (*shaded area*). This record of the growth hormone in the blood of a preadolescent child was collected by Jordan W. Finkelstein and his associates at Montefiore Hospital in the Bronx.

plaint in adolescents; in a few cases it is so extreme that it is termed anorexia nervosa. The disorder is usually attributable to adverse interpersonal relations between parent and child, particularly between mother and daughter. The clinical similarities between adolescent anorexia nervosa and infant and child deprivation dwarfism have long interested investigators. For example, adolescent girls with anorexia nervosa may stop menstruating; the adverse emotional climate evidently halts secretion of the pituitary hormones that mediate ovarian function. It now appears that some patients with anorexia nervosa also respond to insulin stimulation with a subnormal release of growth hormone.

Because it can be difficult to distinguish between anorexia nervosa and organic disorders of the pituitary, John Landon and his associates at St. Mary's Hospital in London recently tested the pituitary function of five patients with anorexia nervosa. All five showed the reaction typical of individuals with impaired pituitary function: after injections of insulin their level of blood sugar was excessively low. Two of the five also showed the reaction that typifies many instances of deprivation dwarfism: the concentration of growth hormone in the blood did not increase. The investigators also noted that before the injection of insulin the concentration of growth hormone in their patients' blood was significantly higher than normal. This paradoxical finding is not unlike the reaction observed among the younger deprivation-dwarfism patients in Michigan.

The significance of the St. Mary's findings is not yet clear, but they could prove to be important clues in unraveling the relations among the higher brain centers, the hypothalamus and the pituitary. We may be observing here a series of differing, age-mediated physiological

responses to what are essentially identical psychosocial stimuli.

An important new direction for future investigation is suggested by the recent discovery of a connection between the release of growth hormone and individual modes of sleep. This connection was uncovered in 1965 by W. M. Hunter and W. M. Rigal of the University of Edinburgh, who observed that the total amount of growth hormone secreted during the night by older children was many times greater than the amount secreted during the day. Soon thereafter Hans-Jürgen Quabbe and his colleagues at the Free University of Berlin measured the amount of growth hormone secreted by adult volunteers during a 24-hour fast and detected a sharp rise that coincided with the volunteers' period of sleep. Pursuing this coincidence, Yasuro Takahashi and his co-workers at Washington University and Yutaka Honda and his colleagues at the University of Tokyo found that the rise in growth-hormone concentration occurs in adults during the first two hours of sleep, and that it equals the increase produced by insulin stimulation. If the subject remains awake, the growth hormone is not secreted. Honda and his associates propose that activation of the cerebral cortex somehow inhibits the secretion of growth hormone, whereas sleep—particularly the sleep that is accompanied by a high-voltage slow-wave pattern in encephalograph readings—induces the secretion of a growth-hormone-releasing factor in the hypothalamus.

Collecting such data calls for the frequent drawing of blood samples from sleeping subjects through an indwelling catheter, with the result that studies of growth-hormone concentration in infants and young children have been relatively

few. What findings there are, however, fall into a pattern. For example, there appears to be no correlation between the concentration of growth hormone in the blood of normal newborn infants and the infants' cycle of alternate sleep and wakefulness. Such a correlation does not appear until after the third month of life. In normal children between the ages of five and 15 the maximum growth-hormone concentration is found about an hour after sleep begins. Maturation therefore appears to be a factor in establishing the correlation. Whether there is any link between these maturation-dependent responses and similar responses in instances of deprivation dwarfism is not clear.

The existence of a cause-and-effect relation between deprivation dwarfism and abnormal patterns of sleep had been suggested by Joseph Schutt-Aine and his associates at the Children's Hospital in Pittsburgh. They and others found that in children with deprivation dwarfism there were spontaneous and transient decreases in reserves of ACTH, the hormone that stimulates the secretion of the adrenal-cortex steroid that raises the level of blood sugar in the bloodstream. They also found that the decrease in ACTH reserve was accompanied by a temporary lowering of the child's blood-sugar level. Taking a position much like Honda's with respect to the growth hormone, Schutt-Aine and his colleagues suggest that any preponderance of inhibitory cerebral-cortex influences on the hypothalamus would tend to interfere with the normal release of ACTH and other pituitary hormones. An abnormal sleep pattern, they conclude, could lead to such a preponderance.

Is it in fact possible to attribute the retarded growth of psychosocially deprived children to sleep patterns that in-

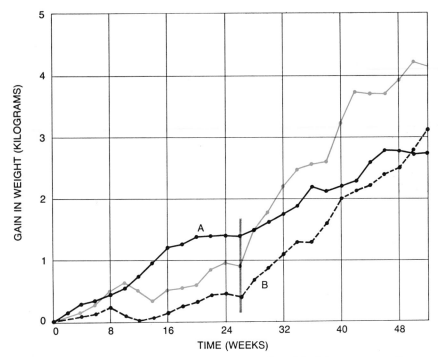

QUALITY OF CARE proved more important than quality of food in two postwar German orphanages studied by Elsie M. Widdowson. For six months during 1948 the 50-odd war orphans in each home received nothing but basic rations, yet the children in Orphanage *A*, supervised by a kindly matron, gained more weight than most of those in Orphanage *B*, whose matron was a stern disciplinarian. An exception was a group of favorites of the stern matron at *B* (*color*); they did better than their companions. After six months the matron at *B* was transferred to *A* and brought her favorites with her. Simultaneously the children at *A* were given extra rations, whereas the children at *B* remained on the same basic diet. (The transition is indicated by the vertical gray line.) Relieved of the stern matron's discipline, the children at *B* began to show a sharp increase in weight; those at *A* showed a weight gain that averaged somewhat less than it had during the preceding six months in spite of the larger ration. Again matron's favorites were an exception: their gain was greatest of any.

hibit the secretion of growth hormone? Certainly there is evidence that deprivation dwarfism and sleep abnormalities, both of commission and omission, often go together. The infants observed by Spitz and Wolf alternated between insomnia and stupor. One of the six thin dwarfs that Patton and I studied slept as much as 18 hours a day; another spent the hours while his family slept roaming the dark house. The tube-fed 15-month-old in Rochester, when admitted to the hospital, appeared to use sleep as a means of withdrawing from the world.

Georg Wolff and John W. Money of the Johns Hopkins Hospital have attempted a quantitative assessment of this question by studying the sleep patterns of a group of children with deprivation dwarfism. Analysis of their data suggests that the sleep pattern of children with deprivation dwarfism is disturbed in periods of subnormal growth and undisturbed in periods of normal growth. Thus far, however, the data are insufficient to establish whether or not there is an abnormal pattern in the secretion of growth hormone by sleeping children with deprivation dwarfism.

It has been proposed that the human infant is born with an innate, species-specific repertory of responses that includes clinging, sucking, "following" with the eyes, crying and smiling. These are the responses that John Bowlby of the Tavistock Institute of Human Relations in London identifies as having survival value for the infant; he believes their existence is a product of natural selection. In Bowlby's view the primary function of the mother is to integrate these responses into "attachment behavior," a more mature and more complicated pattern. In addition there evidently are "sensitive" periods in the course of human development, such as those familiar from animal experimentation. Exactly when these periods occur in human infancy, however, and just what conditions and experiences are necessary if the child is to develop normally remain uncertain. One conclusion nevertheless seems clear. Deprivation dwarfism is a concrete example—an "experiment of nature," so to speak—that demonstrates the delicacy, complexity and crucial importance of infant-parent interaction.

NORMAL MOTHER-INFANT RELATION among monkeys involves close bodily contact between the two. This pair and three similar pairs were used in a study of the relative importance of maternal and peer relations in the social development of the young. Each pair was housed alone, but the infants had access to a common playpen. In this situation the young developed normally.

14

SOCIAL DEPRIVATION IN MONKEYS

HARRY F. AND MARGARET KUENNE HARLOW
November 1962

*Maternal care has long been known to influence
the emotional development of infants. New studies
with rhesus monkeys suggest that peer relations may
play an even more decisive role*

In *An Outline of Psychoanalysis*, published posthumously in 1940, Sigmund Freud was able to refer to "the common assertion that the child is psychologically the father of the man and that the events of his first years are of paramount importance for his whole subsequent life." It was, of course, Freud's own historic investigations, begun a half-century before, that first elucidated the role of infantile experiences in the development of the personality and its disorders. The "central experience of this period of childhood," he found, is the infant's relation to his mother. Freud's ideas have now shaped the thinking of two generations of psychologists, psychiatrists and psychoanalysts. Much evidence in support of his deep insights has been accumulated, particularly from clinical studies of the mentally ill. Contemporary writers stress inadequate or inconsistent mothering as a basic cause of later disorders such as withdrawal, hostility, anxiety, sexual maladjustment, alcoholism and, significantly, inadequate maternal behavior!

The evidence from clinical studies for this or any other view of human personality development is qualified, however, by an inherent defect. These studies are necessarily retrospective: they start with the disorder and work backward in time, retracing the experiences of the individual as he and his relatives and associates recall them. Inevitably details are lost or distorted, and the story is often so confounded as to require a generous exercise of intuition on the part of the investigator. Nor does evidence obtained in this manner exclude other possible causes of personality disorder. Against arguments in favor of a biochemical or neurological causation of mental illness, for example, there is no way to show that the patient began life with full potentiality for normal development. Given

the decisive influence ascribed to the mother-infant relation, there may be a tendency in the reconstruction of the past to overlook or suppress evidence for the influence of other significant early relations, such as the bonds of interaction with other children. Little attention has been given, in fact, to child-to-child relations in the study of personality development. Yet it can be supposed that these play a significant part in determining the peer relations and the sexual role of the adult. Plainly there is a need to study the development of per-

ABNORMAL MOTHER, raised with a cloth surrogate instead of her mother, rejects her infant, refusing to let it nurse. Infants of four such mothers, raised under same conditions as infants of good mothers, developed relatively normally in spite of poor maternal care.

INFANTS PLAY in one of the playpens used in experiments described in two preceding illustrations. Both infants, photographed when they were six months old, had normal mothers.

sonality forward in time from infancy. Ideally the study should be conducted under controlled laboratory conditions so that the effects of single variables or combinations of variables can be traced.

Acceding to the moral and physical impossibility of conducting such an investigation with human subjects, we have been observing the development of social behavior in large numbers of rhesus monkeys at the Primate Laboratory of the University of Wisconsin. Apart from this primate's kinship to man, it offers a reasonable experimental substitute because it undergoes a relatively long period of development analogous to that of the human child and involving intimate attachment to its mother and social interaction with its age-mates. With these animals we have been able to observe the consequences of the deprivation of all social contact for various lengths of time. We have also raised them without mothers but in the company of age-mates and with mothers but without age-mates.

We have thereby been able to make some estimate of the contribution of each of these primary affectional systems to the integrated adult personality. Our observations sustain the significance of the maternal relation, particularly in facilitating the interaction of the infant with other infants. But at the same time we have found compelling evidence that opportunity for infant-infant interaction under optimal conditions may fully compensate for lack of mothering, at least in so far as infant-infant social and heterosexual relations are concerned. It seems possible—even likely—that the infant-

mother affectional system is dispensable, whereas the infant-infant system is the *sine qua non* for later adjustment in all spheres of monkey life. In line with the "paramount importance" that Freud assigned to experience in the first years of life, our experiments indicate that there is a critical period somewhere between the third and sixth months of life during which social deprivation, particularly deprivation of the company of its peers, irreversibly blights the animal's capacity for social adjustment.

Our investigations of the emotional development of our subjects grew out of the effort to produce and maintain a colony of sturdy, disease-free young animals for use in various research programs. By separating them from their mothers a few hours after birth and placing them in a more fully controlled regimen of nurture and physical care we were able both to achieve a higher rate of survival and to remove the animals for testing without maternal protest. Only later did we realize that our monkeys were emotionally disturbed as well as sturdy and disease-free. Some of our researches are therefore retrospective. Others are in part exploratory, representing attempts to set up new experimental situations or to find new techniques for measurement. Most are incomplete because investigations of social and behavioral development are long-term. In a sense, they can never end, because the problems of one generation must be traced into the next.

Having separated the infant from its mother, our procedure was to keep it alone in a bare wire cage in a large room with other infants so housed. Thus each

little monkey could see and hear others of its kind, although it could not make direct physical contact with them. The 56 animals raised in this manner now range in age from five to eight years. As a group they exhibit abnormalities of behavior rarely seen in animals born in the wild and brought to the laboratory as preadolescents or adolescents, even after the latter have been housed in individual cages for many years. The laboratory-born monkeys sit in their cages and stare fixedly into space, circle their cages in a repetitive stereotyped manner and clasp their heads in their hands or arms and rock for long periods of time. They often develop compulsive habits, such as pinching precisely the same patch of skin on the chest between the same fingers hundreds of times a day; occasionally such behavior may become punitive and the animal may chew and tear at its body until it bleeds. Often the approach of a human being becomes the stimulus to self-aggression. This behavior constitutes a complete breakdown and reversal of the normal defensive response; a monkey born in the wild will direct such threats and aggression at the approaching person, not at itself. Similar symptoms of emotional pathology are observed in deprived children in orphanages and in withdrawn adolescents and adults in mental hospitals.

William A. Mason, now at the Yerkes Laboratories of Primate Biology, compared the behavior of six of these animals, which were then two years old and had been housed all their lives in individual cages, with a matched group of rhesus monkeys that had been captured in the wild during their first year of life and housed together in captivity for a while before being individually housed in the laboratory. The most striking difference was that all the animals that had been born in the wild—and not one of the laboratory-born animals—displayed normal sex behavior. That the laboratory-born animals were not lacking in sex drive was indicated by the fact that the males frequently approached the females and the females displayed part of the pattern of sexual presentation. But they did not orient themselves correctly and they did not succeed in mating. Moreover, the monkeys born in the wild had apparently learned to live with others in a stable hierarchy of dominance, or "pecking order"; consequently in the pairing test they fought one another less and engaged more often in social grooming. They would also release a companion from a locked cage more frequently than did the laboratory-born animals, which usually ignored their caged partner's plight.

The severity of the affliction that grips these monkeys raised in the partial isolation of individual wire cages has become more apparent as they have grown older. They pay little or no attention to animals in neighboring cages; those caged with companions sit in opposite corners with only rare interaction. No heterosexual behavior has ever been observed between male and female cagemates, even between those that have lived together for as long as seven years.

When efforts have been made to bring about matings, by pairing animals during the female's estrus, they have sometimes fought so viciously that they have had to be parted. Attempts to mate the socially deprived animals with sexually adequate and experienced monkeys from

MOTHERLESS INFANTS, raised from birth by cloth surrogates, play in a specially constructed playroom supplied with equipment for climbing and swinging. These animals, plus one other not seen in this photograph, were kept in individual cages and brought together in the playroom for 20 minutes a day. Although they had no maternal care whatever, they developed normally in every respect.

the breeding colony have been similarly frustrated.

In the summer of 1960 we undertook to devise a group-psychotherapy situation for 19 of these animals—nine males and 10 females—by using them to stock the monkey island in the municipal zoo in Madison, Wis. This was their first experience outside the laboratory, and they had much to learn in order to survive. They had to learn to drink water from an open trough instead of from a tube in the wall of a cage, to compete for food in a communal feeding situation, to huddle together or find shelter from inclement weather, to climb rocks and avoid the water surrounding the island. Most difficult of all, they had to learn to live together. Within the first few days they made all the necessary physical adjustments. The three casualties—a male that

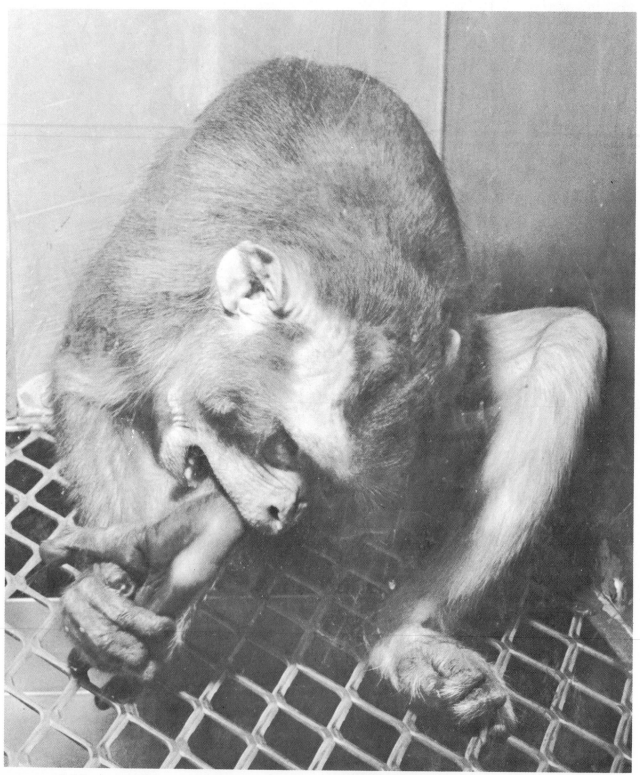

MONKEYS RAISED IN PARTIAL ISOLATION from birth to six months develop severe abnormalities of behavior. This animal, now full-grown, bites itself at the approach of the photographer. Animals raised in isolation often display such self-punishing behavior when a human being appears. They defend themselves adequately, however, against other monkeys and are often extremely aggressive.

EXPERIMENTAL CONDITION	PRESENT AGE	BEHAVIOR				
		NONE	LOW	ALMOST NORMAL	PROBABLY NORMAL	NORMAL
RAISED IN ISOLATION						
TOTAL — CAGE-RAISED FOR 2 YEARS	4 YEARS					
TOTAL — CAGE-RAISED FOR 6 MONTHS	14 MONTHS					
TOTAL — CAGE-RAISED FOR 80 DAYS	10½ MONTHS					
PARTIAL — CAGE-RAISED FOR 6 MONTHS	5 TO 8 YEARS					
PARTIAL — SURROGATE-RAISED FOR 6 MONTHS	3 TO 5 YEARS					
RAISED WITH MOTHER						
NORMAL MOTHER; NO PLAY WITH PEERS	1 YEAR					
MOTHERLESS MOTHER; PLAY IN PLAYPEN	14 MONTHS					
NORMAL MOTHER; PLAY IN PLAYPEN	2 YEARS					
RAISED WITH PEERS						
FOUR RAISED IN ONE CAGE; PLAY IN PLAYROOM	1 YEAR					
SURROGATE-RAISED; PLAY IN PLAYPEN	2 YEARS					
SURROGATE-RAISED; PLAY IN PLAYROOM	21 MONTHS					

■ PLAY
□ DEFENSE
▨ SEX

RESULTS OF EXPERIMENTS are summarized. The monkey's capacity to develop normally appears to be determined by the seventh month of life. Animals isolated for six months are aberrant in every respect. Play with peers seems even more necessary than mothering to the development of effective social relations.

drowned and two females that were injured and had to be returned to the laboratory—resulted from the stress of social adjustment. Fighting was severe at first; it decreased as effective dominance relations were established and friendship pairs formed. Grooming appeared in normal style and with almost normal frequency. A limited amount of sex behavior was observed, but it was infantile in form, with inadequate posturing by both females and males. In the hope of promoting therapy along this line we introduced our largest, strongest and most effective breeding-colony male to the island around the middle of summer. He immediately established himself at the head of the dominance order. But in spite of his considerable persistence and patience he did not succeed in starting a single pregnancy.

Back in the laboratory these animals ceased to groom and fought more frequently. In pairings with breeding-colony monkeys, not one male has achieved a normal mount or intromission and only one female has become pregnant. After two years we have had to conclude that the island experience was of no lasting value.

As the effects of the separation of these monkeys from their mothers in infancy were first becoming apparent in 1957 we were prompted to undertake a study of the mother-infant affectional bond. To each of one group of four animals separated from their mothers at birth we furnished a surrogate mother: a welded wire cylindrical form with the nipple of the feeding bottle protruding from its "breast" and with a wooden head surmounting it. The majority of the animals, 60 in all, were raised with cozier surrogate mothers covered by terry cloth. In connection with certain experiments some of these individuals have had both a bare-wire and a cloth-covered mother. The infants developed a strong attachment to the cloth mothers and little or none to the wire mothers, regardless of which one provided milk. In fright-inducing situations the infants showed that they derived a strong sense of security from the presence of their cloth mothers [see the article "Love in Infant Monkeys," by Harry F. Harlow, beginning on page 94]. Even after two years of separation they exhibit a persistent attachment to the effigies.

In almost all other respects, however, the behavior of these monkeys at ages ranging from three to five years is indistinguishable from that of monkeys raised in bare wire cages with no source of contact comfort other than a gauze diaper pad. They are without question socially and sexually aberrant. No normal sex behavior has been observed in the living cages of any of the animals that have been housed with a companion of the opposite sex. In exposure to monkeys from the breeding colony not one male and only one female has shown normal mating behavior and only four females have been successfully impregnated. Compared with the cage-raised monkeys, the surrogate-raised animals seem to be less aggressive, whether toward themselves or other monkeys. But they are also younger on the average, and their better dispositions can be attributed to their lesser age.

Thus the nourishment and contact comfort provided by the nursing cloth-covered mother in infancy does not produce a normal adolescent or adult. The surrogate cannot cradle the baby or communicate monkey sounds and gestures. It cannot punish for misbehavior or attempt to break the infant's bodily attachment before it becomes a fixation. The entire group of animals separated from their mothers at birth and raised in individual wire cages, with or without surrogate, must be written off as potential breeding stock. Apparently their early social deprivation permanently impairs their ability to form effective relations with other monkeys, whether the opportunity was offered to them in the second six months of life or in the second to the fifth year of life.

One may correctly assume that total social isolation, compared with the partial isolation in which these subjects were reared, would produce even more devastating effects on later personality development. Such disastrous effects have been reported in the rare cases of children who have been liberated after months or years of lonely confinement in a darkened room. We have submitted a few monkeys to total isolation. Our purpose was to establish the maximum of social deprivation that would allow survival and also to determine whether or not there is a critical period in which social deprivation may have irreversible effects.

In our first study a male and a female were housed alone from birth for a period of two years, each one in its own cubicle with solid walls. Their behavior could be observed through one-way vision screens and tested by remote control. The animals adapted to solid food slowly, but they had normal weight and good coats when they were removed from the isolation boxes at the end of two years. Throughout this period nei-

ther animal had seen any living being other than itself.

They responded to their liberation by the crouching posture with which monkeys typically react to extreme threat. When placed together, each one crouched and made no further response to the other. Paired with younger monkeys from the group raised in partial isolation, they froze or fled when approached and made no effort to defend themselves from aggressive assaults. After another two years, in which they were kept together in a single large cage in the colony room, they showed the same abnormal fear of the sight or sound of other monkeys.

We are now engaged in studying the effects of six months of total social isolation. The first pair of monkeys, both males, has been out of isolation for eight months. They are housed, each monkey in its own cage, in racks with other monkeys of their age that were raised in the partial isolation of individual wire cages. For 20 minutes a day, five days a week, they are tested with a pair of these monkeys in the "playroom" of the laboratory. This room we designed to stimulate the young monkeys to a maximum of activity. It was not until the 12th and 27th week respectively that the two totally deprived monkeys began to move and climb about. They now circulate freely but not as actively as the control animals. Although frequently attacked by the

controls, neither one has attempted to defend itself or fight back; they either accept abuse or flee. One must be characterized as extremely disturbed and almost devoid of social behavior. The other resembles a normal two-month-old rhesus infant in its play and social behavior, and the indications are that it will never be able to make mature contacts with its peers.

A considerably more hopeful prognosis is indicated for two groups of four monkeys raised in total isolation for the much shorter period of 80 days. In their cubicles these animals had the contact comfort of a cloth-covered surrogate. They were deficient in social behavior during the first test periods in the playroom. But they made rapid gains; now, eight months later, we rate them as "almost normal" in play, defense and sex behavior. At least seven of the eight seem to bear no permanent scars as the result of early isolation.

Our first few experiments in the total isolation of these animals would thus appear to have bracketed what may be the critical period of development during which social experience is necessary for normal behavior in later life. We have additional experiments in progress, involving a second pair that will have been isolated for six months and a first pair that will have been isolated for a full year. The indications are that six months of isolation will render the animals per-

"TOGETHER-TOGETHER" EXPERIMENT involved raising four motherless infants in one cage and giving them 20 minutes a day in the playroom. At one year of age they are normal, but during their early months they spent most of the time huddled in this position.

manently inadequate. Since the rhesus monkey is more mature than the human infant at birth and grows four times more rapidly, this is equivalent to two or three years for the human child. On the other hand, there is reason to believe that the effects of shorter periods of early isolation, perhaps 60 to 90 days or even more, are clearly reversible. This would be equivalent to about six months in the development of the human infant. The time probably varies with the individual and with the experiences to which it is exposed once it is removed from isolation. Beyond a brief period of neonatal grace, however, the evidence suggests that every additional week or month of social deprivation increasingly imperils social development in the rhesus monkey. Case studies of children reared in impersonal institutions or in homes with indifferent mothers or nurses show a frightening comparability. The child may remain relatively unharmed through the first six months of life. But from this time on the damage is progressive and cumulative. By one year of age he may sustain enduring emotional scars and by two years many children have reached the point of no return.

In all of these experiments in partial and total isolation, whether unwitting or deliberate, our animals were deprived of the company of their peers as well as of their mothers. We accordingly undertook a series of experiments designed to distinguish and compare the roles of mother-infant and infant-infant relations in the maturation of rhesus monkey behavior. Our most privileged subjects are two groups of four monkeys each, now two years old, that were raised with their mothers during the first 18 and 21 months respectively and with peers from the first weeks. Each mother-infant pair occupied a large cage that gave the infant access to one cell of a four-unit playpen. By removing the screens between the playpens we enabled the infants to play together in pairs or as foursomes during scheduled observation periods each day. In parallel with these two groups we raised another group of four in a playpen setup without their mothers but with a terrycloth surrogate in each home cage.

From the time the mothers let them leave their home cages, after 20 or 30 days, the mothered infants entered into more lively and consistent relations with one another than did the four motherless ones. Their behavior evolved more rapidly through the sequence of increasingly complex play patterns that reflects the maturation and learning of the infant

GROUP PSYCHOTHERAPY for monkeys raised in isolation in the laboratory was attempted by removing them to the semiwild conditions of the zoo after they reached maturity. Here their behavior improved; they began to play together and groom one another. But when they were returned to the laboratory, they reverted to their earlier abnormal behavior.

monkey and is observed in a community of normal infants. The older they grew and the more complex the play patterns became, the greater became the observable difference between the mothered and the motherless monkeys. Now, at the end of the second year, the 12 animals are living together in one playpen setup, with each original group occupying one living cage and its adjoining playpen. All are observed in daily interaction without the dividing panels. The early differences between them have all but disappeared. Seven of the eight mothered animals engage in normal sexual activity and assume correct posture. The deviant is a male, and this animal was the social reject in its all-male group of four. Of the two motherless males, one has recently achieved full adult sexual posture and the other is approaching it. The two motherless females appear normal, but it remains to be seen whether or not their maternal behavior will reflect their lack of mothering.

Observation of infants with their mothers suggests reasons for the differences in the early social and sexual behavior of these playpen groups. From early in life on the infant monkey shows a strong tendency to imitate its mother; this responding to another monkey's behavior carries over to interaction with its peers. It is apparent also that sexual activity is stimulated by the mother's grooming of the infant. Finally, as the mother begins occasionally to reject its offspring in the third or fourth month,

the infant is propelled into closer relations with its peers. These observations underlie the self-evident fact that the mother-infant relation plays a positive role in the normal development of the infant-infant and heterosexual relations of the young monkey.

That the mother-infant relation can also play a disruptive role was demonstrated in another experiment. Four females that had been raised in the partial isolation of individual wire cages—and successfully impregnated in spite of the inadequacy of their sexual behavior—delivered infants within three weeks of one another. This made it possible to set up a playpen group composed of these "motherless" mothers and their infants. The maternal behavior of all four mothers was completely abnormal, ranging from indifference to outright abuse. Whereas it usually requires more than one person to separate an infant from its mother, these mothers paid no attention when their infants were removed from the cages for the hand-feeding necessitated by the mothers' refusal to nurse. Two of the mothers did eventually permit fairly frequent nursing, but their apparently closer maternal relations were accompanied by more violent abuse. The infants were persistent in seeking contact with their mothers and climbed on their backs when they were repulsed at the breast. In play with one another during the first six months, the infants were close to the normally mothered animals in maturity of play, but they played less.

In sexual activity, however, they were far more precocious. During the eight months since they have been separated from their mothers, they have exhibited more aggression and day-to-day variability in their behavior than have the members of other playpen groups. The two male offspring of the most abusive mothers have become disinterested in the female and occupy the subordinate position in all activities.

More study of more babies from motherless mothers is needed to determine whether or not the interrelations that characterize this pilot group will characterize others of the same composition. There is no question about the motherless mothers themselves. The aberration of their maternal behavior would have ensured the early demise of their infants outside the laboratory. As for the infants, the extremes of sexuality and aggressiveness observed in their behavior evoke all too vivid parallels in the behavior of disturbed human children and adolescents in psychiatric clinics and institutions for delinquents.

Another pilot experiment has shown that even normal mothering is not enough to produce socially adequate offspring. We isolated two infants in the exclusive company of their mothers to the age of seven months and then brought the mother-infant pairs together in a playpen unit. The female infant took full advantage of the play apparatus provided, but in three months the male was never seen to leave its home cage, and its mother would not permit the female to come within arm's reach. Social interaction of the infants was limited to an occasional exchange of tentative threats. For the past two months they have been separated from their mothers, housed in individual cages and brought together in the playroom for 15 minutes each day. In this normally stimulating environment they have so far shown no disposition to play together. Next to the infants that have been raised in total isolation, these are the most retarded of the infants tested in the playroom.

It is to the play-exciting stimulus of the playroom that we owe the unexpected outcome of our most suggestive experiment. The room is a relatively spacious one, with an eight-foot ceiling and 40 square feet of floor space. It is equipped with movable and stationary toys and a wealth of climbing devices, including an artificial tree, a ladder and a burlap-covered climbing ramp that leads to a platform. Our purpose in constructing the playroom was to provide the monkeys with opportunities to move

about in the three-dimensional world to which, as arboreal animals, they are much more highly adapted than man. To assess the effects of different histories of early social experience we customarily turn the animals loose in the room in groups of four for regularly scheduled periods of observation each day.

The opportunities afforded by the playroom were most fully exploited by two groups of four infants that otherwise spent their days housed alone in their cages with a cloth surrogate. In terms of "mothering," therefore, these monkeys were most closely comparable to the four that were raised with surrogates in the playpen situation. These animals were released in the playroom for 20 minutes a day from the first month of life through the 11th, in the case of one group, and through the second year in the case of the other. In contrast with all the other groups observed in the playroom, therefore, they did their "growing up" in this environment. Even though their exposure to the room and to one another was limited to 20 minutes a day, they enacted with great spirit the entire growth pattern of rhesus-monkey play behavior.

They began by exploring the room and each other. Gradually over the next two or three months they developed a game of rough-and-tumble play, with jumping, scuffling, wrestling, hair-pulling and a little nipping, but with no real damage, and then an associated game of flight and pursuit in which the participants are alternately the threateners and the threatened. While these group activities evolved, so did the capacity for individual play exploits, with the animals running, leaping, swinging and climbing, heedless of one another and apparently caught up in the sheer joy of action. As their skill and strength grew, their social play involved shorter but brisker episodes of free-for-all action, with longer chases between bouts. Subsequently they developed an even more complex pattern of violent activity, performed with blinding speed and integrating all objects, animate and inanimate, in the room. Along with social play, and possibly as a result or by-product, they began to exhibit sexual posturing—immature and fleeting in the first six months and more frequent and adult in form by the end of the year. The differences in play activity that distinguish males and females became evident in the first two or three months, with the females threatening and initiating rough contact far less frequently than the males and withdrawing from threats and approaches far more frequently.

Thus in spite of the relatively limited opportunity for contact afforded by their daily schedule, all the individuals in these two groups developed effective infant-infant play relations. Those observed into the second year have shown the full repertory of adult sexual behavior. At the same chronological age these motherless monkeys have attained as full a maturity in these respects as the infants raised with their mothers in the playpen.

Another group of four motherless animals raised together in a single large cage from the age of two weeks is yielding similar evidence of the effectiveness of the infant-infant affectional bond. During their first two months these animals spent much of their time clinging together, each animal clutching the back of the one just ahead of it in "choo-choo" fashion. They moved about as a group of three or four; when one of them broke away, it was soon clutched by another to form the nucleus of a new line. In the playroom the choo-choo linkage gave way to individual exploratory expeditions. During periods of observation, whether in their home cage or in the playroom, these animals have consistently scored lower in play activity than the most playful groups. We think this is explained, however, by the fact that they are able to spread their play over a 24-hour period. At the age of one year they live amicably together. In sex behavior they are more mature than the mother-raised playpen babies. No member of the group shows any sign of damage by mother-deprivation.

Our observations of the three groups of motherless infants raised in close association with one another therefore indicate that opportunity for optimal infant-infant interaction may compensate for lack of mothering. This is true at least in so far as infant-infant and sexual relations are concerned. Whether or not maternal behavior or later social adjustment will be affected remains to be seen.

Of course research on nonhuman animals, even monkeys, will never resolve the baffling complex roles of various kinds of early experience in the development of human personality. It is clear, however, that important theoretical and practical questions in this realm of interest can be resolved by the use of monkeys. The close behavioral resemblance of our disturbed infants to disturbed human beings gives us the confidence that we are working with significant variables and the hope that we can point the way to reducing the toll of psychosocial trauma in human society.

15

BRAIN CHANGES IN RESPONSE TO EXPERIENCE

MARK R. ROSENZWEIG, EDWARD L. BENNETT AND MARIAN CLEEVES DIAMOND
February 1972

*Rats kept in a lively environment for 30 days show
distinct changes in brain anatomy and chemistry
compared with animals kept in a dull environment. The
implications of these effects for man are assessed*

Does experience produce any observable change in the brain? The hypothesis that changes occur in brain anatomy as a result of experience is an old one, but convincing evidence of such changes has been found only in the past decade. It has now been shown that placing an experimental animal in enriched or impoverished environments causes measurable changes in brain anatomy and chemistry. How these changes are related to learning and memory mechanisms is currently being studied by an interdisciplinary approach that involves neurochemical, neuroanatomical and behavioral techniques.

The earliest scientific account of brain changes as a result of experience that we have been able to find was written in the 1780's by an Italian anatomist, Michele Gaetano Malacarne. His experimental design is worth describing briefly, since it resembles the one we are using in our laboratory at the University of California at Berkeley. He worked with two dogs from the same litter and with two parrots, two goldfinches and two blackbirds, each pair of birds from the same clutch of eggs. He trained one member of each pair for a long period; the other member of the pair was left untrained. He then killed the animals and examined their brains. He reported that there were more folds in the cerebellum of the trained animals than in that of the untrained ones. Although his study was noted by some of his contemporaries, we have not found any evidence that others attempted to carry out similar experiments. Knowledge of Malacarne's experiment quickly faded away.

During the 19th century there was considerable interest in the relation between the size of the human head and intellectual ability and training. In the 1870's Paul Broca, a famous French physician and anthropologist, compared the head circumference of medical students and male nurses and found that the students had larger heads. Since he believed the two sets of young men were equal in ability, he concluded that the differences in head size must have been due to the differences in training. Clearly Broca's logic was not impeccable, and there are other possible explanations for the differences he found. His critics pointed to the lack of correspondence between skull size and brain volume, the important roles of age and body size in determining brain size and the relative stability of the size of the brain in comparison with the size of most other organs. By the beginning of the 20th century not only had experimenters failed to prove that training resulted in changes in the gross anatomy of the brain but also a consensus had developed that such changes could not be detected, and so the search was generally abandoned.

With the development of new biochemical tools and techniques in the 1950's, some investigators began to ask if chemical changes in the brain following training could be detected. They looked for changes at the synapses that transmit impulses from one nerve cell to another or for changes in the nucleic acids (RNA and DNA) of nerve cells. The techniques used to find chemical or anatomical changes in the brain following experience are not difficult in principle but they must be carried out with precision because many of the changes that occur are not large. Here is how a basic experiment is conducted with laboratory rats of a given strain. (In our experiments we have worked with several strains of rats and with laboratory mice and gerbils; we have observed similar effects in all these animals.) At a given age, often at weaning, sets of three males are taken from each litter. Usually males are taken from each litter. Usually

a dozen sets of three males are used in an experiment. This yields stabler and more reliable results than working with a single set, as Malacarne did.

The use of rodents for these studies is convenient for several reasons. Brain dissection is simpler in rodents than it is in carnivores or primates because the cerebral cortex of rodents is smooth and not convoluted like the cortex of higher mammals. The gray cortex can be stripped away from the underlying white matter more readily in rodents than it can in higher mammals. Rodents are small, inexpensive and bear large litters, so that littermates with the same genetic background can be assigned to different conditions. In addition, geneticists have developed inbred lines of rats and mice, and working with these inbred lines gives us further control over the genetic background.

The three male rats from each litter are assigned at random so that one rat remains in the standard laboratory colony cage, one rat is placed in an enriched environment and the third is put in an impoverished environment. It should be noted that "enriched" and "impoverished" are not used in an absolute sense but only in relation to the standard laboratory colony environment that is the usual baseline for studies in anatomy, biochemistry, physiology, nutrition and behavior.

In the standard laboratory conditions a few rats live in a cage of adequate size with food and water always present [*see illustration on following page*]. In the enriched environment several rats live in a large cage furnished with a variety of objects they can play with. A new set of playthings, drawn out of a pool of 25 objects, is placed in the cage every day. In the impoverished environment each rat lives alone in a cage. Originally the isolated rats were kept in a separate quiet room, but this turned out to be unnecessary.

At the end of a predetermined experimental period, which can be from a few days to several months, the rats are sacrificed and their brains are removed. The brain dissection and analysis of each set of three littermates are done in immediate succession but in a random order and identified only by code number so that the person doing the dissection does not know which cage the rat comes from. With practice a skillful worker can do dissections with considerable precision and reliability. To delineate the various cortical regions a small plastic calibrated T square is used [*see illustration on page 120*]. Samples removed from a cortical region are weighed to the nearest tenth of a milligram and then placed on dry ice. The samples are kept frozen until chemical analysis is performed to determine the activity of the neurotransmitter enzymes in them.

If the rat brains are to be used for anatomical studies, the animal is anesthetized and perfused with a fixative solution. Later sections of the brain are prepared for microscopy.

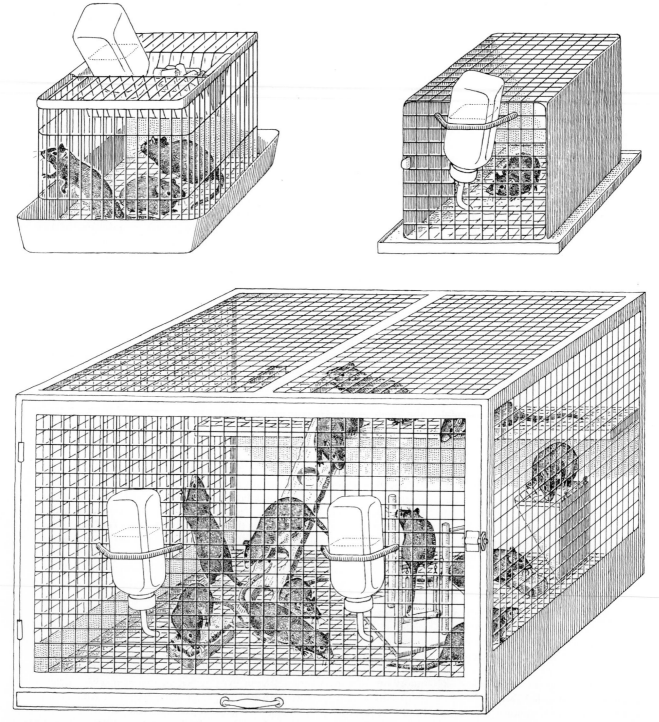

THREE LABORATORY ENVIRONMENTS that produce differences in brain anatomy of littermate rats are depicted. In the standard laboratory colony there are usually three rats in a cage (*upper left*). In the impoverished environment (*upper right*) a rat is kept alone in a cage. In the enriched environment 12 rats live together in a large cage furnished with playthings that are changed daily. Food and water are freely available in all three environments. The rats typically remain in the same environment for 30 days or more.

In the 1950's we had been attempting to relate individual differences in the problem-solving behavior of rats to individual differences in the amount of the enzyme acetylcholinesterase in the brain. (At the time and until 1966 the psychologist David Krech was a member of the research group.) The enzyme rapidly breaks down acetylcholine, a substance that acts as a transmitter between nerve cells. The excess transmitter must be neutralized quickly because nerve impulses can follow each other at a rate of hundreds per second. This enzymatic activity is often measured in terms of tissue weight, and so in our early experi-

ments we recorded the weight of each sample of brain tissue we took for chemical analysis. We found indications that the level of brain acetylcholinesterase was altered by problem-solving tests, and this led us to look for effects of more extensive experience. To our surprise we found that different experiences not only affected the enzymatic activity but also altered the weight of the brain samples.

By 1964 we had found that rats that had spent from four to 10 weeks in the enriched or the impoverished environments differed in the following ways: rats with enriched experience had a

greater weight of cerebral cortex, a greater thickness of cortex and a greater total activity of acetylcholinesterase but less activity of the enzyme per unit of tissue weight. Moreover, rats with enriched experience had considerably greater activity of another enzyme: cholinesterase, which is found in the glial cells and blood capillaries that surround the nerve cells. Glial cells (named from the Greek word for "glue") perform a variety of functions, including transportation of materials between capillaries and nerve cells, formation of the fatty insulating sheath around the neural axons and removal of dead neural tissue.

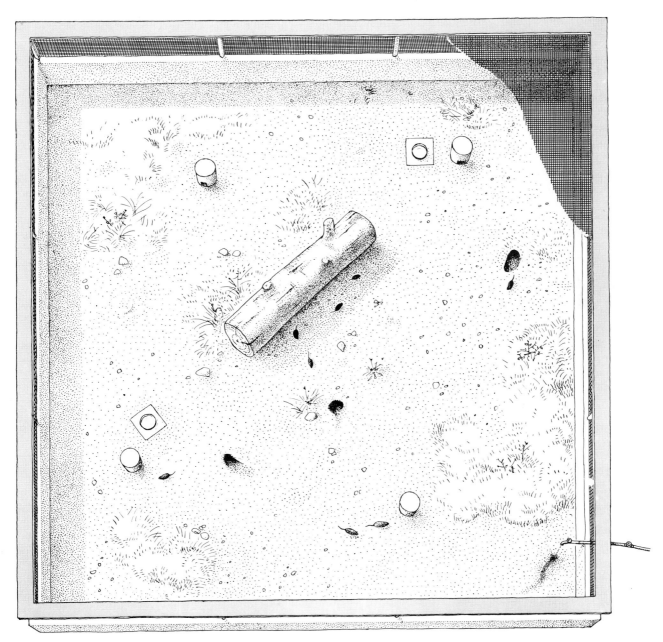

SEMINATURAL ENVIRONMENT for studying the effects of experience on the brain is provided by outdoor enclosures at the **Field Station for Research in Animal Behavior at the University of California at Berkeley. The enclosures have a concrete base 30 feet** by 30 feet with a screen over the top. Inbred laboratory rats thrive in the outdoor setting when food and water are provided. The rats revert to burrowing, something that their ancestors, which had lived in laboratory cages, had not done for more than 100 generations.

We later found that there were more glial cells in rats from the enriched environment than there were in rats from the impoverished one, and this may account for the increased activity of cholinesterase. Although differences in experience did not change the number of nerve cells per unit of tissue, the enriched environment produced larger cell bodies and nuclei. These larger cell bodies indicate higher metabolic activity. Further chemical measures involving RNA and DNA pointed in the same direction. The amount of DNA per milligram of tissue decreased, presumably because the bulk of the cortex increased as the number of neurons, whose nuclei contain a fixed amount of DNA, remained relatively constant. The amount of RNA per milligram remained virtually unchanged, yielding a significant increase in the ratio of RNA to DNA, and this suggests a higher metabolic activity. In most of the experiments the greatest differences between enriched and impoverished experience were found in the occipital cortex, which is roughly the rear third of the cortical surface.

We do not know why the occipital region of the cortex is affected by enriched experience more than other regions. At first we thought that differences in visual stimulation might be responsible, but when we used blinded rats, the occipital cortex still showed significant differences between littermates from the enriched and the impoverished environments. We found the same effects when normal rats were placed in the different environments and kept in darkness for the entire period. This is not to say that deprivation of vision did not have an effect on the anatomy and chemistry of the brain. The occipital cortex of rats that were blinded or kept totally in the dark gained less weight than the occipital cortex of littermates that were raised in standard colony conditions with a normal light-dark cycle, but this did not prevent the occurrence of the enrichment-impoverishment effect.

Although the brain differences induced by environment are not large, we are confident that they are genuine. When the experiments are replicated, the same pattern of differences is found repeatedly. For example, in 16 replications between 1960 and 1969 of the basic enriched-environment-v.-impoverished-environment experiment, using the same strain of rat exposed to the experimental conditions from the age of 25 to 105 days, each experiment resulted in a greater occipital-cortex weight for the rats in the enriched environment. Twelve

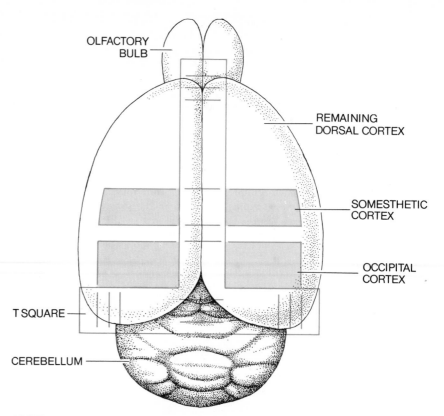

CORTICAL AREAS of a rat brain are located for dissection with the aid of a calibrated plastic T square to ensure uniform samples. The desired sections are removed, weighed and stored on dry ice. The remaining cortex and the subcortex also are weighed and frozen.

of the 16 replications were significantly at better than the .05 level, that is, for each of the 12 experiments there was less than one chance in 20 that the difference was due simply to chance or biological variability. For weight of the total cortex, 13 of the 16 experiments showed significant differences [see top illustration on opposite page].

The most consistent effect of experience on the brain that we found was the ratio of the weight of the cortex to the weight of the rest of the brain: the subcortex. It appears that the cortex increases in weight quite readily in response to an enriched environment, whereas the weight of the rest of the brain changes little. Moreover, since rats with larger bodies tend to have both a heavier cortex and a heavier subcortex than smaller rats, the ratio of the cortex to the rest of the brain tends to cancel the influence of body weight. For animals of a given strain, sex, age and environment the cortex/subcortex ratio tends to be the same even if the animals differ in body weight. When the environment is such that the cortex grows, the cortex/subcortex ratio shows the change very clearly and reliably. On this measure 14 of the 16 experiments were significant at the .01 level.

One of the major problems for mea-

suring the effects of experience on the brain is finding an appropriate baseline. Initially we took the standard laboratory colony condition as the baseline, as most other investigators have. The cortex/subcortex-weight ratio in rats from the enriched environment is greater than the ratio in rats from the standard colony environment, and this ratio in turn is greater than the ratio in rats from the impoverished environment. Where thickness of cortex is concerned, both environmental enrichment and impoverishment are effective but on different regions of the cortex.

Suppose that the natural environment in which the animals evolved were taken as the baseline. Compared with the laboratory environments, even the enriched one, a natural environment may be much richer in learning experiences. For inbred laboratory animals, however, it is no longer clear what the natural environment is. Laboratory rats and mice have been kept for more than 100 generations in protected environments, and inbreeding has made their gene pool different from the natural one. For this reason we have begun to study wild deer mice (Peromyscus). The mice are trapped in the San Francisco area and brought to our laboratory; some are kept in almost

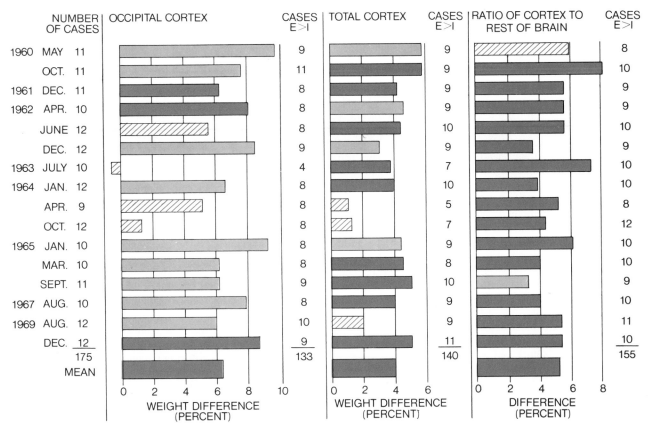

BRAIN-WEIGHT DIFFERENCES between rats from enriched environments and their littermates from impoverished environments were replicated in 16 successive experiments between 1960 and 1969 involving an 80-day period and the same strain of rat. For the occipital cortex, weight differences in three of the replications were significant at the probability level of .01 or better (*dark colored bars*), nine were significant at the .05 level (*light colored bars*) and four were not significant (*hatched bars*). The ratio of the weight of the cortex to the rest of the brain proved to be the most reliable measure, with 14 of the 16 replications significant at the .01 level.

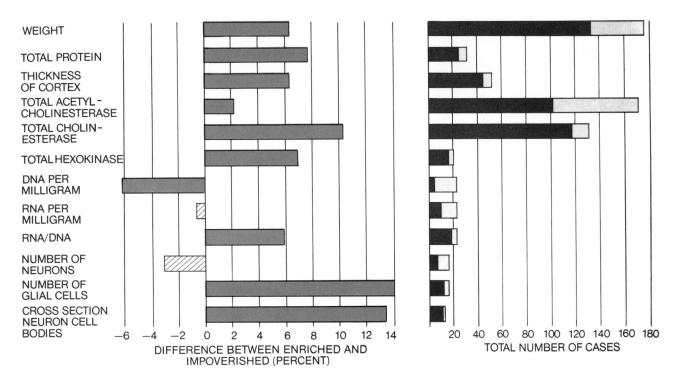

OCCIPITAL CORTEX of rats kept in enriched or impoverished environments from 25 to 105 days showed the effects of the different experiences. The occipital cortex of rats from the enriched environment, compared with that of rats from the impoverished one, was 6.4 percent heavier. This was significant at the .01 level or better, as were most other measures (*dark colored bars*). Only two measures were not significant (*hatched bars*). The dark gray bars on the right show the number of cases in which the rat from the enriched environment exceeded its littermate from the impoverished environment in each of the measures that are listed.

natural conditions at an outdoor station and others are put into laboratory cages. The work with deer mice is still in progress, but we have also placed laboratory rats in the outdoor setting. We found that when food is provided, laboratory rats can thrive in an outdoor enclosure even in a wet winter when the temperature drops to the freezing point. When the ground was not too wet, the rats dug burrows, something their ancestors had not done for more than 100 generations. In each of eight experiments the rats kept for one month in the outdoor setting showed a greater brain development than their littermates that had been kept in enriched laboratory cages. This indicates that even the enriched laboratory environment is indeed impoverished in comparison with a natural environment.

It is possible that the brain changes we found are not the result of learning and memory but are due to other aspects of the experimental situation, such as the amount of handling and stress, or perhaps an altered rate of maturation. For example, simply handling rats, particularly young ones, is known to increase the weight of their adrenal glands. Rats in the enriched environment are handled each day when they are removed from their cage while their playthings are being changed, whereas rats in the impoverished environment are handled only once a week for weighing. We tested the effects of handling on brain changes some years ago. Some rats were handled for several minutes a day for either 30 or 60 days; their littermates were never handled. There were no differences between the handled rats and the nonhandled ones in brain weight or brain-enzyme activity. More recently rats from both the enriched and the impoverished environments were handled once a day and the usual brain differences developed.

Stress was another possible cause of the cerebral effects. Rats from the impoverished environment might have suffered from "isolation stress" and rats from the enriched environment may have been stressed by "information overload." To test this notion Walter H. Riege subjected rats to a daily routine of stress. The rats were briefly tumbled in a revolving drum or given a mild electric shock. The stress produced a significant increase in the weight of the adrenal glands but did not give rise to changes in the brain measures that we use. It seems clear that stress is not responsible for the cerebral changes we have found.

It was also possible, since some of the brain changes we have found go in the same direction as changes that occur in

normal maturation, that enriched experience simply accelerates maturation or that isolation retards it. Changes in the depth of the cerebral cortex and certain other changes resulting from an enriched environment go in the opposite direction to what is found in normal growth. The cortical thickness of standard colony rats reaches a maximum at 25 days after birth and then decreases slightly with age, whereas enriched experience causes cortical thickness to increase even in year-old rats. In fact, Riege has found that an enriched environment will produce as great an increase in brain weight in fully mature rats as it does in young rats, although the adult rats require a longer period of environmental stimulation to show the maximum effect.

The effect of enriched environment on very young rats has been tested by Dennis Malkasian. He puts sets of three litters of six-day-old rat pups and their mother either into an unfurnished cage or into a cage containing play objects. Brains were taken for anatomical analysis at 14, 19 and 28 days of age. At each age pups from the enriched environment showed a greater thickness of cerebral cortex, and in some parts of the cortex the differences were larger than those found in experiments with rats examined after weaning.

When we first reported our results other investigators were understandably skeptical, since the effect of experience on the brain had not been previously demonstrated. After our findings had been replicated, some investigators began to think that the brain may be so plastic that almost any treatment can modify it, for example merely placing a rat for 15 minutes a day in any apparatus other than its home cage. This does not happen; although cerebral changes are easier to induce than we had supposed at first, a moderate amount of experience is still necessary. We recently demonstrated that two hours of daily enriched experience over a 30-day period is sufficient to produce the typical changes in brain weight. On the other hand, placing a group of 12 rats in a large unfurnished cage for two hours a day for 30 days did not bring about significant changes in our usual brain measures. Moreover, putting rats alone in large cages with play objects for two hours a day is not very effective, probably because a single rat does not play with the objects much and tends to rest or to groom itself. The enriched environment will produce cerebral changes in a single rat if the rat is stimulated to interact with the objects. This can be done by

giving the rat a moderate dose of an excitant drug or by putting it into the enriched environment during the dark part of its daily cycle (rats are nocturnal animals). A recent experiment indicates that cerebral changes can also be achieved by putting the rat into the enriched environment after several hours of food deprivation and placing tiny pellets of food on and in the play objects.

There can now be no doubt that many aspects of brain anatomy and brain chemistry are changed by experience. Some of our most recent efforts have been directed toward determining the changes that occur at the synaptic level in the occipital cortex, a region of the brain that shows relatively large changes with experience in enriched environments. Over the past few years Albert Globus of the University of California at Irvine has been counting the number of dendritic spines in brain sections from rats that have been exposed to an enriched environment or an impoverished one in our laboratory. Most of the synaptic contacts between nerve cells in the cortex are made on the branchlike dendrites of the receiving cell or on the dendritic spines, which are small projections from the dendrites. Globus made his counts on the cortical neuron called a pyramidal cell [see top illustration on opposite page]. He found more spines, particularly on the basal dendrites, in rats exposed to an enriched environment than in littermates from the impoverished environment.

An even more detailed view of changes in the synaptic junctions has come out of a study we have done in collaboration with Kjeld Møllgaard of the University of Copenhagen, who spent a year in our laboratory. He prepared electron micrographs of brain sections from the third layer of the occipital cortex of rats. Measurement of the synaptic junctions revealed that rats from enriched environments had junctions that averaged approximately 50 percent larger in cross section than similar junctions in littermates from impoverished environments. The latter, however, had more synapses per unit area [see illustration on page 124].

William T. Greenough, Roger West and T. Blaise Fleischmann of the University of Illinois have also found that there is increased synaptic contact in enriched-experience rats. Some other workers have reported that increased size of synapse is associated with a decreased number of synapses, whereas decreased size of synapse is associated with an increased number. It seems that memory

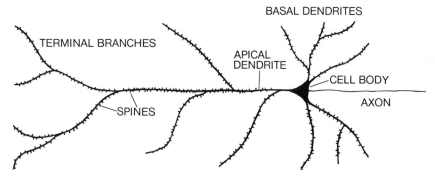

DENDRITIC SPINES, tiny "thorns," or projections, from the dendrites of a nerve cell, serve as receivers in many of the synaptic contacts between neurons. The drawing is of a type of cortical neuron known as the pyramidal cell. Rats from an enriched environment have more spines on these cells than their littermates from an impoverished environment.

or learning may be encoded in the brain either by the selective addition of contacts between nerve cells or by the selective removal of contacts, and that both processes may go on at the same time.

Does an enriched environment or an impoverished environment alter learning ability? Although some studies suggest that experience in an enriched environment usually improves subsequent learning, the effects are often short-lived. The result depends on many factors, for example the measure of learning that is used, the age at which the enriched experience is provided and the type of task that is learned. Early enrichment may improve subsequent learning of one task, have no effect on another task and actually impair learning in a third. Perhaps we should not expect much transfer of capacity among entirely different kinds of behavior. Nor should we expect experience in an enriched environment to lead to an increase in "general ability"; every environment is specific and so are abilities. Harry F. Harlow of the University of Wisconsin has shown that early problem-solving in monkeys may have the deleterious effect of fixating infantile behavior patterns; such monkeys may never reach the efficient adult performance that they would have attained without the early training. Again, this result is specific and should be generalized only with caution.

Formal training of rats, such as teaching them to press a lever in response to a signal or to run a maze, produces changes in brain anatomy and chemistry, but the type of training seems to determine the kind of changes. Victor Fedorov and his associates at the Pavlov Institute of Physiology near Leningrad found changes in brain weight and in the activity of acetylcholinesterase and cholinesterase after prolonged training of rats, but the pattern of changes is different from what we found with enriched and impoverished environments. In our laboratory we have given rats daily formal training in either operant-conditioning devices or in a series of mazes for a month or more and have found changes in brain weight and brain enzymes. These changes, however, were rather small and also had a pattern different from the changes induced by environmental experience. This is clearly a problem that requires more research.

The effect of experimental environments on the brains of animals has sometimes been cited as bearing on problems of human education. We should like to sound a cautionary note in this regard. It is difficult to extrapolate from an experiment with rats under one set of conditions to the behavior of rats under another set of conditions, and it is much riskier to extrapolate from a rat to a mouse to a monkey to a human. We have found generally similar brain changes as a result of experience in several species of rodents, and this appears to have fostered the assumption that similar results may be found with carnivores and with primates, including man. Only further research will show whether or not this is so. Animal research raises questions and allows us to test concepts and techniques, some of which may later prove useful in research with human subjects.

If this research leads to knowledge of how memories are stored in the brain, it will have obvious implications for the study of conditions that favor learning and memory and also of conditions that impair learning and the laying down of memories. Among the unfavorable conditions that are of great social concern are mental retardation and senile decline in ability to form new memories. Clues to the prevention or amelioration of these conditions could be of great social value. Let us also consider two other areas into which such research on brain plasticity may extend.

One of these areas concerns the effects of malnutrition on the development of the brain and of intelligence. Some investigators, such as R. H. Barnes and David A. Levitsky of the Cornell University Graduate School of Nutrition, have proposed that certain effects of malnutrition may actually be secondary effects of environmental impoverishment. That is,

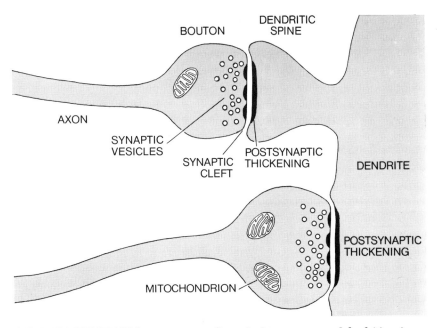

SYNAPTIC JUNCTIONS between nerve cells can be between axon and dendritic spine or between axon and the dendrite itself. The vesicles contain a chemical transmitter that is released when an electrical signal from the axon reaches the end bouton. The transmitter moves across the synaptic cleft and stimulates the postsynaptic receptor sites in the dendrite. The size of the postsynaptic membrane is thought to be an indicator of synaptic activity.

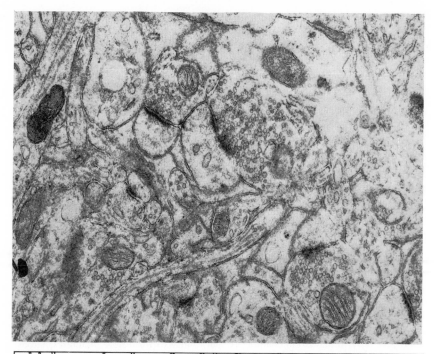

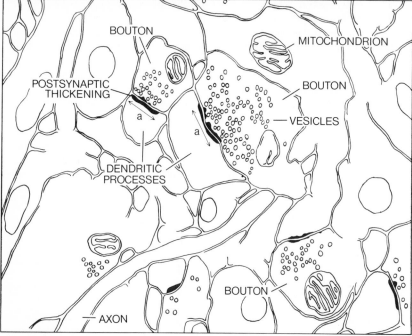

BRAIN SECTION from the occipital cortex of a rat is enlarged 37,000 times in this electron micrograph by Kjeld Møllgaard. The map identifies some of the components. Measurement of the postsynaptic thickening is shown in the map of the section by the arrow (*a*). The number of synaptic junctions was also counted. It was found that rats reared in an enriched environment had junctions approximately 50 percent larger than littermates from an impoverished environment, and the latter had more junctions, although smaller ones, per unit area.

cation on the postmortem examination of the brain of a blind deaf-mute, Laura Bridgman. It was found that the parts of her cortex that were involved in vision and hearing were thin and lacked the pattern of folding found in the normal human brain. In contrast, the region of her cortex devoted to touch had a normal appearance. It would be of interest to see if such results could be generalized by a large-scale modern postmortem study of brains of people who had been deprived of one or more senses. It would be even more interesting to find out if heightened employment of a sense leads to supranormal development of the associated brain region. Would musicians as a group, for example, show an enhanced development of the auditory cortex?

The human brain, because of the specialization of the two cerebral hemispheres, is more likely to provide answers to such questions than animal brains. Spoken words are analyzed in the auditory region of the left cerebral hemisphere, whereas music is analyzed in the auditory region of the right hemisphere. (These hemispheric functions are reversed in a few people.) The relative development of different regions in the same brain could be measured, so that the subjects would be their own control. In recent investigations Norman Geschwind and Walter Levitsky of the Harvard Medical School have found that 65 percent of the human brains they examined showed a greater anatomical development of the auditory area in the left hemisphere, 11 percent showed a greater auditory development in the right hemisphere and 24 percent showed equal development on the two sides. On the other hand, behavioral and physiological tests indicate that 96 percent of the people tested have left-hemisphere speech dominance and presumably have a greater development of the auditory area on that side. Is it possible that people with musical training account for most of the cases in which size of the right auditory area equals or exceeds the size of the left? In order to find out investigators will have to measure sufficient numbers of brains of individuals whose major abilities and disabilities are known. In fact, such a program was proposed 100 years ago by Broca, but the techniques available then were not adequate to carrying out the project. Today the results of our animal studies can serve as a guide, and investigators can look more penetratingly for the anatomical and chemical changes in the human brain that are correlated with experience and learning.

since a prominent effect of malnutrition is to make the person or animal apathetic and unresponsive to the environment, the individual then suffers from lack of stimulation, and this may be the direct cause of some of the symptoms usually associated with malnutrition. Current research suggests that some of the effects of malnutrition may be offset by programs of environmental stimula-

tion or increased by environmental impoverishment.

Another possibly beneficial result of our research findings would be to stimulate a resurgence of attempts to determine relations between experience and brain anatomy in man. This was a topic of some interest late in the 19th century, and a number of reports were published. For example, in 1892 there was a publi-

16

INTELLIGENCE AND RACE

WALTER F. BODMER AND LUIGI LUCA CAVALLI-SFORZA
October 1970

Do the differences in I.Q. scores between blacks and whites have a genetic basis? Two geneticists, reviewing the evidence, suggest that the question cannot be answered in present circumstances

To what extent might behavioral differences between social classes and between races be genetically determined? This question is often discussed, although generally not at a scientific level. Recently attention has been focused on the average differences in intelligence, as measured by I.Q., between black and white Americans by the educational psychologist Arthur R. Jensen and the physicist William Shockley. We are geneticists who are interested in the study of the interaction between heredity and environment. Our aim in this article is to review, mainly for the nongeneticist, the meaning of race and I.Q. and the approaches to determining the extent to which I.Q. is inherited. Such a review can act as a basis for the objective assessment of the evidence for a genetic component in race and class I.Q. differences.

We should first define what we mean by terms such as "heredity," "intelligence" and "race." Heredity refers to those characteristics of an individual that are inherited from past generations. The primary functional unit of heredity is the gene. The human genome—the complete set of genes in an individual—consists of perhaps as many as 10 million genes. Some of these genes and their expression can now be analyzed at the biochemical level. Complex behavioral traits such as intelligence, however, are most probably influenced by the combined action of many genes. The inheritance of differences known to be deter-

mined by one gene or a few genes can be reliably predicted, but the tools for dealing with the inheritance of more complex characteristics are still relatively ineffective.

What is intelligence? A rigorous, objective definition of such a complicated characteristic is not easy to give, but for the purposes of this discussion one can focus on qualities that can actually be observed and measured. One instrument of measurement for intelligence is a test such as the Stanford-Binet procedure. Such a test is devised to measure a capacity to learn or, more generally, the capacity to benefit from experience.

Intelligence tests are based on the solution of brief problems of various kinds and on the response to simple questions. The total score is standardized for a given age by comparing it with the values of a large sample of a given reference population (such as native-born American whites). The final standardized score, which is called the intelligence quotient, is usually computed so that it is given on a scale for which the average of the reference population is 100, and for which the spread is such that about 70 percent of the individuals have I.Q.'s in the range of 85 to 115 and 5 percent have I.Q.'s either below 70 or above 130 (corresponding to a standard deviation of about 15 points).

The Stanford-Binet test and other procedures yield results that correspond

reasonably well to one another. More ambitious attempts have been made to measure the "general intelligence factor." There is a tendency among the more optimistic psychologists to consider such tests as measuring an "innate" or potential ability. Any given test, however, depends on the ability acquired at a given age, which is inevitably the result of the combination of innate ability and the experience of the subject. Intelligence tests are therefore at most tests of achieved ability.

This limitation is confirmed by the dependence of all intelligence tests on the particular culture of the people they are designed to test. The transfer of tests to cultures different from the one for which they were designed is usually difficult, and sometimes it is impossible. Attempts to design tests that are genuinely "culture-free" have so far failed.

A check on the usefulness of I.Q. measurements is provided by examining their reliability (equivalent to short-term consistency), their stability (equivalent to long-term consistency) and their validity. For the Stanford-Binet test the average difference between repeat tests after a short time interval ranges from 5.9 points at an I.Q. of 130 to 2.5 for I.Q.'s below 70, indicating a fairly high reproducibility. The long-term consistency of the test is less impressive, particularly if the age at the first test is lower than five or six. Repetitions of testing after a period of years may show large discrepancies (up to 20 to 30 I.Q. points), and these differences increase with the number of years between tests.

There is at present no definition of intelligence that is precise enough to answer questions of validity in general terms. The validity of a particular test must therefore be related to its predictive aims. If the aim is to predict future school performance, then the validity is measured by how well I.Q. predicts that performance. The prediction will be on a probability basis, meaning that a higher I.Q. will usually but not always be associated with better school performance. There is, in fact, fairly general agreement that there is a high correlation between intelligence tests and success in school. The same is true for success in jobs and, in general, in society. I.Q. tests do have some predictive value on a probability basis, although this is limited to performance in contemporary American and European society. In this sense I.Q. tests do have some validity.

Races are subgroups that emerge within the same species. Like other species, the human species is made up of individuals whose genetic composition is so similar that in principle any male can mate with any female and give rise to fertile progeny. In the course of evolution this highly mobile species has spread over the entire surface of the earth. Even today, however, most individuals live out their lives within a small area. This pattern, together with geographic and other barriers, leads to considerable reproductive isolation of groups living in different regions.

Ecological factors, such as geology, climate and flora and fauna, may differ widely in the different habitats of a species. Natural selection, that is, the preferential survival and reproduction of individuals better fitted to their local environment, inevitably creates differences among these somewhat localized groups. In addition the isolation of one group from another allows differences to arise by the random sampling to which genes are subject from generation to generation; this process results in what is called random genetic drift.

Isolated subgroups of the same species therefore tend to differentiate. The process is a slow one: hundreds—more probably thousands—of generations may be necessary for biological differences to become easily noticeable. When sufficient time has elapsed for the differences to become obvious, we call the subgroups races.

In man biological differentiation is usually accompanied or preceded by cultural differentiation, which is a much faster process than biological evolution. The two kinds of differentiation inevitably interact. Cultural differences may contribute to perpetuation of the geographic barriers that lead to reproductive isolation. For example, religious differences may promote reproductive isolation. In the U.S. differences in skin color, which reflect biological differentiation, usually reduce the chances of marriage between groups. This effect, however, is probably a direct psychological consequence not of the difference in skin color but of the parallel cultural divergence.

The relative contributions of biological and cultural factors to complex characteristics such as behavioral differences, including those that distinguish one race from another, are exceedingly difficult to identify. In this connection it is instructive to consider characteristics in which differences can easily be attributed to biological factors. It is clear, for example, that differences in skin color are mostly biological. There is a predominantly nongenetic factor—tanning—that operates during the life of an individual; it is a short-term physiological adaptation and is generally reversible. Apart from this adaptation, most of the differences in skin color both within and among races are genetic.

There are many differences among individuals that are totally under genetic control, that is, they are not subject to even the small physiological adaptation mentioned for skin color. These genetic differences are called genetic polymorphisms when the alternative versions of the genes determining them each occur within a population with a substantial frequency. Such genetic traits are generally detected by chemical or immunological tests, as in the case of the "blood groups." (There are three genes, A, B and O, that determine the ABO blood type.)

The frequencies of polymorphic genes vary widely among races. For example, in Oriental populations the frequencies of the A, B and O genes are respectively 49 percent, 18 percent and 65 percent; in Caucasian populations they are 29 percent, 4 percent and 68 percent. Such polymorphisms are a valuable aid in understanding the nature and magnitude of the biological similarities and differences among races, since they show what kinds of factor can be due solely to heredity. The inheritance of the more conspicuous face and body traits, however, is complex and not well understood, which decreases their value for the biological study of races.

The analysis of genetic polymorphisms demonstrates three very important features of the nature and extent of genetic variation within and among races. First, the extent of variation with-

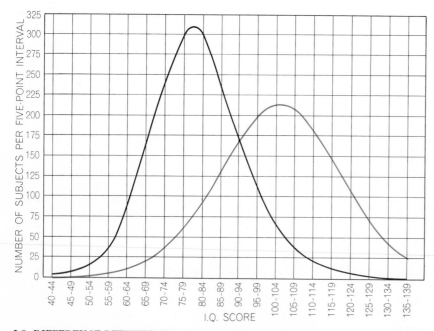

I.Q. DIFFERENCE BETWEEN U.S. BLACKS AND WHITES emerges from a comparison of the I.Q. distribution in a representative sample of whites (*colored curve*) with the I.Q. distribution among 1,800 black children in the schools of Alabama, Florida, Georgia, Tennessee and South Carolina (*black curve*). Wallace A. Kennedy of Florida State University, who surveyed the students' I.Q., found that the mean I.Q. of this group was 80.7. The mean I.Q. of the white sample is 101.8, a difference of 21.1 points. The two samples overlap distinctly, but there is also a sizable difference between the two means. Other studies show a difference of 10 to 20 points, making Kennedy's result one of the most extreme reported.

in any population generally far exceeds the average differences between populations. Second, the differences between populations and races are mostly measured by differences in the relative frequencies of a given set of genes rather than by qualitative differences as to which gene is present in any particular population. Thus any given genetic combination may be found in almost any race, but the frequency with which it is found will vary from one race to another. Third, the variation from race to race is mostly not sharp but may be almost continuous at the boundaries between races. This is the consequence of hybridization's occurring continuously at these boundaries in spite of isolation, or of the formation of hybrid groups by recent migration followed by the more complete mixing of formerly isolated groups.

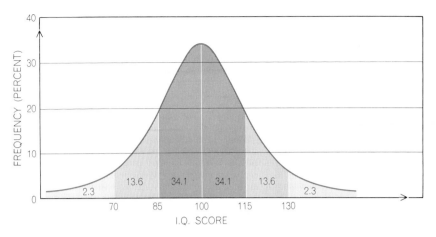

NORMAL DISTRIBUTION OF I.Q. for a population whose mean is 100 is shown by curve. The standard deviation, that is, the usual measure of variation, is about 15 points and the distance in either direction from this mean is measured in multiples of the standard deviation. Thus about 34 percent have an I.Q. with a value that lies between 85 and 100, another 34 percent of the population have an I.Q. score of 100 to 115 points (*dark color*). Those with very high or low scores are a smaller part of population: about 2 percent have an I.Q. below 70, whereas another 2 percent have an I.Q. above 130 (*light color*).

As we have noted, intelligence must be a complex characteristic under the control of many genes. Extreme deviations from normal levels, as in cases of severe mental retardation, can, however, be attributed to single gene differences. Such deviations can serve to illustrate important ways in which genetic factors can affect behavior. Consider the disease phenylketonuria. Individuals with this disease receive from both of their parents a mutated version of the gene controlling the enzyme that converts one amino acid, phenylalanine, into another, tyrosine. That gene allows phenylalanine to accumulate in the blood and in the brain, causing mental retardation. The accumulation can be checked early in life by a diet deficient in phenylalanine.

The difference between the amounts of phenylalanine in the blood of people with phenylketonuria and that in the blood of normal people, which is closely related to the primary activity of the gene causing phenylketonuria, clearly creates two genetic classes of individuals [*see bottom illustration on next page*]. When such differences are compared with differences in I.Q., there is a slight overlap, but individuals afflicted with phenylketonuria can be distinguished clearly from normal individuals. This simply reflects the fact that the phenylketonuric genotype, that is, the genetic constitution that leads to phenylketonuria, is associated with extreme mental retardation. If differences in head size and hair color in phenylketonuric individuals and normal individuals are compared, however, they show a considerable overlap. Although it can be said that the phenylketonuric genotype has

on the average a significant effect on both head size and hair color, measurements of these characteristics cannot be used to distinguish the phenylketonuric genotype from the normal one. The reason is that the variation of head size and hair color is large compared with the average difference. Thus the genetic difference between phenylketonuric and normal individuals contributes in a major way to the variation in blood phenylalanine levels but has only a minor, although significant, effect on head size and hair color.

The phenylketonuric genotype is very rare, occurring with a frequency of only about one individual in 10,000. It therefore has little effect on the overall distribution of I.Q. in the population. It is now known, however, that a large fraction of all genes are polymorphic. Among the polymorphic genes must be included many whose effect on I.Q. is comparable to the effect of the phenylketonuric genotype on head size or hair color. These genotype differences cannot be individually identified, but their total effect on the variation of I.Q. may be considerable.

The nature of phenylketonuria demonstrates another important point: The expression of a gene is profoundly influenced by environment. Phenylketonuric individuals show appreciable variation. This indicates that the genetic difference involved in phenylketonuria is by no means the only factor, or even the major factor, affecting the level of phenylalanine in the blood. It is obvious that dietary differences have a large effect, since a phenylalanine-deficient diet

brings the level of this amino acid in the blood of a phenylketonuric individual almost down to normal. If an individual receives the phenylketonuric gene from only one parent, his mental development is not likely to be clinically affected. Nevertheless, he will tend to have higher than normal levels of phenylalanine in his blood. The overall variation in phenylalanine level is therefore the result of a combination of genetic factors and environmental factors. Measuring the relative contribution of genetic factors to the overall variation is thus equivalent to measuring the relative importance of genetic differences in determining this type of quantitative variation.

When we turn to the analysis of a complex characteristic such as I.Q., which is influenced by many genes each contributing on the average a small effect, we can expect the characteristic to be even more strongly affected by the previous history of the individual and by a host of other external, nongenetic or in any case unrelated factors, which can together be called the "environment." It is necessary to resort to statistical analysis in order to separate the effects of these various factors. Consider an experiment of nature that allows the separation, at least roughly, of environmental factors from genetic factors. This is the occurrence of two types of twins: twins that are "identical," or monozygous (derived from only a single zygote, or fertilized egg, and therefore genetically identical), and twins that are "fraternal," or dizygous (derived from two separate zygotes and therefore genetically different).

Clearly the difference between the

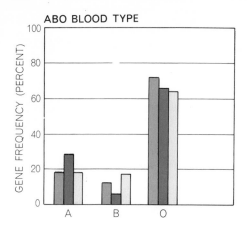

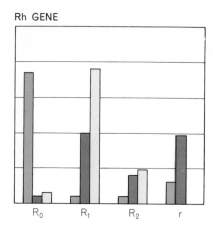

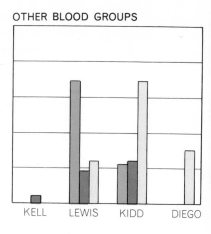

FREQUENCIES OF POLYMORPHIC GENES among Africans, Caucasians and Orientals provide a means of differentiating these three races. (A polymorphic gene is one of a group that accounts for variability in a particular characteristic.) About half of the

two members of a monozygous pair is determined only by environmental factors. It would seem that the distribution of such differences among a number of pairs might tell us how much two individuals can differ because of environmental factors alone. The members of monozygous pairs do not generally have identical I.Q.'s. The members of a given twin pair can differ by as much as 20 I.Q. points, although in the majority of cases they differ by less than 10. Hence environmental differences can have an effect on I.Q. whose average magnitude is comparable to, or slightly larger than, the difference between the I.Q. scores of the same individual who has been tested more than once over a period of time.

To see whether or not, and if so to what extent, genetic differences are found, we turn to dizygous twins. Here we know that in addition to the environment genetic factors also play a role in differentiating the members of a pair. The differences in I.Q. among dizygous pairs show a greater spread than those among monozygous pairs, indicating that the addition of genetic diversity to the purely environmental factors increases, on the average, the overall difference between members of a pair. Hence genetic factors that can contribute to the differentiation of I.Q.'s also exist among normal individuals.

It might seem that the twin data could easily provide a measure of the relative importance of genetic variation and environmental variation. A comparison of the average difference between the members of a monozygous pair and the average difference between the members of a dizygous pair should be a good index of the comparative importance of genetic factors and environmental ones. (A minor technical point should be mentioned here. As is customary in all modern statistical analysis, it is better to consider not the mean of the differences but the mean of their squares. This is comparable to, and can easily be transformed into, a "variance," which is a well-known measure of variation.)

There are two major contrasting reasons why such a simple measure is not entirely satisfactory. First, the difference between members of a dizygous pair represents only a fraction of the genetic differences that can exist between two individuals. Dizygous twins are related to each other as two siblings are; therefore they are more closely related than two individuals taken at random from a population. This implies a substantial reduction (roughly by a factor of two) in the average genetic difference between dizygous twins compared with that between two randomly chosen individuals. Second, the environmental difference between members of a pair of twins encompasses only a fraction of the total environmental difference that can exist between two individuals, namely the difference between individuals belonging to the same family. This does not take into account differences among families, which are likely to be large. Within the family the environmental differences between twins are limited. For instance, the effect of birth order is not taken into account. Differences between ordinary siblings might therefore tend to be slightly greater than those between dizygous twins. It also seems possible

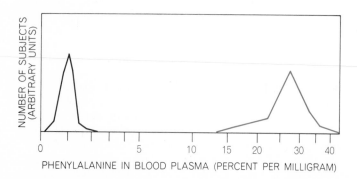

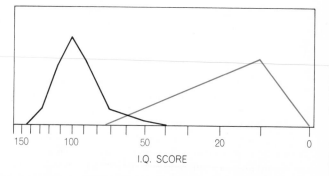

PHENYLALANINE LEVELS in blood plasma shown in first set of curves at left distinguish those who carry a double dose of the defective gene that causes high phenylalanine levels (*colored curve*), a condition called phenylketonuria, from those with normal phenylalanine levels (*dark curve*). Second set of curves shows that this genotype has a direct effect on intelligence: phenylketonurics (*colored curve*) have low I.Q.'s because accumulation of phenylalanine and its by-products in blood and nerve tissue damages the brain. Individuals with functioning gene (*dark curve*) have normal I.Q.'s. In the third set phenylalanine levels are related

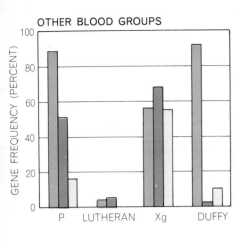

OTHER BLOOD GROUPS

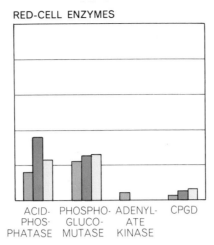

RED-CELL ENZYMES

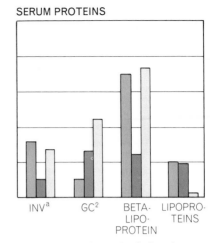

SERUM PROTEINS

polymorphic systems in man are shown. Average differences in frequencies between Africans (*color*) and Caucasians (*dark color*) are 22 percent, those between Africans and Orientals (*light color*) are 30 percent, those between Caucasians and Orientals are 22 percent.

that the environmental differences between monozygous twins, who tend to establish special relations with each other, are not exactly comparable to those between dizygous twins. In short, whereas the contrast between monozygous and dizygous twin pairs minimizes genetic differences, it also tends to maximize environmental differences.

In order to take account of such difficulties one must try to use all available comparisons between relatives of various types and degrees, of which twin data are only a selected case. For technical reasons one often measures similarities rather than differences between two sets of values such as parent I.Q.'s and offspring I.Q.'s. Such a measure of similarity is called the correlation coefficient. It is equal to 1 when the pairs of values in the two sets are identical or, more generally, when one value is expressible as a linear function of the other. The correlation coefficient is 0 when the pairs of measurements are completely independent, and it is intermediate if there is a relation between the two sets such

that one tends to increase when the other does.

The mean observed values of the correlation coefficient between parent and child I.Q.'s, and between the I.Q.'s of pairs of siblings, are very nearly .5. This is the value one would expect on the basis of the simplest genetic model, in which the effects of any number of genes determine I.Q. and there are no environmental influences or complications of any kind. It seems probable, however, that the observed correlation of .5 is coincidental. Complicating factors such as different modes of gene action, tendencies for like to mate with like and environmental correlations among members of the same family must just happen to balance one another almost exactly to give a result that agrees with the simplest theoretical expectation. If we ignored these complications, we might conclude naïvely (and in contradiction to other evidence, such as the observation of twins) that biological inheritance of the simplest kind entirely determines I.Q.

Instead it is necessary to seek a means

of determining the relative importance of environmental factors and genetic factors even taking account of several of the complications. In theory this measurement can be made by computing the quotients known as heritability estimates. To understand what such quotients are intended to measure, consider a simplified situation. Imagine that the genotype of each individual with respect to genes affecting I.Q. can be identified. Individuals with the same genotype can then be grouped together. The differences among them would be the result of environmental factors, and the spread of the distribution of such differences could then be measured. Assume for the sake of simplicity that the spread of I.Q. due to environmental differences is the same for each genotype. If we take the I.Q.'s of all the individuals in the population, we obtain a distribution that yields the total variation of I.Q. The variation within each genotype is the environmental component. The difference between the total variation and the environmental component of variation leaves a component of the total variation

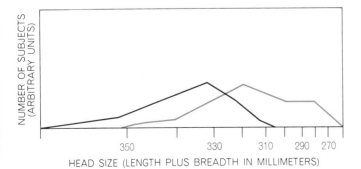

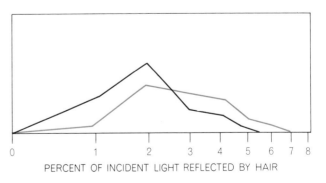

to head size (displayed as the sum of head length and breadth), and in the fourth set phenylalanine levels are related to hair color (displayed as the percentage of light with a wavelength of 700 millimicrons reflected by the hair). In both cases it is obvious that the phenylketonuric genotype has a significant effect on each of these

characteristics: the reflectance is greater and the head size is smaller (*colored curves*) among phenylketonurics than they are among normal individuals (*dark curves*). Yet the distribution of these characteristics is such that they cannot be used to distinguish those afflicted with phenylketonuria from those who are not.

that may be accounted for by genetic differences. This component, when expressed as a fraction of the total variance, is one possible measure of heritability.

In practice, however, the estimation of the component of the total variation that can be accounted for by genetic differences (from data on correlations between relatives) always depends on the construction of specific genetic models, and is therefore subject to the limitations of the models. One problem lies in the fact that there are a number of alternative definitions of heritability depending on the genetic model chosen, because the genetic variation may have many components that can have quite different meanings. A definition that includes only those parts of the genetic variation generally considered to be most relevant in animal and plant breeding is often used. This is called heritability in the narrow sense. If all genetic sources of variation are included, then the heritability estimate increases and is referred to as heritability in the broad sense.

The differences between these esti-

mates of heritability can be defined quite precisely in terms of specific genetic models. The resulting estimates of heritability, however, can vary considerably. Typical heritability estimates for I.Q. (derived from the London population in the early 1950's, with data obtained by Sir Cyril Burt) give values of 45 to 60 percent for heritability in the narrow sense and 80 to 85 percent for heritability in the broad sense.

A further major complication for such heritability estimates has the technical name "genotype-environment interaction." The difficulty is that the realized I.Q. of given genotypes in different environments cannot be predicted in a simple way. A given genotype may develop better in one environment than in another, but this is not necessarily true for any other genotype. Even if it is true, the extent of the difference may not be the same. Ideally one would like to know the reaction of every genotype in every environment. Given the practically infinite variety of both environments and genotypes, this is clearly impossible. Moreover, in man there is no way of con-

trolling the environment. Even if all environmental influences relevant to behavioral development were known, their statistical control by appropriate measurements and subsequent statistical analysis of the data would still be extremely difficult. It should therefore be emphasized that because estimates of heritability depend on the extent of environmental and genetic variation that prevails in the population examined at the time of analysis, they are not valid for other populations or for the same population at a different time.

In animals and plants the experimental control of the environment is easier, and it is possible to explore "genotype-environment" interactions. An interesting experiment was conducted by R. Cooper and John P. Zubek of the University of Manitoba with two lines of rats in which genetic differences in the rats' capacity to find their way through a maze had been accumulated by artificial selection. The two lines of rats had been selected to be either "bright" or "dull" at finding their way through the maze. When rats from these lines were raised for one generation in a "restricted" environment that differed from the "normal" laboratory conditions, no difference between the lines could be found. Both bright and dull animals performed at the same low level. When they were raised in a stimulating environment, both did almost equally well [*see illustration page 135*]. Since the difference between the lines is genetic, the effect of environmental conditions should be reversible in future generations. This experiment is particularly relevant to differences in I.Q. because of the structure of human societies. If "ghetto" children tend to have I.Q. scores lower, and the children of parents of high social and economic status to have scores higher, than the level one would expect if both groups of children were reared in the same environment, then heritability estimates may be biased upward.

The only potential safeguard against such bias is provided by the investigation of the same genotype or similar genotypes in different environments. In man this can be done only through the study of adopted children. A particularly interesting type of "adoption" is that in which monozygous twins are separated and reared in different families from birth or soon afterward. The outcome is in general a relatively minor average decrease in similarity. Following the same line of reasoning, the similarity between foster parents and adopted children can be measured and contrasted with that between biological parents and their

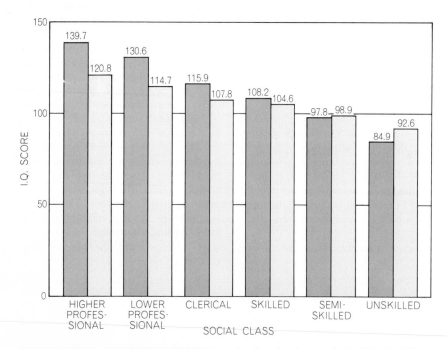

SOCIAL CLASS AND INTELLIGENCE are closely related, a study by Sir Cyril Burt of the University of London indicates. Set of bars at left shows the mean I.Q. for higher professionals (*dark bar*) is 139.7, children of higher professionals have a mean I.Q. of 120.8 (*light bar*). Second set of bars shows that lower professionals have a mean I.Q. of 130.6, children of lower professionals have a mean I.Q. of 114.7. Third set shows that clerical workers have a mean I.Q. of 115.9, their children have a mean I.Q. of 107.8. Fourth set shows that skilled workers have a mean I.Q. of 108.2, their children have a mean I.Q. of 104.6. Fifth set shows that semiskilled workers have a mean I.Q. of 97.8, their children have a mean I.Q. of 98.9. Sixth set shows that unskilled workers have a mean I.Q. of 84.9, their children have a mean I.Q. of 92.6. Mean I.Q.'s of wives (*not shown*) correlate well with husbands'. Above the mean children's I.Q. tends to be lower than that of parents. Below it children's I.Q. tends to be higher. Social mobility maintains distribution because those individuals with high I.Q.'s tend to rise whereas those with low I.Q.'s tend to fall.

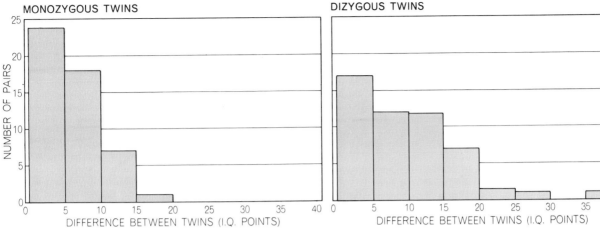

MONOZYGOUS TWINS

DIZYGOUS TWINS

NUMBER OF PAIRS

DIFFERENCE BETWEEN TWINS (I.Q. POINTS)

DIFFERENCE BETWEEN TWINS (I.Q. POINTS)

EXPERIMENT OF NATURE based on I.Q. data collected by Horatio H. Newman of the University of Chicago gives a rough measurement of the relative influence of heredity and environment on intelligence. Chart at left shows I.Q. differences between the members of 50 pairs of monozygous twins, that is, twins who developed from the same egg and have identical genotypes. I.Q. differences between members of these pairs tend to be low: 24 pairs (or almost half of the sample) show a difference of from zero to five points. Only one pair shows a difference of between 15 and 20 points. The mean difference between the members of each pair is 5.9 points. Since the genotypes in each pair are identical it appears that the environmental effect tends to be small. Second chart shows I.Q. differences between 45 pairs of dizygous twins, that is, twins with different genotypes who developed from separate eggs. In this case the mean difference in I.Q. between the members of these pairs is about 10 points. Thus a fairly large difference appears to be attributable to heredity. Such a comparison does not separate the effects of heredity and environment precisely. Members of monozygous pairs have very similar environments, whereas genotypes of dizygous twins are less different on the average by a factor of two than those of unrelated individuals. Comparison thus underestimates effect of heredity but also minimizes environmental influence.

children. A few such studies have been conducted. They show that the change of family environment does indeed have an effect, although it is not as great as that of biological inheritance. The correlation between foster parents and their adopted children is greater than 0, but it is undoubtedly less than that between biological parents and their offspring.

A complete analysis of such data is almost impossible because environmental variation among families and genotype-environment interactions of various kinds must be responsible for the observed effects in ways that make it difficult to disentangle their relative importance. Adoption and rearing apart take place in conditions far from those of ideal experiments, and so any conclusions are bound to be only semiquantitative. On the basis of all the available data, with allowance for these limitations, the heritability of intelligence, as measured by I.Q., is still fairly high. It must be kept in mind, however, that the environmental effects in such studies are generally limited to the differences among and within families of a fairly homogeneous section of the British or American population. They cannot be extrapolated to prediction of the effects of greater differences in environment, or of other types of difference.

There are significant differences in mean I.Q. among the various social classes. One of the most comprehensive and widely quoted studies of such differences and the reasons for their apparent stability over the years was published by Burt in 1961 [*see illustration on opposite page*]. His data come from schoolchildren and their parents in a typical London borough. Socioeconomic level was classified, on the basis of type of occupation, into six classes. These range from Class 1, including "university teachers, those of similar standing in law, medicine, education or the church and the top people in commerce, industry or civil service," to Class 6, including "unskilled laborers, casual laborers and those employed in coarse manual work." There are four main features of these data:

1. Parental mean I.Q. and occupational class are closely related. The mean difference between the highest and the lowest class is over 50. Although occupational class is determined mostly by the father, the relatively high correlation between the I.Q.'s of husband and wife (about .4) contributes to the differentiation among the classes with respect to I.Q.

2. In spite of the significant variation between the parental mean I.Q.'s, the residual variation in I.Q. among parents within each class is still remarkably large. The mean standard deviation of the parental I.Q.'s for the different classes is 8.6, almost three-fifths of the standard deviation for the entire group. That standard deviation is about 15, and it is usual for the spread of I.Q.'s in any group.

3. The mean I.Q. of the offspring for each class lies almost exactly between the parental mean I.Q.'s and the overall population mean I.Q. of 100. This is expected because it is only another way of looking at the correlation for I.Q. between parent and child, which as we have already seen tends to be about .5 in any given population.

4. The last important feature of the data is that the standard deviations of the I.Q. of the offspring, which average 13.2, are almost the same as the standard deviation of the general population, namely 15. This is another indication of the existence of considerable variability of I.Q. within social classes. Such variability is almost as much as that in the entire population.

The most straightforward interpretation of these data is that I.Q. is itself a major determinant of occupational class and that it is to an appreciable extent inherited (although the data cannot be used to distinguish cultural inheritance from biological). Burt pointed out that, because of the wide distribution of I.Q. within each class among the offspring and the regression of the offspring to the population mean, appreciable mobility among classes is needed in each generation to maintain the class differences with respect to I.Q. He estimated that to maintain a stable distribution of I.Q. differences among classes, at least 22 percent of the offspring would have to change class, mainly as a function of I.Q., in each generation. This figure is

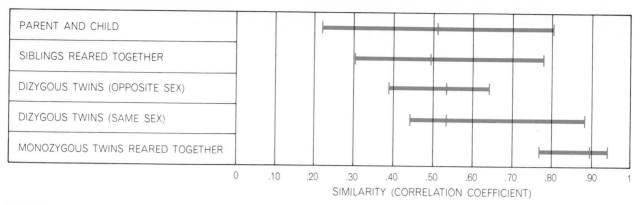

SIMILARITY (CORRELATION COEFFICIENT)

CORRELATION COEFFICIENTS are calculations of similarity, for example, between the I.Q.'s of two sets of relatives such as parents and children. A coefficient of 1 indicates identity, 0 indicates independence of one value from the other. These data were collected from published literature by L. Erlenmeyer-Kimling and Lissy F. Jarvik of the New York State Psychiatric Institute to derive measurements of comparative effects of heredity and environment, taking into account all possible effects of relatedness between individuals. The horizontal line at top indicates that the coefficients of samples of parents and children from different studies range from about .20 to .80. Second horizontal line indicates that coefficients for siblings reared together range from .30 to about .78. Range for dizygous (fraternal) twins of opposite sex is .38 to .65; for dizygous twins of same sex it is .43 to .88. The mean (*vertical line intersecting each horizontal line*) for each of these four sets of relatives is about .50. Monozygous (identical) twins, however, have a range of .77 to .92 with a mean of .89. Mean coefficient of .50 is that which would be expected if there were no environmental effects in I.Q. Since other evidence indicates that environment exerts a significant effect, these calculations must be further refined.

well below the observed intergenerational social mobility in Britain, which is about 30 percent.

Fears that there may be a gradual decline in I.Q. because of an apparent negative correlation between I.Q. and fertility have been expressed ever since Francis Galton pointed out this correlation for the British ruling class in the second half of the 19th century. If there were such a persistent association, if I.Q. were at least in part genetically determined and if there were no counteracting environmental effects, such a decline in I.Q. could be expected. The fact is that no significant decline has been detected so far. The existing data, although they are admittedly limited, do not support the idea of a persistent negative correlation between I.Q. and overall reproductivity.

The existence of culturally, and often racially, reproductively isolated subgroups within a human population almost inevitably leads to social tensions, which are the seeds of racism. This has been true throughout the history of mankind, and is by no means unique to the present tensions among different racial groups such as those between blacks and whites in the U.S. Conflicts between religious groups, such as Protestants and Catholics in Northern Ireland, are examples of the same type of social tension. Cultural divergence is often accompanied by relative economic deprivation in one group or the other, which aggravates the tensions between them.

The striking outward differences between blacks and whites, mainly of course the color of their skin, must be a major extra factor contributing to the racial tensions between them. If the cultural differences between the Protestants and Catholics of Ireland disappeared, there would be no way of telling the two groups apart. The same is not true for black and white Americans. Many generations of completely random mating would be needed to even out their difference in skin color.

Such mating has not taken place in the U.S. The average frequency of marriages between blacks and whites throughout the U.S. is still only about 2 percent of the frequency that would be expected if marriages occurred at random with respect to race. This reflects the persistent high level of reproductive isolation between the races, in spite of the movement in recent years toward a strong legal stand in favor of desegregation. Hawaii is a notable exception to this separation of the races, although even there the observed frequency of mixed marriages is still only 45 to 50 percent of what would be expected if matings occurred at random.

The socioeconomic deprivation of one racial group with respect to another inevitably raises the question of whether or not the difference has a significant genetic component. In the case of U.S. blacks and whites the question has recently been focused on the average difference in I.Q. Many studies have shown the existence of substantial differences in the distribution of I.Q. in U.S. blacks and whites. Such data were obtained in an extensive study published by Wallace A. Kennedy of Florida State University and

his co-workers in 1963, based on I.Q. tests given to 1,800 black children in elementary school in five Southeastern states (Florida, Georgia, Alabama, Tennessee and South Carolina). When the distribution these workers found is compared with a 1960 sample of the U.S. white population, striking differences emerge. The mean difference in I.Q. between blacks and whites is 21.1, whereas the standard deviation of the distribution among blacks is some 25 percent less than that of the distribution among whites (12.4 v. 16.4). As one would expect, there is considerable overlap between the two distributions, because the variability for I.Q., like the variability for most characteristics, within any population is substantially greater than the variability between any two populations. Nevertheless, 95.5 percent of the blacks have an I.Q. below the white mean of 101.8 and 18.4 percent have an I.Q. of less than 70. Only 2 percent of the whites have I.Q.'s in the latter range.

Reported differences between the mean I.Q.'s of blacks and whites generally lie between 10 and 20, so that the value found by Kennedy and his colleagues is one of the most extreme reported. The difference is usually less for blacks from the Northern states than it is for those from the Southern states, and clearly it depends heavily on the particular populations tested. One well-known study of Army "Alpha" intelligence-test results, for example, showed that blacks from some Northern states achieved higher average scores than whites from some Southern states, although whites always scored higher than blacks from the same state. There are many uncertainties and variables that influence the outcome of I.Q. tests, but the observed mean differences between U.S. blacks and whites are undoubtedly more or less reproducible and are quite striking.

There are two main features that clearly distinguish I.Q. differences among social classes described above from those between blacks and whites. First, the I.Q. differences among social classes relate to the environmental variation within the relatively homogeneous British population. It cannot be assumed that this range of environmental variation is comparable with the average environmental difference between black and white Americans. Second, and more important, these differences are maintained by the mobility among occupational classes that is based to a significant extent on selection for higher I.Q. in the higher occupational classes. There is clearly no counterpart of this mobility with respect to the differences between U.S. blacks and whites; skin color effectively bars mobility between the races.

The arguments for a substantial genetic component in the I.Q. difference between the races assume that existing heritability estimates for I.Q. can reasonably be applied to the racial difference. These estimates, however, are based on observations within the white population. We have emphasized that heritability estimates apply only to the population studied and to its particular environment. Thus the extrapolation of existing heritability estimates to the racial differences assumes that the environmental differences between the races are comparable to the environmental variation within them. Since there is no basis for making this assumption, it follows that there is no logical connection between heritabilities determined within either race and the genetic difference between them. Whether or not the variation in I.Q. within either race is entirely genetic or entirely environmental has no bearing on the question of the relative contribution of genetic factors and environmental factors to the differences between the races.

A major argument given by Jensen in favor of a substantial genetic component in the I.Q. difference is that it persists even when comparisons are made between U.S. blacks and whites of the same socioeconomic status. This status is defined in terms of schooling, occupation and income, and so it is necessarily a measure of at least a part of the environmental variation, comparable to the class differences we have discussed here.

Taken at face value—that is, on the assumption that status is truly a measure of the total environment—these data would indicate that the I.Q. difference is genetically determined. It is difficult to see, however, how the status of blacks and whites can be compared. The very existence of a racial stratification correlated with a relative socioeconomic deprivation makes this comparison suspect. Black schools are well known to be generally less adequate than white schools, so that equal numbers of years of schooling certainly do not mean equal educational attainment. Wide variation in the level of occupation must exist within each occupational class. Thus one would certainly expect, even for equivalent occupational classes, that the black level is on the average lower than the white. No amount of money can buy a black person's way into a privileged upper-class white community, or buy off more than 200 years of accumulated racial prejudice on the part of the whites, or reconstitute the disrupted black family, in part culturally inherited from the days of slavery. It is impossible to accept the idea that matching for status provides an adequate, or even a substantial, control over the most important environmental differences between blacks and whites.

Jensen has suggested other arguments in defense of his thesis that the average I.Q. difference between blacks and whites is entirely genetic or mostly so, and he has challenged readers of his paper in the *Harvard Educational Review* to consider them. One is a set of data on blacks that is quite similar to those we have cited for whites; it shows the filial regression of I.Q. or related measurements as a function of the social class of the parents. The only conclusion one can draw is that among blacks the inheritance of I.Q. must also be fairly high. No conclusion can be drawn from these data concerning environmental differences between blacks and whites that affect I.Q., and it is this that is the real issue.

Jensen also discusses differences between the races in rates of early motor development, and in other developmental rates, which are believed to be correlated with I.Q. The argument must, by implication, be that developmental rates are determined mostly by genetic factors. Environmental influences on such rates are widely recognized, so that this information does not help to clarify the situation concerning I.Q. Moreover, Jensen makes the statement, based on the well-known "Coleman report," that American Indians, in spite of poor schooling, do not show the same I.Q. gap as blacks. According to the Coleman report, however, American Indians typically go to schools where whites are in the majority, which is not the case for most of the schools attended by black children. (The actual difference between whites and Indians may be greater, be-

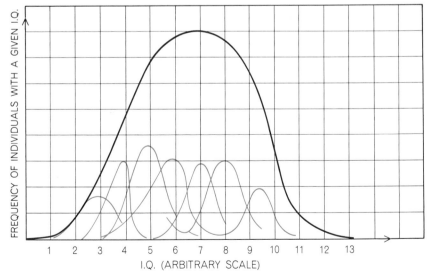

HERITABILITY is a measure of the relative effects of heredity and environment on characteristics such as I.Q. The heritability estimate is based on the assumption that a population consists of several groups each distinguished by a different genotype and I.Q. distribution (*colored curves*). The total of these I.Q. distributions equals the I.Q. spread for the population (*black curve*). By definition those in each group have the same genotype, thus any variation in a group is environmental. Heredity's effect on the total I.Q. distribution can be calculated by averaging together the I.Q. spread of each group and subtracting the result from the total I.Q. spread. The remainder is the total variation due to genetic factors.

cause the sample may not have adequately represented the 70 to 80 percent of American Indians who live on reservations.) The differences between Indians and blacks or whites are clearly no easier to assess than those between blacks and whites.

Jensen states that because the gene pools of whites and blacks are known to differ and "these genetic differences are manifested in virtually every anatomical, physiological and biochemical comparison one can make between representative samples of identifiable racial groups ... there is no reason to suppose that the brain should be exempt from this generalization." As geneticists we can state with certainty that there is no a priori reason why genes affecting I.Q., which differ in the gene pools of blacks and whites, should be such that on the average whites have significantly more genes increasing I.Q. than blacks do. On the contrary, one should expect, assuming no tendency for high-I.Q. genes to accumulate by selection in one race or the other, that the more polymorphic genes there are that affect I.Q. and that differ in frequency in blacks and whites, the less likely it is that there is an average genetic difference in I.Q. between the races. The same argument applies to the differences between any two racial groups.

Since natural selection is the principal agent of genetic change, is it possible that this force has produced a significant I.Q. difference between American blacks and whites? Using the simple theory with which plant and animal breeders predict responses to artificial selection, one can make a rough guess at the amount of selection that would have been needed to result in a difference of about 15 I.Q. points, such as exists between blacks and whites. The calculation is based on three assumptions: that there was no initial difference in I.Q. between Africans and Caucasians, that the heritability of I.Q. in the narrow sense is about 50 percent and that the divergence of black Americans from Africans started with slavery about 200 years, or seven generations, ago. This implies a mean change in I.Q. of about two points per generation. The predictions of the theory are that this rate of change could be achieved by the complete elimination from reproduction of about 15 percent of the most intelligent individuals in each generation. There is certainly no good basis for assuming such a level of selection against I.Q. during the period of slavery.

It seems to us that none of the above arguments gives any support to Jensen's conclusion. The only observation that could prove his thesis would be to compare an adequate sample of black and white children brought up in strictly comparable environments. This seems practically impossible to achieve today.

What can be said concerning environmental differences that are known or suspected to affect I.Q.? First it should be mentioned that, in spite of high I.Q. heritability estimates, the mean intrapair I.Q. difference found by Horatio H. Newman and his co-workers at the University of Chicago between monozygotic twins reared apart was 8 and the range was from 1 to 24. Therefore even within the white population there is substantial environmental variation in I.Q.

The following known environmental effects are also worth mentioning:

1. There is a systematic difference of as much as five I.Q. points between twins and nontwins, irrespective of socioeconomic and other variables. This reduction in the I.Q. of twins could be due either to the effects of the maternal environment *in utero* or to the reduced attention parents are able to give each of two very young children born at the same time.

2. It has been reported that the I.Q. of blacks tested by blacks was two to three points higher than when they were tested by whites.

3. Studies of the effects of protein-deficient diets administered to female rats before and during pregnancy (conducted by Stephen Zamenhof and his co-workers at the University of California School of Medicine in Los Angeles) have shown a substantial reduction in total brain DNA content of the offspring and hence presumably a reduction in the number of brain cells. The reductions were correlated with behavioral deficiencies and in man could be the basis for substantial I.Q. differences. There can be no doubt that in many areas the poor socioeconomic conditions of blacks are correlated with dietary deficiency. Dietary deficiencies in early childhood are likely to have similar consequences.

4. The very early home environment has long been thought to be of substantial importance for intellectual development. There are clear-cut data that demonstrate the detrimental effects of severe early sensory deprivation. There can be little doubt that both the lower socio-

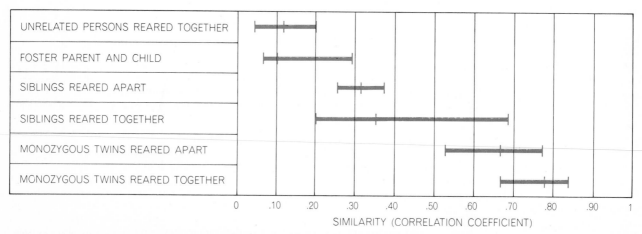

EFFECTS OF ENVIRONMENT can be measured by comparing correlation coefficients of individuals with similar genetic backgrounds reared in different environments and those with different backgrounds reared in the same environment. Published data collected by Erlenmeyer-Kimling and Jarvik show that unrelated persons reared together have coefficients that range from about .15 to slightly over .30. Coefficients for foster-parents and children range from .16 to almost .40. Siblings reared apart have coefficients that range from more than .30 to more than .40. Siblings reared together have coefficients that range from .30 to almost .80. Monozygous twins reared apart have coefficients that range from more than .60 to above .80, and monozygous twins reared together have coefficients of more than .70 to more than .90. It appears that environment affects intelligence but not as strongly as heredity does.

economic status of U.S. blacks and a cultural inheritance dating back to slavery must on the average result in a less satisfactory home environment; this may be particularly important during the preschool years. Here again animal experiments support the importance of early experience on brain development.

5. Expectancy of failure usually leads to failure.

In his *Harvard Educational Review* article Jensen chooses to minimize environmental effects such as these. We believe, however, that there is no evidence against the notion that such influences, among other environmental factors, many of which doubtless remain to be discovered, could explain essentially all the differences in I.Q. between blacks and whites.

We do not by any means exclude the possibility that there could be a genetic component in the mean difference in I.Q. between races. We simply maintain that currently available data are inadequate to resolve this question in either direction. The only approach applicable to the study of the I.Q. difference between the races is that of working with black children adopted into white homes and vice versa. The adoptions would, of course, have to be at an early age to be sure of taking into account any possible effects of the early home environment. The I.Q.'s of black children adopted into white homes would also have to be compared with those of white children adopted into comparable white homes. To our knowledge no scientifically adequate studies of this nature have ever been undertaken. It is questionable whether or not such studies could be done in a reasonably controlled way at the present time. Even if they could, they would not remove the effects of prejudice directed against black people in most white communities. We therefore suggest that the question of a possible genetic basis for the race I.Q. difference will be almost impossible to answer satisfactorily before the environmental differences between U.S. blacks and whites have been substantially reduced.

Apart from the intrinsic difficulties in answering this question, it seems to us that there is no good case for encouraging the support of studies of this kind on either theoretical or practical grounds. From a theoretical point of view it seems unlikely that such studies would throw much light on the general problem of the genetic control of I.Q., because any racial difference would be a small fraction of the total variation in I.Q. The mere fact that even the rela-

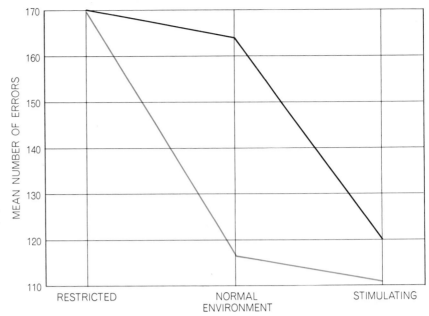

GENOTYPE-ENVIRONMENT INTERACTION is measured in these results from an experiment carried out by R. Cooper and John P. Zubek of the University of Manitoba. The experiment involved two strains of rats: those that were bred to be "bright," that is, clever at finding their way through a maze, and those that were "dull." In a normal environment bright rats (*colored curve*) made only 120 errors, whereas dull rats made about 168 errors. When both strains were raised in a restricted environment, however, both made about 170 errors. When raised in a stimulating environment, both kinds of rats did equally well.

tively crude studies on the inheritance of I.Q. conducted so far have not taken advantage of racial differences suggests that these are not the most convenient differences to investigate. Much basic work on the biology and biochemistry of mental development under controlled conditions, making use of known genetic differences, is needed before a fuller understanding of the inheritance of I.Q. can be achieved.

Perhaps the only practical argument in favor of research on the race I.Q. difference is that, since the question that the difference is genetic has been raised, an attempt should be made to answer it. Otherwise those who now believe—we think on quite inadequate evidence—that the difference is genetic will be left to continue their campaigns for an adjustment of our educational and economic systems to take account of "innate" racial differences.

A demonstration that the difference is not primarily genetic could counter such campaigns. On the other hand, an answer in the opposite direction should not, in a genuinely democratic society free of race prejudice, make any difference. Our society professes to believe there should be no discrimination against an individual on the basis of race, religion or other a priori categorizations, including sex. Our accepted ethic holds that each individual should be given equal and maximum opportunity, ac-

cording to his or her needs, to develop to his or her fullest potential. Surely innate differences in ability and other individual variations should be taken into account by our educational system. These differences must, however, be judged on the basis of the individual and not on the basis of race. To maintain otherwise indicates an inability to distinguish differences among individuals from differences among populations.

We are not unaware of the dangers of either overt or implicit control of scientific inquiry. The suppression of Galileo and the success of T. D. Lysenko are two notorious examples of the evils of such control. Most investigators, however, do accept certain limitations on research on human beings, for example in the right of an individual not to be experimented on and in the confidentiality of the information collected by organizations such as the Bureau of the Census. In the present racial climate of the U.S. studies on racial differences in I.Q., however well intentioned, could easily be misinterpreted as a form of racism and lead to an unnecessary accentuation of racial tensions. Since we believe that, for the present at least, no good case can be made for such studies on either scientific or practical grounds, we do not see any point in particularly encouraging the use of public funds for their support. There are many more useful biological problems for the scientist to attack.

BIBLIOGRAPHIES

When the articles in this volume appeared in the SCIENTIFIC AMERICAN, they were accompanied by these bibliographies.

I PRENATAL DEVELOPMENT AND CAPACITY OF THE NEWBORN

1. The Eye and the Brain

R. W. Sperry

MECHANISM OF NEURAL MATURATION. R. W. Sperry in *Handbook of Experimental Psychology.* John Wiley & Sons, Inc., 1951.

PATTERNING OF CENTRAL SYNAPSES IN REGENERATION OF THE OPTIC NERVE IN TELEOSTS. R. W. Sperry in *Physiological Zoology,* Vol. 21, No. 4, pages 351–361; October, 1948.

2. The Visual Cortex of the Brain

D. H. Hubel

DISCHARGE PATTERNS AND FUNCTIONAL ORGANIZATION OF MAMMALIAN RETINA. Stephen W. Kuffler in *Journal of Neurophysiology,* Vol. 16, No. 1, pages 37–68; January, 1953.

INTEGRATIVE PROCESSES IN CENTRAL VISUAL PATHWAYS OF THE CAT. David M. Hubel in *Journal of the Optical Society of America,* Vol. 53, No. 1, pages 58–66; January, 1963.

RECEPTIVE FIELDS, BINOCULAR INTERACTION AND FUNCTIONAL ARCHITECTURE IN THE CAT'S VISUAL CORTEX. D. H. Hubel and T. N. Wiesel in *Journal of Physiology,* Vol. 160, No. 1, pages 106–154; January, 1962.

THE VISUAL PATHWAY. Ragnar Granit in *The Eye, Volume II: The Visual Process,* edited by Hugh Davson. Academic Press, 1962.

3. The "Visual Cliff"

E. J. Gibson and R. D. Walk

BEHAVIOR OF LIGHT- AND DARK-REARED RATS ON A VISUAL CLIFF. E. J. Gibson, T. J. Tighe and R. D. Walk in *Science,* Vol. 126, No. 3,262, pages 80–81; July 5, 1957.

THE MECHANISM OF VISION. XI. A PRELIMINARY TEST OF INNATE ORGANIZATION. K. S. Lashley and J. T. Russell in *Journal of Genetic Psychology,* Vol. 45, No. 1, pages 136–144; September, 1934.

SPACE PERCEPTION OF TORTOISES. R. M. Yerkes in *The Journal of Comparative Neurology,* Vol. 14, No. 1, pages 17–26; March, 1904.

VISUALLY CONTROLLED LOCOMOTION AND VISUAL ORIENTATION IN ANIMALS. James J. Gibson in *The British Journal of Psychology,* Vol. 49, Part 3, pages 182–194; August, 1958.

4. Brain Damage by Asphyxia at Birth

W. F. Windle

AN EXPERIMENTAL APPROACH TO PREVENTION OR REDUCTION OF THE BRAIN DAMAGE OF BIRTH ASPHYXIA. William F. Windle in *Developmental Medicine and Child Neurology,* Vol. 8, No. 2, pages 129–140; April, 1966.

BRAIN DAMAGE AT BIRTH: FUNCTIONAL AND STRUCTURAL MODIFICATIONS WITH TIME. William F. Windle in *The Journal of the American Medical Association,* Vol. 209, No. 9, pages 1967–1972; November 25, 1968.

MEMORY DEFICIT IN MONKEYS BRAIN DAMAGED BY ASPHYXIA NEONATORUM. Jeri A. Sechzer in *Experimental Neurology,* Vol. 24, No. 4, pages 497–507; August, 1969.

5. The Visual World of Infants

T. G. R. Bower

NATIVISM AND EMPIRICISM IN PERCEPTION. J. E. Hochberg in *Psychology in the Making: Histories of Selected Research Problems,* edited by Leo Postman. Alfred A. Knopf, Inc., 1962.

THE PERCEPTION OF THE VISUAL WORLD. James J.

Gibson, Houghton Mifflin Company, 1950.
SLANT PERCEPTION AND SHAPE CONSTANCY IN IN-
FANTS. T. G. R. Bower in *Science*, Vol. 151, No. 3712, pages 832–834; February 18, 1966.

II   CRITICAL EVENTS IN THE SHAPING OF BASIC SYSTEMS

6. Sex Differences in the Brain

S. Levine

HORMONES AND SEXUAL BEHAVIOR. William C. Young, Robert W. Goy and Charles H. Phoenix in *Science*, Vol. 143, No. 3603, pages 212–218; January 17, 1964.

SEX HORMONES, BRAIN DEVELOPMENT AND BRAIN FUNCTION. Geoffrey W. Harris in *Endocrinology*, Vol. 75, No. 4, pages 627–651; October, 1964.

SEXUAL DIFFERENTIATION OF THE BRAIN AND ITS EXPERIMENTAL CONTROL. G. W. Harris and S. Levine in *The Journal of Physiology*, Vol. 181, No. 2, Pages 379–400; November, 1965.

7. Stimulation in Infancy

S. Levine

DIFFERENTIAL MATURATION OF AN ADRENAL RESPONSE TO COLD STRESS IN RATS MANIPULATED IN IN-FANCY. Seymour Levine, Morton Alpert and George W. Lewis in *The Journal of Comparative and Physiological Psychology*, Vol. 51, No. 6, pages 774–777; December, 1958.

EFFECTS OF EARLY EXPERIENCE UPON THE BEHAVIOR OF ANIMALS. Frank A. Beach and Julian Jaynes in *Psychological Bulletin*, Vol. 51, No. 3, pages 239–263; May, 1954.

A FURTHER STUDY OF INFANTILE HANDLING AND ADULT AVOIDANCE LEARNING. Seymour Levine in *Journal of Personality*, Vol. 25, No. 1, pages 70–80; September, 1956.

INFANTILE EXPERIENCE AND RESISTANCE TO PHYSIO-LOGICAL STRESS. Seymour Levine in *Science*, Vol. 126, No. 3,270, page 405; August 30, 1957.

8. Arrested Vision

A. H. Riesen

THE DEVELOPMENT OF VISUAL PERCEPTION IN MAN AND CHIMPANZEE. Austin H. Riesen in *Science*, Vol. 106, No. 2744, pages 107–108; August 1, 1947.

9. The Origin of Form Perception

R. L. Fantz

EFFECTS OF EARLY EXPERIENCE UPON THE BEHAVIOR OF ANIMALS. Frank A. Beach and Julian Jaynes in *Psychological Bulletin*, Vol. 51, No. 3, pages 239–263; May, 1954.

FORM PREFERENCES IN NEWLY HATCHED CHICKS. Robert L. Fantz in *The Journal of Comparative and Physiological Psychology*. Vol. 50, No. 5, pages 422–430; October, 1957.

ON THE STIMULUS SITUATION RELEASING THE BEG-GING RESPONSE IN THE NEWLY HATCHED HERRING GULL CHICK. N. Tinbergen and A. C. Perdeck in *Behavior*, Vol. 3, Part 1, pages 1–39; 1950.

PATTERN VISION IN YOUNG INFANTS. Robert L. Fantz in *The Psychological Record*, Vol. 8, pages 43–47; 1958.

THE PERCEPTION OF THE VISUAL WORLD. James J. Gibson. Houghton Mifflin Company, 1950.

10. Plasticity in Sensory-Motor Systems

R. Held

MOVEMENT-PRODUCED STIMULATION IN THE DEVEL-OPMENT OF VISUALLY GUIDED BEHAVIOR. Richard Held and Alan Hein in *Journal of Comparative & Physiological Psychology*, Vol. 56, No. 5, pages 872–876; October, 1963.

NEONATAL DEPRIVATION AND ADULT REARRANGEMENT: COMPLEMENTARY TECHNIQUES FOR ANALYZING PLASTIC SENSORY-MOTOR COORDINATIONS. Richard Held and Joseph Bossom in *The Journal of Com-parative and Physiological Psychology*, Vol. 54, No. 1, pages 33–37; February, 1961.

PLASTICITY IN HUMAN SENSORIMOTOR CONTROL. Richard Held and Sanford J. Freedman in *Science*, Vol. 142, No. 3591, pages 455–462; October 25, 1963.

III   ENVIRONMENTAL DETERMINANTS OF COMPLEX BEHAVIOR

11. "Imprinting" in a Natural Laboratory

E. H. Hess

"IMPRINTING" IN ANIMALS. Eckhard H. Hess in *Scien-tific American*, Vol. 198, No. 3, pages 81–90; March, 1958.

IMPRINTING IN BIRDS. Eckhard H. Hess in *Science*, Vol. 146, No. 3648, pages 1128–1139; November 27, 1964.

INNATE FACTORS IN IMPRINTING. Eckhard H. Hess and Dorle B. Hess in *Psychonomic Science*, Vol. 14, No. 3, pages 129–130; February 10, 1969.

Development of Species Identification in Birds: An Inquiry into the Prenatal Determinants of Perception. Gilbert Gottlieb. University of Chicago Press, 1971.

Natural History of Imprinting. Eckhard H. Hess in *Integrative Events in Life Processes: Annals of the New York Academy of Sciences*, Vol. 193, in press.

12. Love in Infant Monkeys

H. F. Harlow

The Development of Affectional Responses in Infant Monkeys. Harry F. Harlow and Robert R. Zimmermann in *Proceedings of the American Philosophical Society*, Vol. 102, pages 501–509; 1958.

The Nature of Love. Harry F. Harlow in *American Psychologist*, Vol. 12, No. 13, pages 673–685; 1958.

13. Deprivation Dwarfism

L. I. Gardner

Growth Failure in Maternal Deprivation. Robert Gray Patton and Lytt I. Gardner. Charles C Thomas, Publisher, 1963.

Emotional Deprivation and Growth Retardation Simulating Idiopathic Hypopituitarism, II: Endocrinologic Evaluation of the Syndrome. G. F. Powell, J. A. Brasel, S. Raiti and R. M. Blizzard in *The New England Journal of Medicine*, Vol. 276, No. 23, pages 1279–1283; June 8, 1967.

Short Stature Associated with Maternal Deprivation Syndrome: Disordered Family Environment as Cause of So-called Idiopathic Hypopituitarism. Robert Gray Patton and Lytt I. Gardner in *Endocrine and Genetic Diseases of Childhood*, edited by L. I. Gardner. W. B. Saunders Company, 1969.

Growth Hormone in Newborn Infants during Sleep-Wake Periods. Bennett A. Shaywitz, Jordan Finkelstein, Leon Hellman and Elliot D. Weitzman in *Pediatrics*, Vol. 48, No. 1, pages 103–109; July, 1971.

14. Social Deprivation in Monkeys

H. F. Harlow and M. K. Harlow

Affectional Responses in the Infant Monkey. Harry F. Harlow and Robert R. Zimmermann in *Science*, Vol. 130, No. 3373, pages 421–432; August 21, 1959.

Determinants of Infant Behaviour. Edited by B. M. Foss. Methuen & Co., Ltd., 1961.

The Development of Learning in the Rhesus Monkey. Harry F. Harlow in *Science in Progress: Twelfth Series*, edited by Wallace R. Brode, pages 239–269. Yale University Press, 1962.

The Heterosexual Affectional System in Monkeys. Harry F. Harlow in *American Psychologist*, Vol. 17, No. 1, pages 1–9; January, 1962.

Love in Infant Monkeys. Harry F. Harlow in *Scientific American*, Vol. 200, No. 6, pages 68–74; June, 1959.

15. Brain Changes in Response to Experience

M. R. Rosenzweig, E. L. Bennett, and M. C. Diamond

Chemical and Anatomical Plasticity of Brain. Edward L. Bennett, Marian C. Diamond, David Krech and Mark R. Rosenzweig in *Science*, Vol. 146, No. 3644, pages 610–619; October 30, 1964.

Effects of Environment on Development of Brain and Behavior. Mark R. Rosenzweig in *Biopsychology of Development*, edited by Ethel Tobach. Academic Press, 1971.

Environmental Influences on Brain and Behavior of Year-Old Rats. Walter H. Riege in *Developmental Psychobiology*, Vol. 4, No. 2, pages 157–167; 1971.

Quantitative Synaptic Changes with Differential Experience in Rat Brain. Kjeld Møllgaard, Marian C. Diamond, Edward L. Bennett, Mark R. Rosenzweig and Bernice Lindner in *International Journal of Neuroscience*, Vol. 2, No. 2, pages 113–128; August, 1971.

16. Intelligence and Race

W. F. Bodmer and L. L. Cavalli-Sforza

Introduction to Quantitative Genetics. D. S. Falconer. Oliver and Boyd, 1960.

Intelligence and Social Mobility. Cyril Burt in *The British Journal of Statistical Psychology*, Vol. 14, Part 1, pages 3–24; May, 1961.

Monozygotic Twins Brought Up Apart and Brought Up Together: An Investigation into the Genetic and Environmental Causes of Variation in Personality. James Shields. Oxford University Press, 1962.

Genetics and Intelligence: A Review. L. Erlenmeyer-Kimling and Lissy F. Jarvik in *Science*, Vol. 142, No. 3598, pages 1477–1479; December 13, 1963.

How Much Can We Boost IQ and Scholastic Achievement? Arthur R. Jensen in *Harvard Educational Review*, Vol. 39, No. 1, pages 1–123; Winter, 1969.

Discussion: How Much Can We Boost IQ and Scholastic Achievement? *Harvard Educational Review*, Vol. 39, No. 2, pages 273–356; Spring, 1969.

WITHDRAWN